UNIVERSITY OF CAMBRIDGE
DEPARTMENT OF APPLIED ECONOMICS

MONOGRAPH 25

TECHNOLOGICAL DIFFUSION
AND THE COMPUTER REVOLUTION
THE UK EXPERIENCE

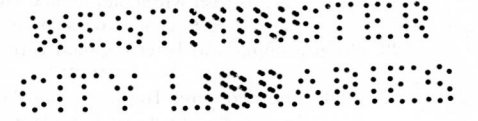

UNIVERSITY OF CAMBRIDGE
DEPARTMENT OF APPLIED ECONOMICS

Monographs

This series consists of investigations conducted by members of the Department's staff and others working in direct collaboration with the Department.

The Department of Applied Economics assumes no responsibility for the views expressed in the Monographs published under its auspices.

The following Monographs are still in print.

TECHNOLOGICAL DIFFUSION AND THE COMPUTER REVOLUTION

THE UK EXPERIENCE

PAUL STONEMAN

Lecturer in Economics, University of Warwick

CAMBRIDGE UNIVERSITY PRESS

CAMBRIDGE

LONDON · NEW YORK · MELBOURNE

Published by the Syndics of the Cambridge University Press
The Pitt Building, Trumpington Street, Cambridge CB2 1RP
Bentley House, 200 Euston Road, London NW1 2DB
32 East 57th Street, New York, NY 10022, USA
296 Beaconsfield Parade, Middle Park, Melbourne 3206, Australia

Library of Congress catalogue card number 75-12136

ISBN: 0 521 20945 5 /7601

First published 1976

Printed in Great Britain
at the
University Printing House, Cambridge
(Euan Phillips, University Printer)

338·06

-5. APR. 1976

DR

To K.T. and G.K.

CONTENTS

LIST OF TABLES AND FIGURES

PREFACE

This monograph is a slightly modified version of a PhD thesis entitled 'On the Change in Technique: A Study of the Spread of Computer Usage in the U.K. 1954–1970' that was presented to the University of Cambridge in 1973. The main purpose of that thesis and thus the present study was to investigate in detail one clearly defined example of a change in technique in an attempt to clarify the forces promoting that change and the effects of the change. A personal fascination with computers and a noticeable lack of a comprehensive study of the UK situation led to the choice of the present example.

When the possibility of publication was mooted my first reaction was to consider that the study ought to be updated. Primarily it seemed desirable to extend the econometric analysis of chapter 7 up to 1974. This soon proved impractical, for the data sources originally used were no longer providing the data in a form that matched our requirements. Rather than try to start again with another data source it was decided to abandon such a full scale updating. This also meant that it would not be of any great benefit to update the other chapters that support chapter 7. The only updating that has been undertaken therefore is the correction of statements that have been overtaken by events. Such modifications have, however, been only minor.

Apart from these updating modifications the other changes to the original text are mainly stylistic. The major changes are to be found in chapter 8, these being made on the advice of an anonymous referee and Professor Reddaway. Although I feel that the chapter is considerably improved, the content is very little changed.

The other acknowledgements I must make are to Dr R. M. Goodwin, who supervised me while writing the original thesis, and with whom I had many interesting and stimulating discussions; SSRC and King's College, Cambridge, who funded my research in Cambridge; Dr D. M. Nuti, the Fellowship Electors of King's College, Cambridge, and the members of the University of Warwick Industrial Economics

Workshop for comments on various earlier drafts of the text; my PhD examiners for their encouragement to publish; Mrs E. Taylor for card punching; Mrs J. Gardner for typing the final draft; and especially my wife for providing the computer programs that were needed for the manipulation of the large data sets that it was necessary to handle, and for her general support and encouragement. Finally, it is apt that I should credit the Cambridge University computer, Titan (prototype Atlas II), and the software supplied by the Department of Applied Economics, Cambridge, for their contribution to this study of computerisation. Of course, all errors that may remain are my responsibility alone.

Coventry   P. STONEMAN
September 1975

1. PREAMBLE

1.1 INTRODUCTION

This monograph reports the results of an analysis into the growth in the production and use of electronic digital computers in the United Kingdom.

The computer has affected modern advanced economies in such a way as to cause the process of the increase in its use to be labelled 'the Information Revolution', thus comparing it to the Industrial Revolution and the Agrarian Revolution. The computer is the embodiment of the automation concept that has been the concern of society for at least a generation. The understanding of this phenomenon would appear to be a socially desirable objective in its own right.

If one can also find that most precious of commodities for the economist – a set of raw data and information that enables an analysis to yield implications – then one also has the resources to perform that analysis. The concern that society has felt with regard to computerisation has led to the compilation of data on the computerisation process of a quality rarely available to the researcher. Moreover, this concern has prompted the House of Commons to conduct enquiries into the state of the UK computer industry. The information arising from its enquiries† provides many insights into the computerisation process. The study of a socially important phenomenon and the existence of the resources to perform that study justify the efforts expended. It is also submitted, however, that the problems with which we shall be concerned can be shown to have relevance outside their immediate context, and that the implications to be drawn from the basic data are of interest in any attempt to relate economic assumptions to reality.

To illustrate this statement it is necessary first to explain more precisely the topics covered in this monograph. Our aim is to provide

† Published as SCST [1970a], SCST [1970b], SCST [1971a], SCST [1971b], SCST [1971c].

an explanation of the spread of computer usage. To achieve this, investigations are made into the nature of computer technology, the development of the technology (technological change), the forces determining the spread of computer usage (technique choice and the diffusion of technology) and the effects of computer usage. These elements constitute the analysis of the computerisation process.

The analysis of the effects of computer usage proceeds on two levels, one of which is concerned with the comparison of an economy in different equilibrium states and the other involving the characteristics of an economy undergoing the process of change from one equilibrium to the other. In chapter 8 an attempt is made to quantify the effects of computer usage on the economy on both levels. It is argued, however, that a theoretical analysis may be more relevant. This analysis proceeds in the appendix. Although it is possible to effect a comparison of states it is found that no adequate framework exists for the analysis of an economy in the process of change. Because it was not possible to improve materially on this position the analysis was relegated to the appendix, but it is possible to illustrate that if one is to analyse an economy undergoing a change in technique then one requires information on the determinants of output in a period, the distribution of the output of capital goods between industries, the choice of capital good, the nature of the innovative process, the nature of the process of technological change and the relative importance of different adjustment mechanisms. These are all matters considered in this study.

It is therefore suggested that, because modern capitalist economies are continually changing technique, if a realistic analysis of these economies is to be carried out then some basic understanding of such problems is essential. It is hoped that this study can contribute to that understanding.

At the same time as the concept of this investigation was developing, Professors W. Leontief and E. H. Phelps Brown in their Presidential Addresses to the American Economic Association (Leontief [1971]) and the Royal Economic Society (Phelps Brown [1972]) respectively, expressed views of the state of economic science that have influenced the approach of this study. Basically they are both concerned with 'the smallness of the contribution that the most conspicuous developments in the last quarter century (in economics) have made to the most pressing problems of the time' (Phelps Brown [1972] p. 1), which they feel is partly the result of 'so many people refining the analysis of economic states which they have no reason to suppose will ever, or have ever, come about' (Hahn [1970] p. 1), and partly the result of the approach of economics: 'In the presentation of a new model, attention nowadays is usually centred on a step-by-step derivation of its formal properties...By the time it comes to interpretation of the substantive *conclusions*, the assumptions on which the model has been based are easily forgotten. But it is precisely the empirical validity of these *assumptions* on which the usefulness of the entire exercise depends.' (Leontief [1971] p. 2.) Leontief thus calls for 'a very difficult and seldom very neat assessment and verification of assumptions in terms of observed facts' (Leontief [1971] p. 2). The method that economists have tended to use to justify their assumptions is to see if the implications of their models are consistent with data (usually time series) on the phenomena under discussion. Phelps Brown objects to this on the grounds that it is difficult to separate causality from contingent relations by the application of refined statistical techniques to small data sets. His argument can be developed further.

It is a familiar concept in the explanation of observable phenomena that two or more theories may have exactly the same implications about an observable phenomenon under all circumstances. The fact that observations on economic phenomena are only available under restricted circumstances increases the likelihood that two theories may be able to generate the same observations. The selection of the 'correct' theory is the problem of identification, and only when we have identified the 'correct' theory do we really have any understanding of the phenomenon being observed.

A theory consists of a model and a structure. The model is the set of the functions relating the variables to each other; the structure is the model with all parameters given numerical values. When a theory is used it is necessary to know which structures are acceptable and whether the model reflects reality. This can only be achieved by returning to basic data to see what *a priori* parameters are acceptable and/or whether direct observation can support the assumptions of which the model is constructed. The problem of model identification does not allow one to do this by implication.

Thus, quoting Phelps Brown, 'For our knowledge of the behaviour of economic agents we must rely mainly on the patient accumulation of direct observations' (Phelps Brown [1972] p. 7). In this study attempts are made, where possible, to use direct observations rather than implication to investigate the subject. It is thus possible to say that some of the results produced are relevant to any attempt to assess and verify the assumptions that underlie economic theory. Comments can thus be made on the nature of technology, the forces moulding technological change, the behaviour of producers in choosing their productive method and on markets in disequilibrium. To generalise, observations are made on technology, the decision making process within the firm and the interactions between producers and suppliers in a market.

Before proceeding, however, it is necessary to indicate why it is felt that observations on the one process, computerisation, should be considered to be a reasonable statistical sample from which to draw implications. One may investigate the problems discussed here by using either a number of observations on one process or single observations on a number of processes. In this study one process is concentrated upon but there are observations upon a large number of agents making decisions with regard to computerisation and thus a statistically significant sample exists for the analysis of decision making behaviour. Moreover, observations are available from a number of different time periods that enable one to construct a reasonably sized sample for the analysis of technology and markets.

Even if it is still argued that the results can only imply things about computerisation it is surely of interest to know about one process rather than none.

This work is thus a study of a socially important phenomenon upon which observations are available, and the results of which can be used either to promote the understanding of economies in the process of change and/or contribute to our understanding of some of the relations that underly economic theory in general.

1.2   THE THEORETICAL FRAMEWORK

A study of this kind must proceed within a conceptual framework in order to advance satisfactorily and logically. However, there is a danger that any framework can so structure the analysis as to make the conclusions simply implications of the framework. Thus a general framework is used, the representation being taken from Lancaster (Lancaster [1968] pp. 98–101). Using this, definitions are provided for the main body of the work, and the explanation of the approach to the study can then be completed.

Let a system involve a total of n commodities, then an activity j is characterised by two n vectors, an input vector $\mathbf{a}^j$ in which a_{ij} is positive if i is an input, zero otherwise, and an output vector $\mathbf{b}^j$ in which b_{ij} is positive if commodity i is an output of that activity and zero otherwise. A commodity which is both an input and an output of the same activity is treated as net so that it appears as either a net input or a net output. Labour is considered as a commodity, and represented in the same way as any other input.

Once any arbitrary labelling of the activities is chosen and any arbitrary choice of the unit level of each activity is made, each activity is defined by its input and output coefficients.

If there are m activities, all the output vectors are assembled into an

$n \times m$ matrix **B**, the output matrix, and all the input vectors into an input matrix **A**, also of order $n \times m$. The matrix $(\mathbf{B} - \mathbf{A})$ is the technology matrix. It is a matrix containing an entry b_{ij} if commodity i is an output of the jth activity, $-a_{ij}$ if commodity i is an input of activity j, and the ijth element is zero if commodity i is neither an input nor an output of activity j.

If the various activities are operated at levels given by the m vector **y** ($\mathbf{y} \geqslant 0$), then the net outputs of the system are given by the vector **x**, where

$$\mathbf{x} = (\mathbf{B} - \mathbf{A})\mathbf{y}.$$

The activity analysis of production is the study of the properties of the set of output vectors and activity vectors, **y**, given assumptions on $(\mathbf{B} - \mathbf{A})$. However, that is not the way this study proceeds – here the model is just a framework.

The advantage of this framework is that the representation of the technology allows that there may be many commodities as outputs of a single activity, or many activities that produce the same commodity or commodities. The existence of alternative activities for a given output introduces substitution into the production process, and the existence of several outputs for a single activity allows for joint production.

This general linear model goes far in bridging the gap between the neoclassical analysis of pure substitution and the input–output analysis of pure complementarity. Moreover the existence of joint production allows for fixed capital goods – a capital good of a specific age is an input and a one year older capital good is an output. Capital goods of different ages are considered as different commodities.

When this model is made operational the coefficients are considered to be fixed, no indivisibilities are allowed, and constant returns to scale are assumed. The definition of these concepts along with others that are to be used, can be made in terms of this framework.

Technology – the total matrix $(\mathbf{B} - \mathbf{A})$ of all activities known, either in use or not. An industry's technology is that subset of the activities that can produce as an output the commodity by which the industry is labelled.

Technique – the reduced form of $(\mathbf{B} - \mathbf{A})$ involving only those activities actually in use (i.e. for which the corresponding element in **y** is non-zero). An industry's technique is the activity or activities actually being used to generate the commodity by which the industry is labelled.

Choice of technique – the process by which the technique is chosen from the technology, i.e. the selection of the non-zero elements of **y**.

Technological change – changes in (usually additions to) the activities comprising the technology.

Change in technique – a change in the activities comprising the technique matrix, or more usually used to define the replacement of just one activity in the matrix for another.

Substitution – a change in technique that is not the direct or indirect result of technological change.

Technical change – a change in technique resulting from technological change, which can be split into

invention – the generation of new technology of which research and development is a part,

innovation – the first application of a new technology,

diffusion – the process from the start to the completion of the change in technique process. It may be considered as the process by which one element in the **y** vector reduces to zero while another increases from zero to generate the output that would have originally been derived from the reducing activity.

Fixed coefficients – the coefficients of every application of an activity at a given level would be the same if all applications were equally efficient.

Constant returns to scale – if a given activity operated at unit level produces output b_i of commodity i and uses a_r of commodity r, the activity can be operated at any level (no indivisibility), μ ($\mu \geqslant 0$) and will produce μb_i of i and use μa_r of r.

1.3   THE OUTLINE

Using the above definitions this study can be labelled as the analysis of that change in technique shown by the spread of computer usage in the UK. The central propositions in this study are concerned with the choice of technique decision; however, prior to analysing a choice decision one must first discuss what the choice is to be made between and how the possibilities of choice arose. Once that choice has been made it is natural to investigate the effects of that choice. With this in mind the study can be neatly compartmentalised.

Chapter 2 consists of a guide to the UK computer environment which acts as a base for all that follows. In chapter 3 the results of an investigation into computer prices and quality over time are reported, which enable one to construct price and quantity series free of quality change for use in later analysis. In the following chapter the technology of computer production and use is discussed, which then leads into the study of technological change in chapter 5. The technique choice decision is analysed in chapter 6 and shown to lead naturally into a study of the diffusion process which is carried out in chapter 7. Chapter 8 consists of attempts to isolate the effect of computer usage in an empirical context. In chapter 9 we bring together the results of the analysis.

Finally, the theoretical reactions to technological change are analysed in the appendix.

Thus the study allows one to use direct observation to comment on an economy's production technology in chapter 4, the forces influencing technological change in chapter 5, decision making within the firm in chapter 6, and market behaviour in chapter 7.

2. THE COMPUTER ENVIRONMENT

2.1 INTRODUCTION

Large sections of this study rely on the observation of computer technology and thus it becomes necessary to provide initially an introduction to the computer and its industrial environment. In this chapter an attempt is made to explain the nature of the computer as a capital good, to define some of the terminology of the technology, to indicate the size of the computer market and to detail the positions, past and present, of the participants in that market.† One of the main difficulties with such a discussion is the fact that computer technology advances so quickly that a detailed survey can soon be out of date. This chapter is therefore made as general as possible; however, because the study is primarily concerned with the time period up to the end of 1970 any failure to take account of very recent changes does not affect the main body of the report.

We begin with a definition of 'computer':

A device –
(a) capable of automatically accepting data, applying a sequence of processes to the data, delivering the results and restarting the cycle without operator intervention; and
(b) having a stored **program** and capability of modifying its own program; and
(c) capable of being programmed to execute a reasonably wide variety of types of computation or other data handling processes, and enabling its users readily to replace one store program by another in the ordinary course of their work (D of E [1972] appendix 1).

As a generic term 'computer' is generally split into analogue and digital computers, although hybrid computers with analogue concepts but digital logic do exist. The analogue machine is based on the principle of measurement and the digital on the principle of counting. In

† The information used in this study is derived mainly from the following sources: SCST [1970a]; SCST [1970b]; SCST [1971a]; SCST [1971b]; SCST [1971c]; CSD [1971]; Hollingdale [1970]; and Rose [1969].

this study the emphasis is on digital machines, for they are the major category in commercial use, the area with which we are mainly concerned and the analogue/hybrid machines represented only 2 % of the overall UK market in 1968 (SCST [1970a] p. 355).

Concentrating on digital machines, the first major distinction to be made is between hardware and software. In general terms, hardware means that part of the total computing system which receives information, stores it, acts upon it, and produces new information. This term derives ultimately from the identification with the electro-mechanical aspects of the computer system, i.e. the actual machinery seen standing in the computer room. Software involves the program of instructions by which the hardware actually operates.

2.2   HARDWARE

The hardware consists of input/output devices, storage (divided between 'working store' and other), the arithmetic unit and the control unit. The working store, arithmetic unit and control unit are often together labelled the central processing unit (CPU), being generally in the same mainframe. It is a common thought process to identify the CPU as 'the computer', but this is misleading in both physical and monetary terms, as will become apparent as the chapter proceeds. The individual pieces of hardware can be discussed in turn.

Input/output devices

The two most common methods used to communicate data to the system are paper tape and punched cards. On the tape or card holes are punched which the tape or card reader converts into electrical impulses, these in turn being recognisable by the CPU. To give some idea of operating performance, the modern punched card reader can read between 600 and 1600 cards per minute, and a modern card punch can generate between 150 and 300 cards per minute at 80 characters per card. Paper tape readers recognise about 1000 characters a second, and an output paper tape can be punched on a modern machine at 100 to 300 characters per second.

However, when the need occurs to input information there is a three stage process, (a) data coding and preparation, (b) the punching of cards or paper tape by punch operators and (c) the reading of the tape or cards into the computer itself. The time consuming tasks are (a) and (b), and even (c) using modern equipment is very slow when compared to the performance time of the CPU. Similarly the times quoted above for punch rates when outputing data are slow in comparison to CPU speeds.

Other input devices do exist and are used to a greater or lesser extent, e.g. Mohawk tapes and Key systems (magnetic tapes onto which data is recorded for input) and automatic document readers. The latter may be sensing either magnetic ink characters (as on cheques), characters printed in a special fount in non-magnetic ink, or a series of pencil or ink marks. All these devices were designed for batch process computing, but in the last few years there have been developments in the field of 'man/machine' interaction, or real time systems, in which a continuous conversation is carried on between the computer and the communicant. This has led to the use of Computer Graphics, the technique of communicating with a computer by means of pictures (graphic displays on cathode ray tubes that can be defined or amended by means of a light pen), and to the addition of remote access terminals to the list of possible hardware. These 'on line' terminals consist of a console or teletype for typing in small amounts of input and receiving output, and should not be confused with remote job entry terminals which also have facilities attached for remote access batch processing. Access to the computer itself is via Post Office transmission links. Terminals are becoming one of the main computer communication devices, and it is predicted that they will experience a phenomenal growth rate – a Scicon survey for the Post Office estimates a need for 51,000 in 1973, and 434,000 by 1980. In April 1970 there was a total population of 8,000 (SCST [1970a] p. 345).

The performance characteristics of these terminals for both input and output depend on the nature of the communication link that is procured from the Post Office – the transmission rates can vary between 110 bits/sec. and 48,000 bits/sec. (a 'bit' is defined below).

Despite the growing popularity of terminals, the most common output device is the line printer, with which any installation that is expected to produce large amounts of hard copy must be equipped. As the name implies it prints one whole line at a time, and high speed versions are quite capable of printing up to 2,000 lines per minute (once again slow in comparison to CPU operating speeds). Other not so widespread methods of recording output are on microfilm or graph plotters, but these are not investigated any further here.

Storage devices

Having input the data to the system the files on which it is held must be stored in the computer system until required. For this purpose a number of different types of storage are provided, each with different operating characteristics and cost. Usually the computer has a store of relatively small capacity and a short access time (the high speed, work-

Table 2.1. *Storage devices – performance*

Characteristic	Type				
	Drum	Exch. disc	Fixed disc	Mag. tape	Core store
Average access time in millisecs	10	100	100	10,000	0.001
Capacity per unit in million characters	5	10	500	100	0.01
Transfer rate (thousands characters/sec.)	1,000	200	200	200	n.a.

SOURCE: Hollingdale [1970] p. 247.

ing, or core store), and a much larger capacity store having a longer access time (the backing store). Consider first the backing store. This usually consists of some combination of magnetic tapes, magnetic discs and magnetic drums. In terms of cost per bit of storage, disc and drum cost almost the same, both are more expensive than tape, but tape, disc, and drum are all three less expensive than core store. Magnetic disc is available in two forms, fixed and exchangeable; both use the same principle of storage but whereas each fixed disc needs its own transport, the exchangeable disc uses the same philosophy as magnetic tape, in that, just as a number of tapes use the same tape deck through sequential loading, disc packs can be sequentially loaded on to the same disc transport.

Comparisons of different types of backing store are provided in table 2.1 and fig. 2.1; the former illustrates performance and the latter cost.

However, these are very average statistics and some differences between manufacturers are found. Also each type of store performs optimally when it is used in a specific manner; for example, because it is wound on a spool, tape needs winding and unwinding as it is searched for characters; this means that if data is randomly distributed over the tape, total access time to find and read a particular document can be long, and the tape is therefore best suited for the storage and processing of data in a sequential manner. All these storage devices use the principle of magnetisation, which is also used by other less common storage devices, e.g. magnetic strips. The reason why the designer is able to use magnetic store is that all computers work in binary digits ('bits'), so one is able to allow north–south magnetisation to correspond to a 1, and south–north magnetisation to a 0, and therefore store all data in binary form.

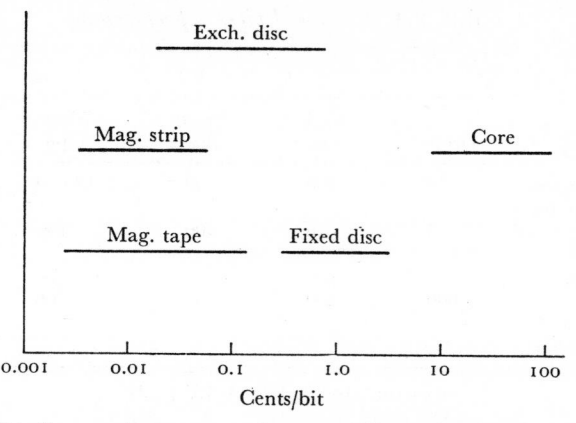

Fig. 2.1. Storage devices – cost. (SOURCE: Sharpe [1969] pp. 438–9.)

The working store, often using the technology of ferrite cores at least until the early 1970s, also makes use of magnetism. The core store consists of a grid of doughnut shaped ferrite cores that can take two magnetisation states, and thus represent one or zero. The grid of cores is threaded with wires that pass electric current, such that three wires pass through each core. Each of two wires carries half the total current, and when they are activated, at the core where they intersect the total current exists; this is just sufficient to magnetise that core in a specific direction. That core then contains one bit of information. To read back this bit there is a sense wire which can sense or read which cores are in a certain state of magnetisation. This technique for storage allows very fast access times but unfortunately is relatively very expensive.

It is useful at this stage, given the principle of working store, to look at the measure of this storage. It is often written that a certain machine has, for example, 64K of store – we should explain what this means. First it refers in most cases only to the capacity of working store, and backing store is separately quantified. The 'K' does not mean 1,000, but stands for 1,024, a binary digit (2^{10}). The units in which store capacity is expressed differs between models, thus 64K can mean

64K bits
64K bytes – 1 byte equals 8 bits
64K characters – a character can be taken to represent a group of six bits
64K words – a word can vary from twelve bits upward.

Thus unless one knows whether it is measured in words (and if so of what length), bits, bytes, or characters, 64K means very little. Moreover, the total amount of working store does not necessarily indicate the working space available, for there is also the matter of how much of this store is taken up by essential software (e.g. the executive, see below).

Having discussed core store, which has been by far the most common type of working store in the 1960s, mention ought to be made of the other types of working store existing in machines using the very latest technology, these include thin film store, electro-plated wire, and the use of integrated circuits (ICs). However, instead of pursuing these developments any further here we will turn to the other elements that constitute the CPU.

The control unit

This unit oversees the entry, exit, and transfer of information from, to and within the system, and does so in accordance with the program instructions. It is in fact a complex master switch.

The arithmetic unit

This final piece of hardware is that part which adds, subtracts, multiplies and divides numbers drawn from store. It can also perform the task of comparison.

Taking CPUs in general, a number of attempts have been made to measure their performance, but for reasons that become apparent no definitive measure exists; those that have been proposed include:

Cycle time – the time taken for the machine to access the contents of a single core location. On the ICL Series 1900A the cycle time varies from 4 micro secs. (micro equals 1/1,000,000) on the 1901A to 750 nano secs. (nano equals 1/1,000,000,000) on the 1906A. However, as different machines have different store widths and different access rates of locations per basic central processor cycle, this measure can yield misleading conclusions.

Add time and multiply time – looking at the ICL Series again, add time varies from 26 micro secs. to 900 nano secs., and multiply time from 88.5 micro secs. to 1.5 micro secs. This, however, is a suspect measure when comparing machines of differing architecture.

Times taken to perform specific instruction mixes – as an example a work load requiring eight hours on a KDF9 was completed in 40 minutes on a 1906A. One particular mix is known as the Post Office Work Unit, this is used quite frequently but favours machines of fixed word length architecture.

Other measures are used but one of the most important considerations is the ability of the central processor to overlap peripheral device operations with computing (simultaneity) for, as was stressed earlier, input/output speeds are slow in comparison to CPU speeds, thus if the CPU can overlap a greater workload can be undertaken in a given time.

2.3 SOFTWARE

In its broadest sense software is the crystallisation of working procedures necessary to instruct the hardware to perform the functions for which it was designed. In more concrete terms it refers to the products, especially the programs, derived from the systems design and programming effort. A useful definition of a program is that it is 'a complete and detailed set of operating instructions [that cause] the computer to perform a particular calculation on any values of numerical data presented to it, and to print [sic] the results of the calculation'.[†] However, software can be separated into 'hard' software, compilers and application software.

Hard software

This is the arrangement of basic instructions that are necessary for the hardware to function in a coherent manner. There is a basic program of these instructions for each model, called the executive or house-keeping system (the software known as the operating system also belongs in this category), that organises the operation of the computer and its peripherals, accepts user programs and protects them from interference in time sharing mode. It also initiates action sequences in the hardware to perform the arithmetic function. The hard software thus provides this general interface between operator, user programs and hardware facilities. The importance of this software is obvious; it is thus usually supplied with the hardware by the mainframe manufacturers. Because the quality of this software can greatly affect a computer's performance, the suppliers stress its efficiency in their sales effort.[‡]

However, ICL also say that because of the complexities of the house-keeping systems on machines in the very large size range the executive takes so much core store as to make these uneconomic in terms of cost per unit of computing power (SCST [1971b] para. 897, p. 162).

The compiler

Every digital computer works entirely in binary digits, thus every program has to be converted into a binary form eventually. The task of the compiler is to carry out this conversion, transforming a program in some programming language (e.g. a procedure orientated language)

---

† Wooldridge [1963] p. 1. My brackets.   ‡ See ICL [1971].

into its equivalent binary form. The compiler often also contains facilities for diagnosing mistakes in programs.

The manufacturers also tend to supply compilers (one for each language likely to be used) with the hardware, and again stress their efficiency (ICL [1971]).

The applications software

In this area there are two main factors, the systems design and programming efforts. The systems analyst's task is to look at an organisation's information requirements and to seek the optimal data flows for satisfying them. He then presents to the programmer the specification for the necessary programs. The completion of the software occurs when the programs are written and tested and the new system is in satisfactory operation. It is in this field of applications software that the computer users make their major software effort, and it is also on these tasks that the software houses concentrate most of their resources.

These three types of software are joint capital inputs with the hardware in the computer activity. As the phrase 'manufacturers' software' implies, and as was mentioned earlier, it was common practice for the hardware supplier to include hard software and compilers in the purchase price, but it was also usual to include a certain amount of applications software. In April 1970, IBM (UK) Ltd, following the lead of its parent corporation, 'unbundled', restricting the amount of software supplied in this way. Other manufacturers have followed suit to differing degrees. When IBM unbundled they reduced the price of the models of their '360' range by 3%. When questioned on whether the total software element in cost was only 3%, IBM replied (SCST [1970a] p. 84) that it was not, and that the software of the 360 was 'in the public domain and will be available to our customers for as long as they want to use it free of charge'. Given that this was their reply it would repay the effort to investigate the proportion of total system cost that is attributable to software. In doing this, unless stated to the contrary, 'computer' refers to the whole system, i.e. hard and software. The major source of information is again evidence to the Select Committee on Science and Technology (SCST) Subcommittees A and D.

Consider first the evidence of J. K. Steward on behalf of ICI Ltd:

We have 28 digital computers in the UK (and) there are 28 process control computers...ICI now has something like 2,000 man years of effort in program software and development, and any change in the future must take into account this investment and that we have got to continue running the business and utilising that vast investment in programs. (SCST [1970a] p. 167.)

The cost of a man year of programming effort is about £5,000 (1970 figures), enabling one to value the total software investment at £10m, and this is supplementary to manufacturers' software. If we value each computer at £200,000, probably an overestimate, giving a total hardware value of £10m, then software represents half the total investment. These figures are rather vague admittedly, but they begin to show one how costs break down into their constituent parts.

The fraction of one half seems to be the generally accepted figure for the relevant ratio of costs of setting up a computer system, see for example Smythe [1970]. Systems Programming Ltd (SCST [1970a] p. 206) quote a prediction that by 1974 the non-hardware sector of the industry in the USA will be about 60 % of the total computer industry, though they give no indication of whether this is by turnover, labour employed, or what measure. *The Economist* of 27 February 1971 further reflects the cost involved in providing software when it says that 'Computers can do many marvellous things, but actually making them do such things is more complicated, more expensive and more accident-prone than is generally believed' (Economist [1971b]).

However, what has happened over the relatively short period of the history of automatic data processing (ADP) is that the proportion of the total computer market going to software has increased, owing to cost reductions in hardware. This trend is considered in a later chapter, but as an example of, and a prediction of the continuation of, this trend, turn once more to Subcommittee D:

In general purpose computer applications, software currently constitutes about 50% of the cost of installation of the complete system. Over the next decade there is likely to be a significant reduction in the hardware cost per unit of computing power which will not be entirely matched by reductions in the cost of software; therefore software will constitute an increasing proportion of total system cost. (SCST [1970a] p. 356.)

The estimates of proportionate costs are, however, approximate, for it seems that many observers differ even as to what constitutes software, some include computer users' effort and some include only the products of manufacturers, software houses and computer bureaux. From an economic viewpoint, however, there is a different question to consider; in the above, care was taken to state that software represented approximately half the total *investment* in an installation. This does not necessarily imply that half the total costs of providing computing services over a long time period are attributable to software. First one must realise that often during the life of the hardware an increasing workload is provided for the machine, thus, for example, it may initially be performing only payroll and stock control functions, then more applications software is provided to increase its applicability to production control, sales analysis, etc. Thus as a machine has a life of about seven years,† while the hardware value depreciates, the total software investment increases.

It would, however, be surprising if this software effort were to be undertaken in the later years of the hardware's life unless it could be used again, for otherwise the short period of software use would not be sufficient to yield a satisfactory return on the investment. Software in fact has certain peculiarities as a capital good, its material aspect is purely the medium on which it is recorded and its value resides in the working procedures that it inters. One would imagine that given a certain task to perform, once the software was available there would be no need to program the task again. Three pieces of evidence (among many) imply that this is not so.

(a) The UK government has 23 payroll programs for the 1900 Series‡
(b) The US government has at least 105 payroll programs.§
(c) There are at least 1,000 payroll applications on the 360 Series.‖

Obviously, one program is not universally valid – even for the same task on the one machine by the same user there are numerous programs. Even if allowance is made for unnecessary duplication owing to poor information the evidence is too strong to support any principle of universality. However, there is some truth in the statement that some tasks are the same across many users, and one program reproduced many times can perform just as well as a number of programs written individually. The software houses make use of this principle; their function is to employ highly qualified systems staff to write a package to perform a certain application. Copies of the package are then sold to computer users (one can note in passing that there is no copyright protection for software). The cost to the user depends on the number of copies sold and the pricing policy of the software houses. Assuming that this pricing policy involves achieving a fixed rate of return on investment then the more copies sold, the lower the price to each user.

There is, however, one problem that is relevant both in the extent to which one program can be used by many computer users and to how long is the life of software. The problem is given the name of 'compati-

† See SCST [1970b] p. 110 and chapter 4, section 3 below.
‡ SCST [1970a] para. 1847, p. 373.
§ SCST [1970a] p. 247.   ‖ SCST [1970a] p. 247.

bility'. Compatibility in hardware refers to the possibility of linking together two pieces of hardware, for example an IBM processor and an ICL disc unit. At the simplest level it may even be in terms of the number of wires to be connected. But it is in software that the real essence of compatibility resides – where the question is, to what extent can software be used on one set of hardware when it was developed for another set? Take as an example a program that was written for a 1900 Series computer in the PLAN language. If that program were to be run on an IBM 360, a PLAN compiler would have to be available for that machine. Such a compiler does not exist. Thus a user owning a 1900 machine and programming in PLAN, changing on obsolescence to an IBM 360 would have to undertake a whole new investment in software. If, however, he were to buy a new 1900 his software would still be of value to him. This has implications for the relative importance of hardware and software in the cost of providing computer services. The point here is that compatibility between computer types allows software a longer life than hardware. This reduces over time the proportion of total cost attributable to software compared to the proportion in the total initial investment. Thus as far as costs are concerned, the greater the element of compatibility in software, the longer is its prospective life and thus the less it will figure in the overall cost of providing computer services. Thus, even if software is half the total investment it may constitute less than half the total cost of providing computer services if the software can be used on a replacement machine.

The importance of compatibility was realised early on in the development of computers, and it was thought that one answer was to develop a universal high level language for which each machine would have its own compiler. This gave rise to Fortran, a mainly scientific language. Uniqueness was not guaranteed and Algol (again scientific) followed. Cobol was produced (a business orientated language), and PL/1 is a later major addition. On most machines compilers exist for all these languages. However, the grand scheme did not live up to the high hopes of its proponents for two principal reasons. First, each manufacturer embellished the basic language, so creating discrepancies between programs written for different machines, and second, the languages are inefficient compared to low level languages though this is partly offset by the fact that it is easier to write in a high level language. Nevertheless, these languages have allowed a greater transference of software than would otherwise have been possible.

One further result of the desire for compatibility has been in the design of hardware. This is reflected in two of the main characteristics of the computer industry, i.e. the design of hardware series or families, and the design of hardware with IBM compatibility. The principle involved in the design of hardware series is that the manufacturer markets a graded family of central processing units and certain peripherals. All peripherals are compatible with any central processor. Moreover the software written for any model in the series of processors is compatible upwards (though not necessarily downwards), although the software may become less efficient the further it is used from the processor for which it was originally written. Two obvious examples of this concept are the ICL 1900 Series and the IBM 360 Series, and to exemplify the philosophy we can quote from ICT advertising literature.

The ICT 1900 Series is more than a range of computers; it is a close linked family of processors, with common data formats, common instruction codes, and common peripheral linkages. The family members are distinguishable by their processing speeds, store ranges, data throughput potentials, multiprogramming and by the number of peripherals they can control. Any processor in the family is compatible with every larger processor; programs written for the smallest machine will run without alteration, though at high speeds, on all other processors in the series. (ICT [1968].)

Turn now to the occurrence of the design of hardware compatible with IBM hard and software. IBM holds, and has held since the mid-1950s, about 70 % of the world market for computers by number and value. Given the principle of compatibility, it is obvious that unless IBM's competitors produce products that are IBM compatible, the present market for extra peripherals and the replacement market for whole systems will be largely closed to them. The first company to use this competitive ploy was Honeywell in the 1960s, advertising their Model 200 as the 'Liberator Concept'. Amongst the British producers, English Electric (now part of ICL) marketed the System 4, which is IBM compatible.

This design of compatible hardware is further strengthened by the fact that IBM design their computer ranges to be compatible with previous series. It would thus seem that the dominant market position of IBM is forcing standards on the industry thereby reducing wasteful duplication of software. However, it can be argued that the standards that IBM sets are good for IBM, but that does not necessarily imply that they are good for the whole industry.

2.4 THE COMPUTER MARKET

In table 2.2 a series on the total computer stock in the UK (1954–70) is presented. This series is based on the data from *Computer Survey* discussed in chapter 7. The size of the market is exemplified by the fact that in 1970 the proportion of GNP spent on data processing was 1.2% (SCST [1970a] para. 74, p. 366).

Table 2.2 *UK computer population 1954–70*

Year	No. of computers installed at the end of each year	Year	No. of computers installed at the end of each year
1954	12	1963	875
1955	23	1964	982
1956	40	1965	1,424
1957	87	1966	1,956
1958	161	1967	2,595
1959	220	1968	3,522
1960	306	1969	4,319
1961	417	1970	5,470
1962	620		

Some observers would disagree with this series on computer population. International Computers Ltd consider, for example, that the 1969 population was only 3,900 (SCST [1970a] para. 6, p. 6). However, as the series does not take account of quality change (a revised series is presented in chapter 7) it should not be taken to imply too much.

In table 2.3 we detail the major participants in the British market, showing manufacturer, country of ownership and the notional value of manufacturers share of sector markets. This value is a weighted average of prices of system configurations. Manufacturers' 1971 model ranges are also shown.

There are other manufacturers in the market, who mainly sell very small machines or have small market shares. They include Marconi–Elliott, Plessey, Digico, Arcturus and Micro Computer Systems, who are all British, and Hewlett Packard and Friden who are foreign owned. Of the larger foreign companies, NCR, IBM, Honeywell, Univac and Burroughs also have varying amounts of productive capacity in this country.

We can extend the market background by illustrating the history of ICL, the major British company. ICL was brought into existence in August 1968 by the government backed merging of the major UK owned computing interests. In fig. 2.2 we show how the British sector arrived at its present state, and to complete the picture the main developments in the life of the US companies are shown in fig. 2.3.

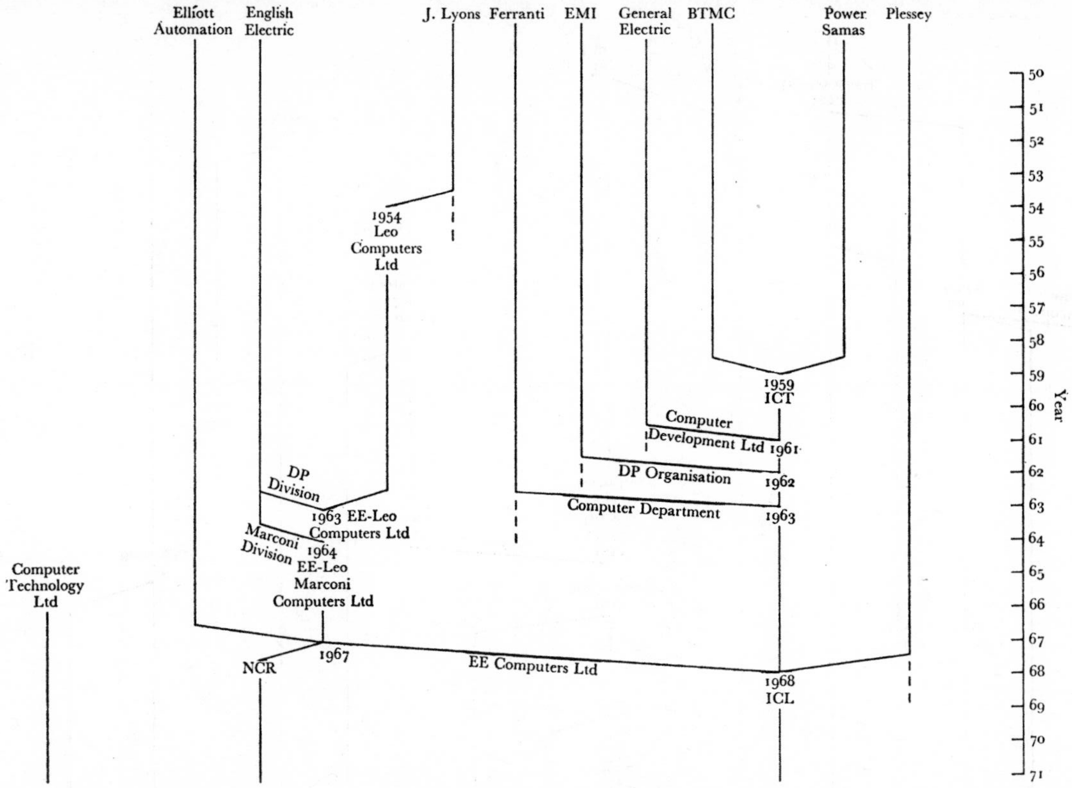

Fig. 2.2. The development of the UK computer manufacturing industry. *Notes.* Pre-1949, IBM and BTMC were linked by Hollerith Franchise. Post-1971, ICL, CII and CDC (of US) were linked by 'Multinational Data', a company for the pooling of research interests. (Dashes indicate that a company continues in non-computer areas) (SOURCES: Sharpe [1969]; Hollingdale [1970]; Smyth [1970]; Rose [1969]; SCST [1970a]; SCST [1970b].)

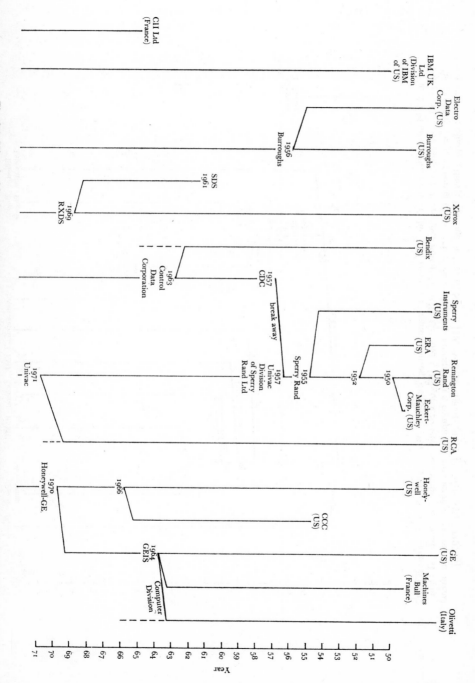

Fig. 2.3. Historical background of major foreign competitors in the UK market. (SOURCES: as for fig. 2.2.)

22

Table 2.3. *The UK market: manufacturers' shares of sector markets*

	Value of manufacturers' installations by sector (£000's)					
Manufacturer	Private	Central govt	Local govt	Public corps	Domi-cile	1971 main model range(s)
ICL	26,588	9,671	2,973	10,065	UK	1900 Series, System 4 Series
Ferranti	262	215	—	290	UK	Argus
GEC/AEI	137	107	—	60	UK	Scientific
Computer Technology	28	14	—	—	UK	Modular One
IBM	24,171	2,399	1,310	250	US	System 3, 360/70 Series
NCR/Elliott	5,272	5,723	812	1,028	US	Century Series
Univac	8,926	—	136	1,500	US	9000 Series, 1100
Burroughs	6,160	—	—	1,500	US	B500–8500
Honeywell	4,591	299	80	1,500	US	H110–8200
CDC	1,275	40	—	—	US	6000, 7000 Series
Digital Eqpt	58	374	14	8	US	PDP Series
STC	—	—	—	100	US	Stantec
Packard/ Raytheon	65	—	—	—	US	703/6, 250, 520
Solartron	102	22	—	—	US	EMR 6000
RCA[a]	—	—	—	634	US	Spectra Series
SDS[b] (1967)	—	44	—	—	US	RXDS Sigma Series
Monroe	—	—	28	—	US	Monrobot
De La Rue Bull[c]	1,104	—	—	—	France	GE Series
Siemag Data	314	—	—	—	Germany	5000
Total UK domiciled	27,015	10,007	2,973	16,415		
Total US domiciled	50,620	8,857	2,380	6,520		
Total others	1,418	—	—	—		
Grand total	79,053	18,864	5,353	16,935		

SOURCES: As for fig. 2.2, plus SCST [1970b] pp. 3–8.
(a) RCA terminated operations in the mainframe field in September 1971, whereupon its interests were taken over by the Univac Division of Sperry Rand Limited.
(b) Merged with Rank Xerox (RXDS), May 1969. RXDS withdrew from mainframe computer manufacture in July 1975.
(c) Merged in 1970 with General Electric, US domiciled, and renamed GEIS. In 1971 GEIS itself merged with Honeywell.

2.5 OTHER ENVIRONMENTAL ASPECTS

To complete the discussion of the computer environment it was felt that there were still three matters that merited consideration. The first of these was to consider predictions that have been made about the future of computer technology and the second was to provide a list of terms, the computer industry being more 'jargonised' than most. These two subjects were not followed up for it was felt that predictions have been adequately covered elsewhere,† and to the extent that definitions are required that have not already been covered we can explain them in the text.

The third area to consider is those aspects of the industry that have not been adequately illustrated above. There are in fact seven main elements in the computer supply industry: (1) the mainframe manufacturers; (2) the terminal and ancillary manufacturers; (3) the communication companies; (4) the service bureaux; (5) the software package vendors; (6) the professional service companies; (7) others. Element (1) has been discussed at some length, and the size of the market and the prospects for the terminal manufacturers (2) has also been covered. Element (3) is really the Post Office, and the predictions are that with the rapid increase in remote access time sharing systems the importance of communication links will come more and more to the fore. As the present links are designed for voice transmission, the computer user explosion will require reciprocal developments in the communication sector – some idea of the problems that this will involve can be gleaned from the evidence to the Select Committee on Science and Technology, Subcommittees A and D, e.g. the Evidence of the Real Time Club (SCST [1970b] pp. 287–9).

Element (7) 'others', concerns such areas as management consultancy, leasing companies, stationery suppliers, and special furnishings where a considerable industry is also growing.

However, the elements to consider here are (4), (5) and (6). A certain amount of discussion has already been carried on about these software aspects of computing, but to show the importance of these sectors to the industry, consider the figures presented in table 2.4, referring to the year 1969, and given in the evidence of the National Computing Centre to the Select Committee (SCST [1970b] p. 10).

Table 2.4. *The computing scene 1969*

No. of computers installed	5,600
No. of establishments with installed computers	4,200
No. of service bureau users	20,000
No. of service bureau users without any computer	14,000
No. of establishments making use of a computer	18,000
No. of computer hardware suppliers in the UK	244
No. of firms providing bureau, software and consultancy	600
No. of firms providing accessories, stationery, etc.	80
No. of people directly involved in computing	152,000
Proportion of total employed in user establishments	57%

† See, for example, CSD [1971] Appendix 2, for such predictions, and its Glossary for the definition of terms.

Most significantly, these figures indicate that elements (4), (5) and (6) make up a very large proportion of the total computer use. Thus any study of computers should take into account the large number of users who do not actually own a computer but make use of bureaux or other such facilities. Similarly there are many users who buy in software rather than use their own staff to provide it. Further evidence indicating the importance of this sector is provided by the Department of Trade and Industry,† their data shows that in the nine months ending in September 1970, computer bureaux alone produced billings to clients for work done of £12½m, an annual increase over the previous year of 37 %. Total employment in this sector was 11,449, and the total value of computer systems in use by bureaux was £50.7m. Explosive growth is also predicted for the future. When we later come to discuss the computerisation process, the importance of these sectors of the industry should not be underestimated.

2.6 Conclusion

The purpose of this chapter has been to introduce the computer and to discuss certain of its major characteristics, to produce an outline of the industry's environment, past and present, and to provide a general framework for later discussion.

† DTI [1971a]. I would like to thank the Department for supplying me with a copy of this document.

3. COMPUTER PRICES AND QUALITY

3.1 INTRODUCTION

The price series is an important indicator to the economist, but it has for long been recognised that because price series are influenced by changes in the quality of the good under consideration a method is needed to correct the series for these changes. Moreover if one can isolate the quality change one can also generate a quantity series free of quality change. This chapter is devoted to correction for the changes in the quality of computers over time, although the quality adjusted quantity index is not constructed until chapter 7. The relation between price and quality is investigated and a quality adjusted price series is constructed. This investigation has been presented at this stage in the study because the relation between price and quality is required in the next chapter as well as much later in chapter 7.

3.2 THE METHOD

The approach has been labelled the 'hedonic' or 'characteristics' method for the construction of price series and is based on

the empirical hypothesis which asserts that the multitude of models and varieties of a particular commodity can be comprehended in terms of a much smaller number of characteristics or basic attributes of a commodity such as 'size', 'power'...In its parametric version it asserts the existence of a 'reasonably well fitting' relation between the prices of different models and the level of their various but not too numerous characteristics.†

Consider a vector $\mathbf{V}_r$ of the level of characteristics, V_r^j of a computer, r, then for a given year, across all computers introduced in that year one estimates the function

$$p_r = \sum_j a_j V_r^j + u_r, \tag{1}$$

† Griliches [1971] p. 4. This book also contains a bibliography of applications of this method.

where p_r is the price of computer r and u_r is the error term. If a logarithmic function yields a better fit the form is

$$\log_e p_r = \sum_j a_j \log_e V_r^j + u_r. \tag{1a}$$

Thus for each year the a_j are the shadow prices of the characteristics for computers introduced in that year. For each year, i, we have a set of a_j estimated by the use of ordinary least squares regression,† $\hat{a}_{ij}$, and for every computer a vector $\mathbf{V}_r$. Thus for every computer for each year one can construct $\sum_j \hat{a}_{ij} V_r^j$, i.e. the predicted price of the computer as if it had been introduced in year i. This number is the computer's quality multiple in terms of the price of the machine if it were to have been introduced in year i. If for every machine one multiplies the number installed by the quality multiple and sums, one has generated the quality adjusted computer stock measured in terms of the predicted price as if all machines had been introduced in year i.

To generate the price series one compares the machines' quality multiples (the predicted price as if they were introduced in the base year i) to their actual prices for different dates.

The following questions arise in applying the procedure.

(a) What are the relevant characteristics?

(b) What is the form of the relationship between characteristics and price?

(c) What weights are to be used in the regression fitting this relationship?

(d) In the construction of the price series how are the observations on each machine to be weighted?

Question (d) is answered in section 4.9 and (a), (b) and (c) in sections 4.3 and 4.5, but before moving on to discuss these questions more ought to be said in general about the regressions of type (1) or (1a) that are to be performed, for they have implications outside the present context that provide the justification for treating the price/quality relationship at this early stage in the work. These relationships have also been interpreted as cost functions from the supply side (Cowling [1970]). By stating that there is a constant relationship between computer price and construction cost, and that the characteristics of the computer system represent its 'size' or 'power' in some general sense, equations (1) or (1a) indicate the relationship for any one year between construction cost and size. They therefore indicate what degree of scale returns exist in the construction of computer systems, in the sense of

---

† Both u_r in (1a) and u_r in (1) must be assumed to satisfy the conditions for the use of Ordinary Least Squares. See Goldberger [1964] p. 162.

how costs increase in the production of bigger (as opposed to more) systems. Moreover by looking at how the coefficients change over time it is possible to investigate how technical progress has affected and been incorporated in computer systems. As these are exactly the questions to be looked at in later chapters it was felt necessary to present this analysis at this stage instead of immediately prior to chapter 7 where the results will be needed again.

3.3 THE RELEVANT CHARACTERISTICS

Although no study has been completed for the period 1954–70, and the UK has been largely ignored, a number of studies have been completed of the price/characteristics relationship for different sub-periods using US data.† These are referred to in the next chapter but some of the characteristics that have been used by other writers are physical space occupied, thousands of fixed point additions per second, minimum working store, maximum working store, number of memory cycles per second, word length, access time, addition time, the ability to perform floating point arithmetic and the use of solid state technology or not. The previous chapter also indicates what characteristics are relevant. A considerable data bank was constructed that for each machine consisted of observations on the following:

Manufacturer.
Date of first installation.
Price in £'000.
The possibility of upgrading within the family or not (dummy
    variables).
Time for fixed point addition in microsecs.
Time for fixed point multiplication in microsecs.
Time for fixed point division in microsecs.
Time for floating point division in microsecs.
Time for floating point multiplication in microsecs.
Time for floating point addition in microsecs.
Addition time without distinction in microsecs.
Multiplication time without distinction in microsecs.
Division time without distinction in microsecs.
Cycle (logic) time in microsecs.
Cycle (store) time in microsecs.
Cycle time without distinction in microsecs.
Minimum store in thousand bits

† For example, Chow [1967] and Sharpe [1969]. Sharpe also presents other studies not
elsewhere published.

Maximum store in thousand bits.
Word length in bits.
Waiting time for delivery in months.
Total floor area in square feet.
To these we have added dummy variables to indicate:
Whether floating point arithmetic is available.
The manufacturer and his domicile.
The year of introduction.

The main problem with this data set is that all the measurements are hardware orientated (with stress on the CPU) and software is ignored. The reason for this is that in general it is not possible to find parameters that indicate software performance (although we can say that certain software characteristics are included, for unbundled software is included in the price and certain performance indicators depend on the presence of efficient software).

The manufacturer dummies have been included in order to investigate whether there are different pricing policies between manufacturers (however, they did not ever appear as significant). The other variables in the list above that need explanation are those arithmetic variables that are 'without distinction'. As will be seen below a number of different data sources were used, one of which separated fixed and floating point arithmetic times whereas the others did not. Thus three figures are generated for the arithmetic operations and, similarly, the cycle times.

3.4 THE DATA

The principal source of the data is *The British Commercial Computer Digest*,[†] but this data is supplemented from *Computers and Automation*[‡] and Smythe.[§] The majority of the data is available for a total of 312 computers with introduction dates ranging from 1952 to 1971. However, in certain cases observations are lacking. Thus what has been done is to estimate, by the use of ordinary least squares regression, equations of type (1a) from which one can estimate the quality index for each machine for which there is complete data. Then the quality index has been regressed on all combinations of the independent variables across the set of machines with full data and the resulting coefficients used to fill the gaps (see section 3.7).

[†] CCL [1962–70]. The same data are available in CCL [1969–71].
[‡] IDC [1961–9]. I would like to thank IBM for making the supplements containing the data available to me.
[§] Smythe [1970], supplemented from Shirley [1969].

There is one variable that needs further explanation and that is price. In some studies annual rental is taken as the dependent variable. However, there is not a constant relationship between price and rental across manufacturers (Sharpe [1969] pp. 380–93); thus if one is to assume a relationship between price and cost, looking at rental would produce warping. The one sum price has thus been used. The published data is on average prices of all installations of that machine, and the data is available for a number of years. Thus the price used is the average of the prices that are published for that machine over the years.

3.5 FUNCTIONAL FORM

In most studies of this type the linear in logs function (1a) has been found to generate the best fit, and it was so here. Thus (1a) is the function fitted to the data. There is, however, the question of what weights to use in the regressions. It was decided to give all observations equal weight, for the only alternative is to use market shares, and as only machines in their year of introduction are being studied, market shares would depend crucially on the time of the year they were introduced. This could mean practically random weights.

3.6 THE RESULTS

In the search for the variables that represented the characteristics with a 'reasonably well fitting' relation to price, the method was to try numerous apparently realistic combinations of the independent variables and to judge their performance by the coefficient of multiple correlation corrected for the number of varables.†

The variables that were finally chosen were the floor area in square feet, the maximum working store in thousand bits, the cycle time without distinction in microsecs., and a constant. The data on these variables can be found in Stoneman [1973] (pp. 302–9). The functional form, as stated, was linear in logs. The results of the regressions are presented in table 3.1. These results are split into two sections, the annual regressions and the pooled regressions. The annual regressions have as their sample only machines installed for the first time in the

---

† An alternative, more systematic method is to use factor analysis (as in Wilkinson [1973]) to identify factors as weighted combinations of variables in the data set, and then to regress price on these factors. In an implicit way this is how the study proceeded although each factor was reduced to one variable – a size factor represented by store size, a speed factor represented by cycle time, a time factor represented by the date of introduction, and floor area the function of which is discussed below. The only real advantage that could have been gained by the use of factor analysis would have been to redefine the speed factor over more indicators, but this would probably have produced problems through data shortages.

specified year, while the pooled regressions combine years. The machines are classified as introduced in year i if they were first installed between July of the previous year and June of year i.

Table 3.1 *Regressions of price on characteristics*

Year	Constant	Cycle time	Floor area	Maximum store	N	R^2	$\bar{R}^2$	$E^{2(a)}$
To 1960	1.07	−0.04	0.71	−0.03	10	0.754	0.590	3.89
	(0.76)[b]	(−0.27)	(1.65)	(−0.10)				
			0.82		10	0.711	0.680	4.55
			(24.2)					
1961	4.71	−0.70	0.40	−0.09	13	0.774	0.674	5.78
	(1.50)	(−1.74)	(1.48)	(—0.27)				
	6.82	−0.77			13	0.718	0.667	7.22
	(18.38)	(−5.3)						
1962	1.61	−0.10	0.41	0.23	16	0.802	0.736	4.37
	(1.81)	(−0.97)	(3.09)	(2.43)				
			0.61	0.25	16	0.743	0.707	5.66
			(7.25)	(2.54)				
1963	1.57	−0.27	0.44	0.22	21	0.835	0.796	4.98
	(2.60)	(−2.56)	(4.97)	(3.10)				
	1.57	−0.27	0.44	0.22	21	0.835	0.796	4.98
	(2.60)	(−2.56)	(4.97)	(3.10)				
1964	−1.94	−0.18	1.02	0.13	13	0.908	0.867	0.964
	(−1.82)	(−1.42)	(4.05)	(1.06)				
	−3.07		1.29		13	0.855	0.829	1.52
	(−3.01)		(8.07)					
1965	1.13	−0.07	0.389	0.22	30	0.606	0.546	15.3
	(1.36)	(−0.57)	(4.93)	(2.13)				
			0.429	0.34	30	0.580	0.550	16.5
			(6.13)	(5.80)				
1966	0.55	−0.12	0.21	0.44	32	0.760	0.730	10.4
	(0.79)	(−0.82)	(3.13)	(4.14)				
			0.21	0.52	32	0.75	0.74	10.7
			(3.20)	(9.70)				
1967	0.199	−0.37	0.55	0.24	32	0.805	0.777	16.01
	(0.28)	(−3.05)	(6.56)	(1.98)				
		−0.35	0.54	0.26	32	0.804	0.784	16.05
		(−3.58)	(6.66)	(4.12)				
1968	−0.83	−0.297	0.57	0.33	27	0.970	0.965	2.20
	(−2.58)	(−3.08)	(13.32)	(5.56)				
	−0.83	−0.297	0.57	0.33	27	0.970	0.965	2.20
	(−2.58)	(−3.08)	(13.32)	(5.56)				

Table 3.1 (*cont.*)

Year	Constant	Cycle time	Floor area	Maximum store	N	R^2	$\bar{R}^2$	$E^{2(a)}$
1969	−1.31 (−1.59)	−0.34 (−0.91)	0.495 (6.27)	0.484 (4.06)	18	0.897	0.867	4.81
	−1.72 (−2.54)		0.495 (6.30)	0.541 (5.37)	18	0.891	0.870	5.10
1970	−0.58 (−0.09)	−0.613 (−1.61)	0.706 (2.37)	0.238 (0.26)	6	0.932	0.796	0.845
			0.938 (22.60)		6	0.811	0.774	2.35
1969 and 1970	−1.19 (−1.8)	−0.51 (−2.21)	0.53 (8.0)	0.45 (4.53)	24	0.913	0.895	6.13
		−0.67 (−2.99)	0.53 (7.7)	0.29 (5.78)	24	0.898	0.884	7.14

(a) The sum of squares of the errors from the regression equation.
(b) The brackets enclose t statistics.

1. *1961 to 1964*
$P = 1.60 \quad -0.19C + 0.42F + 0.25S + 0.08d_{62} \quad -0.33d_{63} \quad -0.49d_{64}$
$\quad (3.22)\ (-3.10)\ (6.22)\ (5.06)\ (0.34)\quad (-1.6)\quad (-2.1)$
$\quad (R^2 = 0.790,\ \bar{R}^2 = 0.764,\ N = 63,\ E^2 = 18.96)$
$P = 1.64 \quad -0.19C + 0.42F + 0.25S \qquad\qquad -0.37d_{63} \quad -0.53d_{64}$
$\quad (3.44)\ (-3.11)\ (6.28)\ (5.09) \qquad\qquad (-2.17)\quad (-2.62)$
$\quad (R^2 = 0.790,\ \bar{R}^2 = 0.768,\ N = 63,\ E^2 = 19.00)$

2. *1954 to 1964*
$P = 1.30 \quad -0.15C + 0.455F + 0.22S + 0.34g_1$
$\quad (3.21)\ (-2.72)\ (6.77)\ (4.55)\ (1.51)$
$\quad (R^2 = 0.755,\ \bar{R}^2 = 0.737,\ N = 73,\ E^2 = 26.29)$
$P = 1.19 \quad -0.12C + 0.47F + 0.22S$
$\quad (2.95)\ (-2.34)\ (7.00)\ (4.54)$
$\quad (R^2 = 0.747,\ \bar{R}^2 = 0.732,\ N = 73,\ E^2 = 27.17)$

3. *1954 to 1964*
$P = 2.03 \quad -0.19C + 0.42F + 0.25S + 0.56d_{58} \quad -1.64d_{59} \quad -0.37d_{60} \quad -0.39d_{61}$
$\quad (2.78)\ (-3.76)\ (6.68)\ (5.56)\ (0.86)\quad (-2.04)\quad (-0.60)\quad (-0.66)$
$\qquad -0.32d_{62} \quad -0.72d_{63} \quad -0.87d_{64}$
$\qquad (-0.54)\qquad (-1.23)\qquad (-1.48)$
$\quad (R^2 = 0.817,\ \bar{R}^2 = 0.784,\ N = 73,\ E^2 = 19.3)$
$P = 1.65 \quad -0.19C + 0.42F + 0.25S + 0.91d_{58} \quad -1.3d_{59} \quad -0.38d_{63} \quad 0.53d_{64}$
$\quad (4.40)\ (-3.8)\ (6.95)\ (5.70)\ (2.64)\quad (-2.30)\quad -2.4)\quad (-2.83)$
$\quad (R^2 = 0.815,\ \bar{R}^2 = 0.793,\ N = 73,\ E^2 = 19.8)$

4. *1965 to 1969*
$P = 0.105 \quad -0.18C + 0.43F + 0.35S \quad -0.17d_{66} \quad -0.205d_{67} \quad -0.42d_{68} \quad -0.16d_{69}$
$\quad (0.29)\ (-2.7)\ (13.4)\ (7.08)\ (-0.95)\quad (-1.15)\quad (-2.21)\quad (-0.76)$
$\quad (R^2 = 0.784,\ \bar{R}^2 = 0.771,\ N = 139,\ E^2 = 62.0)$
$P = \qquad -0.16C + 0.43F + 0.34S$
$\qquad (-3.18)\ (12.6)\ (12.7)$
$\quad (R^2 = 0.776,\ R^2 = 0.771,\ N = 139,\ E^2 = 64.4)$

Table 3.1 (*cont.*)

---

5. *1965 to 1970*

$P =$ 0.12 $-0.19C+0.45F+0.345S$ $-0.180d_{66}$ $-0.21d_{67}$ $-0.42d_{68}$ $-0.165d_{69}$
(0.34) (−3.03) (12.9) (6.9) (−1.0) (−1.2) (−2.25) (−0.77)
$-0.15d_{70}$
(0.47)
($R^2 = 0.794$, $\bar{R}^2 = 0.780$, $N = 145$, $E^2 = 65.4$)

$P =$ $-0.18C+0.45F+0.344S$ $-0.30d_{68}$
(−3.67) (13.17) (12.91) (−2.06)
($R^2 = 0.790$, $\bar{R}^2 = 0.784$, $N = 145$, $E^2 = 65.80$)

---

6. *1954 to 1970*

$P =$ 4.47 $-0.17C+0.47F+0.29S$ $-1.54T$
(5.98) (−4.00) (15.6) (8.5) (−5.80)
($R^2 = 0.770$, $\bar{R}^2 = 0.763$, $N = 218$, $E^2 = 98.5$)

$P =$ 4.47 $-0.17C+0.47F+0.29S$ $-1.54T$
(5.98) (−4.00) (15.6) (8.5) (−5.80)
($R^2 = 0.770$, $\bar{R}^2 = 0.763$, $N = 218$, $E^2 = 98.5$)

---

7. *1954 to 1970*

$P =$ $-0.16C+0.46F+0.32S+1.28g_1+0.92g_2+0.24g_3$
(−3.97) (15.25) (8.60) (3.68) (3.7) (1.05)
($R^2 = 0.772$, $\bar{R}^2 = 0.765$, $N = 218$, $E^2 = 97.1$)

$P =$ $-0.14C+0.46F+0.32S+1.02g_1+0.69g_2$
(−3.96) (15.73) (14.03) (4.15) (5.71)
($R^2 = 0.770$, $\bar{R}^2 = 0.766$, $N = 218$, $E^2 = 97.7$)

---

8. *1954 to 1970*

$P =$ 3.00 $-0.177C+0.450F+0.299S$ $-0.84T$ $-0.034g_2$ $-0.468g_3$
(3.02) (−4.25) (15.20) (8.78) (−1.85) (−0.12) (−1.196)
($R^2 = 0.775$, $\bar{R}^2 = 0.768$, $N = 218$, $E^2 = 95.6$)

$P =$ 3.05 $-0.177C+0.450F+0.299S$ $-0.88T$ $-0.43g_3$
(3.30) (−4.26) (15.24) (8.88) (−2.4) (−2.56)
($R^2 = 0.775$, $\bar{R}^2 = 0.769$, $N = 218$, $E^2 = 95.6$)

In these results, representing logarithms by capital letters and unlogged variables by lower case letters, the following symbols are used:

P log price in £'000
C log cycle time in microsecs
F log floor area in sq. ft.
S log maximum working store in thousand bits
T log introduction date (1952 set to zero)
d_n dummy variable of the year of introduction n
g_i dummy variable for generation i, where generation is decided by the introduction date, 1 is up to 1960; 2 is 1960–4; 3 is 1965–70.†

† This dating of generations is appropriate to the present situation where one is considering the date of first installation as the relevant time variable. In chapters below, especially 7, where one considers the date of first order the second generation is 1960–3 and the third 1964–70. (See chapter 5.)

The results are discussed in three sections: (a) the annual regressions, (b) the regressions pooling subsets of the whole time period and (c) the regressions based on the whole time period, before finally going on to (d) to discuss the choice of the base year for the price and quantity series.

(a) The annual regressions

The table presents the results when all four variables are included and when only significant variables are included (a 95 % significance test is used). The table also includes R^2, corrected and straight, the sample size and the sum of squares of the errors.

The data for the pre-1960 period is pooled because data shortage reduced the sample size. However, when included, time dummies were not significant so it was felt that the pooling made little difference. Otherwise there are sufficient observations for each year, except that the small data base for 1970 is a problem so we have also presented the results of combining 1969 and 1970.

The first comments to be made concern variables that are not included as opposed to the three that are.

(1) A surprising facet of the results was the poor explanatory power of the variables that indicate arithmetic speed and the failure of the floating point arithmetic dummy to be significant. One of the division time variables was significant if included in the pre-1960 regression but its inclusion meant the reduction of the sample size, so it was dropped.

(2) None of the manufacturer dummies were significant when included which indicates similar pricing policy across different manufacturers.†

The poor performance of the arithmetic variables may in fact be the result of the inclusion of the floor area variable, as this is probably a proxy. The importance of this variable is best rationalised by arguing that in a regression for any given year the technology is constant and thus a better machine must be physically bigger (the coefficient is always positive). However, floor area and maximum store are highly correlated – a symptom of the generally high level of multicollinearity present in the regressions. The two variables nevertheless are usually both significant and as the exclusion of either affects R^2 drastically both have been retained.

The movement of R^2 over time is interesting for by visual inspection one can see that it increased from 1961 to 1964, reduces and then increases to 1970. There are three possible explanations for this. First, 1965 is a year of change from the second to the third generation and is thus a mixture of very different machines. Second, families of computers

---

† This is not a conclusive test, for a more thorough method see Muellbauer [1971].

have become more important over time and pricing within families may be more consistent with the hypotheses than between completely different models. Third, over time the number of manufacturers has reduced and thus inter-firm differences may have become less. However, as the family dummies and manufacturer dummies do not reach significance, we cannot be sure of this. One is thus best advised to move on to a detailed discussion of the results.

First, look at the results for the inclusion of all four variables. The constant in the equations seems to fall systematically if not uniformly over time reflecting the fall in price over time of a machine of a given quality. The coefficient on cycle time is everywhere negative indicating that faster machines cost more. The size of the coefficient varies considerably over the years but the pooled regressions would suggest approximately a 20% decrease in price for a 100% increase in cycle time.

Floor area has been discussed already, and it appears as significant in all years except 1961 (a fact probably related to the high coefficient on cycle time for that year). In all cases the coefficient is positive, with a value of about 0.45 as an average, i.e. a doubling of the floor area increases price by 45%.

The final variable, maximum store, is not so consistently significant except in the third generation (excluding 1970 the year of the small sample). In the pre-1960 and the 1961 results the sign is wrong but in both cases the variable is not significant at the 95% level. Once again the effect on price is generally positive, with a doubling of maximum working store increasing price by about 30%.

In the regressions including only the significant variables it can be seen that only in the years of 1963 and 1968 are all four variables represented. In the small sample years of pre-1960 and 1970 only one variable (floor area) is significant. In all cases the coefficients on significant variables are of the expected sign. This shift to the inclusion of only significant variables of course reduces the R^2s but in several cases there is a small improvement in the corrected R^2, though with both of these occurrences the size of the variation is not very great.

(b) The pooled regressions

The idea of pooling the data for several years is to produce results that are independent of any one year, to provide data for the testing of hypotheses about the constancy of coefficients over time, and finally to help provide results for answers to questions that arise in the next chapter.

Taking equation 1 first, the pooling of the data appears to have cleared out the inconvenient anomalies apparent in the 1961 equation.

The significance of the two time dummy variables and their decline over time shows the effect on price as the second generation proceeds. All variables can be seen to have coefficients of the correct sign.

From the errors of this equation and the errors of the individual regressions one can construct a value for the F statistic to test the null hypothesis that the coefficients have remained the same over the period 1961–4 (Chow [1967]). The computed F value is 0.94, whereas the tabulated value at the 95 % level of significance for 9 and 47 degrees of freedom is 2.1; thus the null hypothesis is accepted. The coefficients indicate effects on price of − 19, 42 and 25 per cent for cycle time, floor area and store size respectively.

Equations 2 and 3 are attempts to combine the data on the first and second generations, number 2 using a generation dummy variable (not significant at 95 % level) and number 3 using year dummies (the significance of the early dummies is suspect because there are so few observations). The coefficients of these equations are very similar to those of equation 1 but this could be the result of the predominance of data on second generation machines. Once again in these results the coefficients are of the right sign but in 3 the 1959 dummy appears to be larger than expected. Testing the null hypothesis once again, using equation 2 and the annual regressions including the pre-1960 data, one computes an F value of 1.3; the tabulated value at the 95 % level is 1.9 for 13 and 53 degrees of freedom. Once again the null hypothesis is accepted. Equations 2 and 3 indicate respective effects of the three characteristics on price of approximately − 17 %, 45 % and 24 %.

Turn now to equations 4 and 5, the former excluding the small sample year of 1970 because of its size. The things to note about the results are the insignificance of the constant and the poor showing of the time dummies. The coefficients are of the correct sign and differ little across the two data bases. Effects of − 15 %, 44 % and 34 % are indicated.

Once again we can test the null hypotheses for both the equations. Equation 4 generates an F value when compared to annual regressions 1965 to 1969 of 2.7 with 12 and 119 degrees of freedom whereas the critical 95 % value is 1.83 – the null hypothesis of the constancy of the coefficients over time cannot be accepted. Equation 5 generates an F value of 2.5 and the tabulated value with 15 and 121 degrees of freedom is 1.75 at the 95 % level. Thus the null hypothesis cannot be accepted over this data base either. It is significant that rejection would also occur at the 99 % level of significance. As this rather inconvenient result implies, one cannot really lump together the data in the years 1965 to 1970 and generate one grand regression. Thus the third generation is best represented by the annual results that constitute it.

(c) *The pooled regressions over the whole time period*

These findings on the change in coefficients over time can make rather suspect those types of regression that take data from the whole of the time spectrum and fit one functional form to the whole data set. However, we have presented the results for three such regressions, equations 6, 7 and 8. The only differences are in the manner in which the time influence on price is included. If, for the moment, we forget the problems with changing coefficients and analyse the results, the first observation is that the representation of time has little influence on the R^2s. In each case this statistic is around 77% and the corrected value 76%. Considering the size of the sample (218) this is quite a reasonable result. Many attempts at the inclusion of other variables have made very little difference to the explanatory power. The choice between the three must therefore rest on other factors. All variables have coefficients of the correct sign so that method of choice is no use. We prefer to reject equation 7 for it implies that there is no improvement in quality per unit of price during the second generation whereas equation 1 shows up dummies for 1963 and 1964 as significant. Equation 6 does not come in for this criticism but is not preferred to equation 8 for it is a special case of equation 8 (i.e. it does not include a significant dummy g_3). The final equation 8, which we prefer to accept, may be subject to the same criticism as 7 but the F test on the third generation makes it difficult to say. Equation 8 has the benefit of allowing the first and second generation to be represented as having similar coefficients with the third generation being given an almost zero constant which is indicated by equation 5 as reasonable. If we compare 8 to 4 we find that there is little difference between the coefficients on C, F and S, indicating a fair representation of second generation technology.

Because of the problems of rejection of the null hypothesis it seems only correct to take equation 8 and all the annual regressions and compute the F statistic to see whether (or by how much) the null hypothesis of constant coefficients is rejected. The computed F statistic is 1.75 and the critical value is 1.5 at the 95% level with 37 and 174 degrees of freedom. At the 99% level the critical value is 1.73. Thus one cannot accept the null hypothesis.

Considering what has been said above, if the relation of prices and characteristics over time is to be studied one may do so by lumping together those years prior to 1964, but one must look at the later years separately (it was even tried changing the third generation to start in 1966 but once again the null hypothesis was rejected).

(d) Recommendations

Because the hypothesis of the constancy of coefficients cannot be accepted, the choice of a base year is going to affect the results obtained as regards the quantity and price series. The major problem is that it seems that there is a change in the relative importance of characteristics in the post-1965 period. As a decision has to be made if one is to proceed at all, the apparent constancy in the pre-1965 period has been taken into account and 1963 has been chosen as the base year, using the coefficients apparent from pooled regression 1. This year is chosen as it showed up well in the annual regressions having four significant variables. Thus the actual relation used in the computation of the quality series working to more places of decimals is

$$P_r = 1.269841 - 0.1910122C_r + 0.425034F_r + 0.247165S_r.$$

On this base the series for the 218 machines with the relevant data complete is constructed. The series itself consists of the values of antilog $\hat{P}_r$ i.e. antilog P_r predicted from this equation, and labelled $\hat{p}_r$.

3.7 THE QUALITY SERIES

Using these coefficients the quality multiple for 218 machines was derived. This left about thirty machines that appear in the quantity data but upon which one or more observations on independent variables were lacking and another sixty-four not in the quantity data. Thus, for the sample of 218 with full data, broken down by year of introduction, we performed regressions of predicted price against a constant, the actual price and either nil, one or two of cycle time, floor area, and maximum store. This meant that, as there were observations on price for every machine and often data on some of the other variables, the quality multiple for the machines on which we had incomplete data could be predicted. It was not felt necessary to present the results of these regressions, since a total of seventy-seven were involved.

Thus the sum total of this effort was to generate a quality multiple for every machine that entered the quantity data. This series, covering 250 machines, plus the multiples for the sixty-four machines not in the quantity data can be found in Stoneman [1973] (pp. 302–9).

3.8 THE QUANTITY DATA

In the construction of the price series we shall need to use the data on the number of computers of each type installed in each year. In this section we will discuss this data although we shall not modify it for quality change until chapter 7.

We have data on the number of computers in existence and in which industries they are located. The souce is *Computer Survey*,† the data being broken down by model and year of installation for the period 1954–70. This data refers to numbers at the end of the year. For the years 1963–70 the data is further supplemented by orders broken down by model and these are mid-year based. There is also data on the industry distribution of computers (installed and on order) for the end of each year 1962–70.

There are two problems with this data. The first is that where families of machines appear they are represented by one entry. It is therefore necessary to break these families into individual models. This was done by use of an independent data source. Computer Consultants Limited (in CCL [1962–70]) published data on computer installations broken down by models and not families. Unfortunately this data is not sufficiently complete for the derivation of quantity series but it is adequate to break down families into individual machines. Data for the period 1954–69 was collected from this source involving machines installed and on order at the end of each year. The *Computer Survey* data was thus broken down into models by assuming that a model had the same share of a family's installations in *Computer Survey* aggregate data as in Computer Consultants data. The order data was reduced to models by assuming that the *Computer Survey* mid-year data had the same breakdown as the Computer Consultants data on orders for the end of the previous year. This, however, left 1970 data without any breakdown, so for this year the installations were reduced to models by extrapolating from the previous years installations and orders, and the order data was assumed to have the same composition as in 1969.

At the industry level the installations data was broken down by assuming that each industry had the same model composition of families as was apparent at the aggregate level. This seemed to be the only reasonable approach. As the order data was based at end-year for industries a closer relation existed with Computer Consultants data than at the aggregate level for the data referred to the same date. The order data was reduced to models by assuming that all industry orders had the same model composition of families as was apparent in the

† CS [1962–70]. The data is taken from the summary tables published in the March and July issues 1962–70.

aggregate order data. However, as the order data for 1970 was based on December 1970 and the latest Computer Consultants order data available was December 1969, there were machines on order in the industry data that were not even available at the earlier date; thus the order series could not be extended to 1970.

It should be stated that during the construction of this data considerable discrepancies were found in the *Computer Survey* and Computer Consultants data and even between *Computer Survey* data published in different years. Thus a substantial amount of personal judgement was involved in the construction of the series, but in the absence of better data this was inevitable.

The other major problem with the data is that it was first published in 1962, and the data for aggregate installations in years prior to 1961 does not include machines taken out of service prior to 1962. (The industry data is not affected as that only starts in 1962.) Thus in the construction of the quantity series the data is adjusted by estimating depreciation rates – fortunately the necessary corrections are not large. The question was whether to use the adjusted or unadjusted data for the construction of the price series. It was decided to use the unadjusted data because the adjustment method makes assumptions about market shares which it did not seem desirable to impose on the series, and it was also felt that although no adjustment may lead to errors so could the adjustment method. Series are presented below, however, that show that the effects of adjustment are only minor. The actual adjustment method is explained in chapter 7.

3.9 THE PRICE SERIES

The price series is intended to show how the price of a computer of constant quality has changed over time. We construct for each year, i, $\left(\sum_r p_r w_{ir}\right) / \left(\sum_r \hat{p}_r w_{ir}\right)$, over all models r, where $\hat{p}_r$ is the predicted price of that machine, as if it were to have been introduced in 1963, i.e. the quality multiple, and w_{ir} is the weight to be applied to that machine in year i for the construction of the index. The problem is that we wish to estimate an index of the price facing a buyer in any given year. An estimate of this is an index of the price that buyers are actually paying, i.e. the price of the machines actually installed. This means that the index must weight machine prices by market shares to reflect adequately the price being paid for machines. From the work of other researchers (e.g. Chow [1967]) it was expected to find a series that decreased monotonically over time. However, the results do not support this expectation for although all the weighting schemes tried were different from each other not one of them exhibited this behaviour. This, however, is not the result of any of the weighting systems used, for there are alternative ways to get at the price series and the same result is evident, viz:

(a) To look at the intercepts of the annual price/characteristics regressions – these do not decrease uniformly over time.

(b) To run a regression between price and characteristics over the whole sample and to use the time coefficients as indicating the price series. In the cases where this was tried (the results are not presented) the coefficients on the time dummies did not decrease continually and were often insignificant. Moreover, as was shown above, the F test implied that aggregation across this time scale was not acceptable.

(c) To look at the regressions of predicted price on actual price that were discussed above. Once again the expected behaviour was not evident.

Thus one must turn to the different price series that have been constructed and argue for the choice of one relative to the others. In total, thirteen different weighting systems were used. Some it is argued are theoretically better than others – but they are all based on different concepts of the market and different weighting systems within the market. In each case the index is adjusted to 100 in 1963. Thus all series are directly compatible. It was not felt necessary to list them all but three are presented later. The series fall into five groups.

(a) Machines are only given a non-zero weight in the year of their first installation when the weight is unity. The series indicates falling prices from 1960 to 1969 but fluctuates in the 1954–60 period and rises sharply in 1970. The series is unsuitable since it only includes machines in the first year of their life whereas they are on sale for about four years. Also the weighting means that all machines considered are weighted equally. It is therefore equivalent to a non-weighted index and unsuitable.

(b) Two other series were constructed to allow for the longer current life of machines by giving machines a weight of unity (i) if there are any still in use in the given year or (ii) if there are any in use or on order in that year, and a zero weight elsewhere. This goes some way to correcting the criticism of (a) but does not give bigger weights to machines with bigger market shares. However, the second version is listed below for comparison purposes.

(c) Two more series were constructed using the number of machines (i) installed, (ii) installed or on order, as weights, so defining the market over the whole computer stock and not just the margin of current machines. Although these series have a better weighting system it is felt that the definition of the market is not relevant for present purposes.

(d) As it is desired to define the series over prices that face a buyer at a point in time the series ought to be constructed over current models only. Current was defined in four different ways depending on whether there was in the period under discussion: (i) an increase or (ii) no decrease, in the number of that type of machine (1) installed or (2) installed and on order. The four different combinations define whether the machine has a positive or a zero weight. If the weight is to be non-zero it is either the number installed or the number installed and on order depending on the series. The main criticism of these series is that machines just introduced are given a small weight relative to those that have existed for some time, for the older ones have had the time to build up a number of installations. The two series that include orders correct this to some extent. The series including orders and defining current by no decrease, is presented below.

(e) Finally four more series were constructed where the weights were: (i) the change in the number installed or (ii) the change in the number installed and on order, and in which either (1) negatives are set to zero or (2) negatives are left in. To give machines a negative weight seems to make little sense, and it appears better to include orders. The relevant series is presented below. This is in fact the series that appears to be theoretically nearest to indicating the price facing a buyer at any moment of time, i.e. with weights of the change in the number installed and on order if it is greater than 0, but 0 elsewhere.

Table 3.2. *Price series*

	(b)	(d)	(e)	(d_2)	(e_2)
1954	115.220	160.846	163.219	160.846	163.219
1955	140.311	184.381	205.669	195.757	206.049
1956	154.708	192.647	200.993	192.796	201.501
1957	127.673	177.485	173.639	173.358	173.418
1958	124.504	185.251	196.444	187.925	197.150
1959	108.437	175.530	162.085	176.458	159.915
1960	117.395	130.758	94.631	125.943	91.045
1961	118.788	117.158	103.143	108.046	102.256
1962	106.234	98.760	97.084	98.760	97.084
1963	100.000	100.000	100.000	100.000	100.000
1964	80.845	79.148	64.714	79.148	64.714
1965	64.693	66.049	48.915	66.049	48.915
1966	60.277	47.867	40.346	47.867	40.346
1967	56.496	41.925	40.922	41.925	40.922
1968	55.315	49.481	55.321	49.481	55.321
1969	51.732	48.522	51.064	48.522	51.064
1970	54.769	47.882	47.096	47.882	47.096

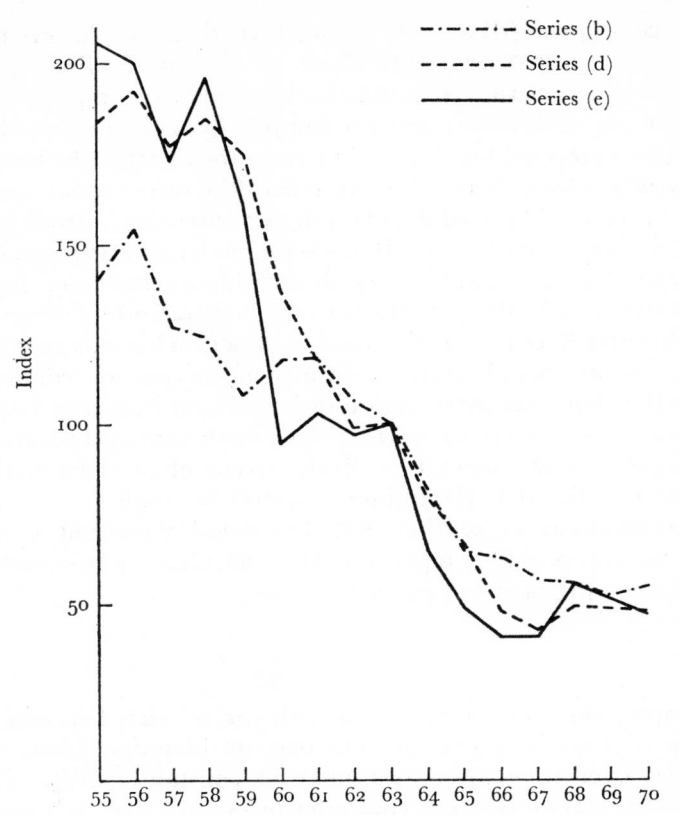

Fig. 3.1. Price series.

In all these calculations the aggregate data was used, where applicable also using aggregate orders for the period 1963–70 (the period for
which data was available).

The three series labelled (b), (d) and (e),† corresponding to the
group from which they come, are shown in table 3.2. Series (d_2) and
(e_2) are the series (d) and (e) when corrections are made to the data to
cover machines taken out of service prior to 1961. In fig. 3.1 we graph
series (b), (d) and (e).

A choice must be made between the three series presented. Series (b)
is rejected since it is a theoretically bad construction; however, its
interest is in the low starting price in 1954, and thus its underestimation
of the price decrease over time.

---

† In the construction of series types (d) and (e) it was assumed that no machines were installed
  in 1953. If one thus wishes the 1954 value may be ignored.

The choice between (d) and (e) is one of whether the relevant market is over present year new installations or the total of all current machines installed. Series (e) tends to have greater amplitude than series (d), for (d) in its construction is damped by the machines already installed. This damping, however, will reduce the effect of the introduction of a new machine. Series (d) will reflect the introduction quickly; however, if a machine is found to be inferior only after introduction it will affect (d) more than (e). It is felt that series (e) is closest to representing the price variable that we want, so we will carry this over into later chapters.

Two points can be made about the general shape of both of these series:

(1) Both series fluctuate in the 1954–8 period. This can possibly be attributed to the switch from scientific prototypes to commercial machines. It is felt that there may also be a small influence from the manipulations necessary to correct for inadequate characteristics data. However, as the machines affected were often those with few installations it is felt that the influence would be small.

(2) The modulations of the 1967–70 period were not expected although they can probably be explained by devaluation because of the international nature of the computer industry.

3.10 Conclusion

In this chapter the concern has been with the relation between computer price and quality. The aim has been to investigate how prices have moved over time for a computer of constant quality, and to investigate the relation between computer price and 'size' at a moment in time. A quality multiple has been constructed for each computer, and this is to be used in chapter 7. Moreover certain results have been presented that are to be used immediately below.

As an attempt to solve an old problem, i.e. the correction of series for quality change, this exercise has been quite successful. This is probably due mainly to the nature of the computer – it being a good the performance of which can quite simply be reduced to certain basic characteristics, although the lack of software performance measures is not encouraging. In comparison to the other main application of this exercise to computers (i.e. the work of Chow on US data), the main differences centre around the nature of the calculated price series, which Chow estimates as falling continuously over time whereas that calculated here does not do so. This study does, however, agree with his result that up to the end of the second generation the relative importance of different characteristics does not change, but by extending into the third generation we have shown that this conclusion will not hold for a longer time period.

4. THE TECHNOLOGY OF COMPUTER PRODUCTION AND USE

4.1 INTRODUCTION

It is now possible to proceed with the main body of our study by building upon the foundation of the previous two chapters. In this chapter economic aspects of the technology of computer production and use are studied. The study is mainly concerned with whether it is justified to represent computer technology by fixed coefficient, constant return to scale activities. In this context these questions can be answered either by looking at the input coefficients in computer using or producing activities, or by seeing how costs of computer production and use vary across applications and scale.

Definitions of scale returns and fixed coefficients have already been provided, but before proceeding there are two matters to be clarified. First, it will be shown in the next chapter that the computer activities have changed considerably over time due to the influence of technological progress; thus in the study of fixed coefficients and scale returns the aim is to detect any systematic patterns across all these activities that reflect on the two major questions.

Second, in the previous chapter the multitude of different models on sale at a moment in time was reflected in the size of the data base; thus, if it is going to be feasible to analyse the characteristics of activities a decision must be made on whether product differentiation reflects the running of different activities or the running of the same activity at a different level. It is considered here as a variation in level not activity. This would mean for example that the construction of a model of size x is considered as running the production activity at a level twice that when a model of size $\frac{1}{2}x$ is produced. However, running an activity at a level to produce two models of size $\frac{1}{2}x$ is also to be considered as running the activity producing a model size $\frac{1}{2}x$ at twice the level. As there need be no reason for the activity to have the same characteristics in both comparisons, the level has to be defined in terms of both number and quality dimensions and both must be studied separately.

The quality dimension has to reflect 'power' or 'size'. In the previous chapter the whole exercise was to isolate characteristics to reflect quality; those characteristics can thus be used in this chapter to reflect the quality dimension. The outcome of the decision to treat model differentiation in this way is to view any differences in input coefficients between the activities representing the production and use of different computer models (that cannot be attributed to technological change and scale) as reflecting non-fixed coefficients rather than different activities. However, as no such differences are in fact isolated the decision is not too crucial.

This chapter continues with a discussion of the production of computers and then the use of computers is investigated. The conclusions are drawn in the fourth section.

4.2   System manufacture

In this context the manufacture of computer systems is defined as the development and construction of hardware and bundled software. Installation costs, except in so far as they are included in computer prices, are considered to be part of the users' inputs. The data available for the study is sparse, but sufficient is available for some conclusions to be drawn.

The subject is approached in the following manner; the computer manufacture process is split into research and development, software production, hardware assembly and then other functions; each element in the total process is discussed separately and then implications are drawn.

The size of the R & D expenditure in the industry is enormous. At present IBM spends about $500m p.a. on R & D, but this represents more than its next seven rivals put together (SCST [1971a] paras. 67, 71, p. xxi). ICL spends about 12% of turnover on R & D (SCST [1971b] para. 873, p. 157). IBM spent in the region of $5,000m, including marketing and leasing capital, on the development of the 360 series, and even then there were teething troubles. These sums tend to include not only the companies' expenditure on hardware development but also on software development.

The research and development process is labour intensive, although computers have been used in the design of computers. The staff involved tends to be highly qualified. This high degree of labour intensity obviates the need to trace through the construction of the machine input. However, despite the labour intensity, computer development is very intensive in capital in terms of invested labour. The time required to develop a new range of machines is about four years. This can be illustrated with reference to ICL. In October 1974, ICL launched their

New Range, and had in June 1973 announced the 2903, assumed to be the smallest machine in this New Range. At the conception of ICL in 1968 one of their objectives was to develop a unified product line to replace the mixture inherited from past takeovers. This new product line was labelled Project 51, but prior to 1970 this was replaced by a new objective, Project 52, now labelled New Range. A development period of four years would thus seem to be implied. The pattern of expenditure over this period is difficult to estimate. On the setting up of ICL the government made available £13½m for R & D distributed over the years 1969–72 by annual payments of £4m, £4m, £3¼m and £2¼m (SCST [1971b] p. 330), but these represent only a quarter of ICLs R & D expenditure† so the time profile need not reflect the expenditure profile. For reasons of software development one can deduce that the major expenditure would be in later years. This conclusion is further supported by the existence of production lags that imply that substantial investment has to be made in building for stock before a machine is launched.

The process of software production is very similar to hardware development being both labour intensive and time intensive. The development time for the software for a new range can be estimated at about three years. This figure is achieved by considering that in the spring of 1971 ICL were advertising for software staff to work on Project 52, and it was launched late in 1974. No figures are available on the relative costs of hardware development and software development – about equal would seem reasonable.

Turning to hardware assembly, it is obvious that production methods must to a greater or lesser degree depend on the nature of the components to be assembled. The components used in computer hardware have proceeded through four stages that also identify the generations of computer hardware:

first generation – use of vacuum tubes
second generation – the use of transistors
third generation – the use of integrated circuits
fourth generation – the use of large scale integration (sometimes labelled the 3½th generation).

Fortunately these different inputs can all be labelled electronic components. From the Census of Production for 1968,‡ one can discover the other inputs. The relevant data is presented in table 4.1.

---

† For the 1971 financial year this was £18m, see SCST [1971b] para. 4, p. 147. The total R & D expenditure on the New Range is estimated at £160m, including launching finance, for the period 1971–8 (CW [1973d]).
‡ The industry is covered by Minimum List Heading 366, (1968 SIC).

Table 4.1. *Purchases by larger establishments in the computer industry (current prices)*

Inputs	1963		1968	
	Value £1000	% of sales	Value £1000	% of sales
Steel	98	0.2	461	0.3
Light metals	55	0.1	316	0.2
Solder	9	0.02	18	0.01
Insulated wires	172	0.4	1,045	1.3
Insulation	7	0.02	31	0.02
Bolts and rivets			312	0.2
Electrical machinery	224	0.5	2,647	2.2
Electrical components	4,277	10.2	35,382	29.6
Other components	2,573	6.1	6,905	5.8
Other materials	668	1.5	4,134	3.7
Packaging	113	0.2	151	0.1
Fuel	214	0.5	669	0.5
Total	8,412	20.1	52,069	43.6
Sales	41,834		119,246	

The main reason for presenting this table is to illustrate two points: that components, especially electrical components, constitute the major part of the industry's purchases; and that the proportion of sales spent on these components increased from 16% to 35% in the five year period between 1963 and 1968. Both facts can be explained by a simple presentation of the computer assembling function.[†]

For the first and second generations the computer manufacturers' activity consisted of the purchase of loose components in the form of condensers, resistors, transistors or valves, etc., and assembling them on to printed circuit boards of their own design and manufacture. The present technology (third and fourth), involves the manufacturer in purchasing integrated semiconductor elements which contain a multiplicity of components in the one chip of silicon. They will also purchase from a specialist manufacturer the thin film supporting matrix on which they assemble the integrated circuits to form the operating units. However, as large scale integration (LSI) proceeds, more circuits are on the silicon chip, such that the manufacturer can purchase a 'functional piece' capable of performing a logical function, rather than a collection of components. Thus the proportions of value added in the production process have varied between component supplier and hardware manufacturer as the technology has developed. Moreover it has always been the tendency for the mainframe companies to buy

† The source for this information is SCST [1970a] pp .367–9.

in the high speed core stores as well as many other sub-assemblies. For example Plessey's supply to the manufacturers: 'capacitors, resistors, connectors, transformers and chokes, printed circuit boards, switches, a wide range of mechanical components and the sheet metal cabinets in which central processors, peripherals, control consoles and the link are housed' (SCST [1971a] p. 289). The Census of Production figures thus reflect the changing nature of the computer manufacturers' role. The size of the assembling function is large though – the total construction time for a machine was and still is about eighteen months.

During the development of the industry the construction methods have not changed significantly until recently. The process was labour intensive, and apart from hand tools, machines only entered as test rigs at the testing stage. Freeman [1965] estimates that in 1965 fixed assets per employee were amongst the lowest in the country, and some British firms estimated a figure of only £500 for the value of fixed assets per employee; the average was probably less than £1,000. The typical installation consisted of a work bench, test gear and inspection machines.

In 1971 ICL received the Queen's Award to Industry for Innovation, and *The Times* report of 21 April states that the 'award is for the company's automated system for designing and producing the 1906A. The computer is so complex that it was designed and is now being substantially produced by computers. The automated scheme was devised and is now being implemented by some 3,000 ICL workers.' This suggests that production methods are changing towards a more machine intensive system.

Because the mainframe manufacturers buy in the majority of their components it is necessary to investigate components manufacture. In their evidence to the Select Committee, Plessey give indications of the nature of the production processes of some of the components that they supply. With reference to ferrite core stores:

Production begins with low grade basic material, the processing of the materials into ferrite powders of appropriate physical and magnetic characteristics and the conversion of the powders into ferrite cores – tiny beads made to exact specifications...
In the production of core planes the main requirement is an adequate supply of labour ...for the weaving of core planes. The description of the process of manufacture of ferrite core planes will have shown that a main requirement is an adequate supply of labour. (SCST [1970a] pp. 290, 294, 295; my ordering.)

By contrast, manufacture of the technically advanced plated wire stores and semiconductor stores now influencing the market require substantial capital investment ...(They) are susceptible to mechanised production processes. The production of integrated circuits in large numbers will secure substantial economies in cost, which, when semiconductor stores are themselves produced in large quantities will be reflected in the prices of semiconductor stores. (SCST [1970a] pp. 290, 295; my ordering.)

This evidence seems to indicate that the production of third generation store is, and has been, a labour intensive process. As technology goes forward the indications are that LSI will encourage greater machine intensity. To carry the investigation into the nature of the production of these machines, although from a capital theoretic viewpoint necessary, is not practicable.

One can also read into Plessey's statements indications of falling price with increasing output of fourth generation components. This could be the result of either machine indivisibilities or increasing returns to scale (assuming cost-plus pricing). In the production of ferrite core stores, however, there are hints that the average cost curve has an upturn after a certain optimal size of store, 'the large store may only be cost effective if we are able to do it with integrated circuits' (SCST [1970a] para. 1620, p. 310). Sharpe [1969] (pp. 374–80) finds that in the production of computer memories there is a certain amount of evidence that would lead one to believe that cost per bit of store is inversely related to memory size and cycle time.

However, there are unfortunately fewer indications of the production processes of the other components. Two sources indicate that certain semiconductors are manufactured by automated processes, and that the manufacture of most electronic components involves a very low ratio of fixed assets per employee (OECD [1968]; Freeman [1965]). For the mechanical components we have no details.

Although the evidence is scarce certain conclusions about component manufacture can be drawn. Computer manufacturers have been buying labour intensive components from their suppliers, these components being produced by a process probably exhibiting increasing returns to scale. However, the production of memory is such that above a certain optimum size and cycle time, cost increases faster than performance. The future holds prospects of increasing returns to scale in the production of LSI components, which will also be more machine intensive, and an increase in the size and a fall in the cycle time of memories at which decreasing performance per unit of cost set in.

The three elements discussed above (hardware and software development and assembly) constitute the major roles of the computer industry, but as with all firms the industry has to incur expenditure on management, administration and marketing. These are fields that tend once again to be labour intensive, although increasing use is being made of business machines – especially computers.

The first conclusion that can be drawn about computer production is that the industry is labour intensive at all stages. To quote from Freeman, 'It seems that in the typical European firm salaries, wages and fringe benefits account for 30–40% of gross output, and in

American firms for a higher proportion (45–50%). In electronic components, payroll costs represented 43% of the total value of all shipments in 1962.' (Freeman [1965].) However, it ought to be stressed that production is also time intensive, for it can take four to five years from the start of R & D to the first installation of a new machine.

With this detail on the production processes it is possible to start the discussion of fixed coefficients and scale returns in computer production. In the investigation no evidence was found to suggest that there are any systematic differences in production methods either between computers or manufacturers that were not the result of technical change or scale economies. From this negative standpoint there would thus seem to be only one activity in use and that activity shows fixed coefficients. A very rough test of this was undertaken by investigating the data available on delivery times. No significant patterns were found, suggesting that each manufacturer has a similar time intensity of production and thus by imputation similar coefficients.

Turning to scale returns, the existence of constant returns to scale would be implied if the coefficients of an activity did not vary as the level varied at which that activity was run. The level at which an activity is run has been defined in two dimensions, the production of more computers and the production of bigger computers. This can be aggregated into the production of more computing power, but there is no reason to believe that the same level of scale economies exists in both directions. To produce ten machines of a given size may cost £x, but to produce one machine ten times the size of the other might not cost £x.

The construction of a number of machines of one type is considered first. To build any number of machines of a specific type there is only a need to perform the R & D and software development once. This represents a fixed expenditure that can be spread over all machines produced and thus the charge on each machine would reduce as the production run increased. The fact that the production process is not very machine intensive does not allow much scope for any other fixed cost scale economies, but it has been shown that there are economies of scale in the production of components thus generating another reason for believing that unit costs fall as the production run increases. To this one can add that in a scientifically based, labour intensive industry one would expect to find 'learning by doing' influences. Although they have not been isolated it is felt that they will contribute to the general picture of increasing returns to scale.

These are exactly the conclusions that Pratten [1971] reached in his study. He quantifies scale returns by stating that average costs for a run of 500 units would be 8% above average costs for a run of 1,000 units. He also specifies 100% of the British market as needed for a manufacturer to generate a sale of 1,000 units. Honeywell consider that 10 % of the world market is necessary for long run profitability (SCST [1970a] para. 93, p. xxvi).

These economies of scale are the result largely of fixed costs incurred in the development of machines. In terms of the framework in chapter 1 there is no role to be played by research, all technology falls like manna from above. However, even if we disregard such fixed-cost-generated scale economies there is still something to be gained from components production and learning by doing, indicating that such economies are also available in such a framework. It may well be that such economies of scale could explain the information in the following exchange:

If I buy a computer today, what percentage of the selling price is represented by the components we are talking about? (Mr. John Clark) The computer itself is about fifty per cent. – (Mr. Hudson) Well I think I would be guessing. It depends on the supplier. In the case of IBM computers its manufacturing cost to selling price is a factor of five to one, so that the total manufacturing cost is only 20% of the selling price anyway. Therefore the component content of that, if it were 25% of that, then on the selling price it comes down to a very small figure. In the case of ICL where unfortunately our margin is not quite so high, it is a significant figure.
Like what? – I should have thought 15% or something of that nature. (SCST [1970a] para. 1669, p. 316.)

That is, whereas IBM who manufacture most of their own components and work on by far the largest scale can cover component costs with 4 % of selling price, ICL can only cover with about 15 %. (Any conflict between these proportions and the Census of Production data can probably be explained by the definitions of components in each case.)

In the analysis of the production of bigger computers one can take two approaches, one depending on a comparison of prices the other on the direct approach. The direct approach is to argue that R & D expenditure would probably not increase in proportion to size, for in essence the development of a small machine would only be slightly different to the development of a large machine; that to produce an equivalent amount of software probably costs only a little less for the small machine than for the large machine; Sharpe's evidence quoted above suggests that costs do not increase proportionately with store size. These comments all indicate that there should be scale returns in the production of bigger machines. However, there is also some conflicting evidence that there is a limit to the size at which costs per unit of computing power fall, e.g. a quote below from ICL shows that they consider that a stage of decreasing returns can be reached.

For various reasons this downturn is not reflected in the approach based on the analysis of price data. The basis of this approach is that computer size can be measured by characteristics representing speed, power, memory size, etc., and that cost of construction can be represented by price. The relationship between cost and size reflects scale returns. A number of studies of this type have been performed.† The original statement of the relationship is known as Grosch's Law,‡ which states that the cost of a machine increases proportionately to the square root of its performance.

To test this proposition it is possible to use the results of the analysis of the previous chapter. Using the terminology of that chapter, the following relationship was fitted cross sectionally for each year, covering machines introduced in that year:

$$P_r = a_0 + a_1 C_r + a_2 F_r + a_3 S_r + u_r.$$

If the sum of the absolute values of the a_j ($j = 1,..., 3$) is greater than unity then decreasing returns to scale are indicated. A sum equal to unity represents constant returns to scale.

If it is assumed that in a given year all machines introduced use the same technology then, given the other assumptions, differences in price must reflect scale economies. Thus if the sums of the coefficients are studied for each year for which results are available those coefficients must reflect scale economies. In table 4.2 the sum of the coefficients for a number of years are presented, where the coefficients are taken from the equations in the previous chapter containing only significant variables (if the variable is not significant its coefficient is not significantly different from zero).

Table 4.2. *Scale returns 1954–70*

Year	Sum of the absolute values of coefficients	Year	Sum of the absolute values of coefficients
pre-1960	0.82	1967	1.15
1961	0.77	1968	1.19
1962	0.86	1969	1.04
1963	0.95	1970	0.94
1964	1.29	1961–4	0.86
1965	0.77	1954–64	0.84
1966	0.73		

† For example, Knight [1966] and studies by Early, Barro & Margolis; J. M. Patrick; N. Jacob and H. Solomon, all reported with another application by Sharpe in Sharpe [1969]. These studies have all used the price characteristics approach, except that of Knight, in which he tries to approach a concept for computing power more directly. His most important conclusion is that increasing returns to scale exist in that performance increases faster than monthly rental, but only up to a certain size of machine. He finds that the IBM STRETCH for example had reached the point of decreasing returns to scale. All these studies refer to US data, whereas ours refers to UK data, but they are all still open to the criticisms levelled against this approach below, i.e. there is no reason to believe that such comparisons of prices reflect comparisons of costs for given output levels.
‡ Dr H. Grosch never published his Law; it is just the name given to the relationship.

The pattern revealed by these results is one of increasing returns to scale prior to 1967 (except for 1964) and decreasing returns for the period 1967–9. However, if we consider the years with only one significant variable (pre-1960, 1961, 1964 and 1970) it is found that only the pre-1960 figure is significantly different from unity, i.e. not within two standard errors of unity. This tends to indicate that the scale returns could be the result of random error rather than a systematic pattern.

An interesting by-product of this analysis was that when the price/characteristics regressions were fitted attempts were made to identify systematic patterns that would reflect higher costs for one manufacturer rather than another. This was done by attempting to introduce dummy variables for each manufacturer in the regressions. No significant dummies were found. If it is assumed that all companies have similar pricing policies and similar costs then fixed coefficients could be implied. Unfortunately the evidence to support these assumptions is very poor.

If the result is accepted, however, what criticisms can be made of these assumptions and, because they are largely the same, of the whole approach of this study of technology through prices? There are two minor objections, first that diseconomies of scale may exist but have not been detected because machines are not built in the area of decreasing returns† – two machines of half the size being more economical. For example ICL say that 'the overheads involved in the pure management of the system...in the super large machine...become very critical and too large' (SCST [1971b] para. 897, p. 162). Second, the measures we have used to measure system size, it has already been stated, are hardware orientated and may not adequately reflect software aspects of system construction.

The major criticism, however, reflects on the assumption that price is proportional to cost across computers of different size and manufacturer. To explain this criticism we must investigate manufacturers' pricing policy. First, it is necessary to discover whether machines produced in the UK differ in price from those manufactured abroad. About 40% of the UK market is supplied from abroad, mainly the United States and Western Europe (see table 2.3 for manufacturer's domicile, although some manufacture is carried on in countries where the manufacturer is not domiciled, especially with IBM). However, a dummy introduced into the price/characteristics regressions indicating that a machine was manufactured by a UK company was not significant at the 95% level. This tends to indicate that the prices on the market do not differ according to country

† See the comments on the work of K. E. Knight in footnote † on p. 53.

of manufacture. The reasons for this are reflected in the following quote.

The pricing policy in our industry we believe is mostly determined by our customers and competitors. We think they are the people who make the most important decisions. The pricing policies here in Britain are decided by our company in Britain after discussion with our various companies throughout the world, and in the light of the computer position that exists in this country and our ability to make profits. (SCST [1970a] para. 544, p. 94.)

IBM say, however, that,

We believe one of the essential elements of this function must be the development oı an international pricing policy, taking into account, on the one hand the limitations set by the tense competition and on the other hand, the return on investment necessary for the continuously rising need to finance future research, development, production and marketing. It is our belief that in such a world market there can only be one basic price structure. (SCST [1970a] p. 67.)

IBM have the power to impose a price structure in this way because of their 60 % share of the world market. However, the fact that they have one price structure, expressed in dollars (which does not affect our results as the exchange rate was fixed for most of the period under consideration), and that they manufacture in several different countries means that their prices in the UK would not reflect UK costs unless they were the same as elsewhere. As wage rates alone differ considerably internationally, IBM prices do not reflect UK costs. But IBM prices do not differ from those of other manufacturers, so the prices of other manufacturers do not reflect UK costs. Therefore in general there is no connection between UK prices and costs.

Even if this is the case, is there still any systematic relationship between the price of a machine and its construction cost as that machine increases in size?

The world's computer companies have all had difficulty with large computer systems either with achieving satisfactory performance or sales. In France, Machines Bull was driven towards bankruptcy by their Gamma 60; General Electric in the US had trouble with the GE 600 model (Rose [1969] pp. 216–17); Ferranti developed ATLAS, which was technically advanced but never sold in any quantity. In each case revenues never covered costs. IBM built the 360/90, a very large machine, to supply an unprofitable but influential section of the US market. A 1968 financial review indicated that the eighteen models constructed would cost $172m but produce a revenue of only $57.9m. However, two smaller models in the 360 range, the 50 and 30 generated a surplus of 39 % and 33 % on sales, according to a 1970 financial review.† Thus the cost of increased size would not be reflected in price.

† *Sunday Times* [1973], a report on the evidence accumulated by CDC to support their anti-trust suit against IBM.

The result of this discussion is that the prices of machines do not reflect UK costs but the pattern imposed by IBM seems to reign. This pattern, we have also shown, has tended to price large machines below their construction cost but allows smaller machines to generate large surpluses. The connection between price and cost is thus broken.

There is one further point to be made that can be used to counteract this argument. It has been shown that there are economies of scale in the production of models of the same type. This would suggest that a comparison of scale returns across machines of different size would have to involve the same number of machines of each type being produced. The nature of the computer market is such that this is not so. Very large machines are uncommon and medium sized machines more common. The advantages of scale economy available to a company that has the same share of the medium as the large machine market are thus much greater for medium machines. Thus their price can be lower or the profits greater. The fact that IBM make more profit per unit in the medium machine market as opposed to the large machine market may thus be the influence of a comparison based on different output levels for each sector.

Taking these four arguments together, the attempts to reach some understanding of costs through looking at prices seems doomed to failure. One must thus rely on the implications of direct observation discussed above. These observations lead to two conclusions: there is no evidence to contradict an assumption of fixed coefficients, once scale returns and technological change are removed from observations; direct observation indicates that increasing returns to scale are expected in the production of both more computers and bigger computers (although decreasing returns may set in with very large machines).

The results with respect to scale returns are important for many of the arguments below, but at this stage there is just one point to be made. It has been shown that there are not any specific relationships between computer price and UK construction costs, but prices tend to fit a pattern based on IBM conceptions of international costs and price structure. It has also been shown that there are increasing returns to scale. This means that a small company without the scale benefits will be at a distinct disadvantage, but if it produces in a low wage environment (the process of production has been shown to be very labour intensive) it can still compete with other producers. The ability of ICL to survive in competition with the American producers may be at least in part due to the wage differential.

Before proceeding to the study of computer use it is necessary to consider whether the criticism of the computer cost/characteristics approach affects the basis of the price and quantity series constructed on the base of the price/characteristics relationships. Fortunately the approach taken to the problem of quality adjustment is concerned only with what faces the customer, not the costs facing the producer. The above criticism reflects only on costs, not prices.

4.3   COMPUTER USE

A study of computer use is a study of the computer input into those activities producing any commodity or commodities with the aid of these machines. To investigate the use of computers it is necessary to know what it is that they produce that the firm requires. To discover what is the product of computer systems, the first objective is to find the areas in which, and the tasks for which, computers are used. Two surveys are of use here, one conducted in 1965 by the Ministry of Labour [1965], updated in 1972 with 1969 data (D of E [1972]),† the other by Miles Roman Ltd in 1971.‡ The 1965 survey covered 388 installations and the pattern of computer usage was found as in table 4.3. Included in this table are the figures for the percentages of installations using their computers for the specific tasks in 1969 compared to 1965. The second survey had a wider coverage but unfortunately only a 9 % response rate. The pattern of use as shown in their replies is presented in table 4.4. Given this wide spread of uses,§ all one can say is that the computer generates 'computing power', a rather vague generalised concept. To put it another way, the machines provide the firm with information processing services.

Table 4.3. *Computer applications* (1)

Tasks	1965		1969
	No. of applications	%	%
Payroll	227	59	69
Management accounting and statistics	208	54	81
Stock control	157	40	64
Financial accounting	157	40	82
Invoicing and billing	140	36	67
General statistics	107	28	60
Production control	75	19	32
Miscellaneous	46	12	45

† I wish to thank the Department of Employment for making a pre-publication copy available to me.
‡ NCC [1972]. I wish to thank Lord Shackleton for making preliminary results of the survey available to me prior to publication through Miles Roman Ltd.
§ Further details of the pattern of computer usage are presented throughout the book, with the most complete coverage in chapter 8, where non-office uses are also discussed.

Table 4.4. *Computer applications* (2)

Tasks	No. of applications
Payments/remittances/nominal ledger	234
Payroll	229
Sales order/invoicing/statements	195
Management information	191
Financial statistics	187
Inventory/stock control	179
Sales/marketing statistics	169
Statistical analysis	160
Profit and loss account/cost ledger	136
Operating/production statistics	97
Billing (banks and insurance)	85
Production control/planning scheduling	80
Engineering design calculations	78
Network analysis	66
Operational research/linear programming	59

In each case the machine is processing information in order to generate more useful information. There is in fact no reason why the same process should not be carried out by hand or with the assistance of accounting machines. The common denominator of the different methods, no matter what the task, is that information processing ability is required, and the measure of that ability is computing power. This, however, implies that computing power has multidimensional aspects: speed, accuracy and capacity.

However, computing power in itself can only have derived value. That value arises from the value of better information which is the result of the application of computing power. The work on the value of information, however, has not yielded very applicable results. Theil [1967]† gives a good example of existing theory; if some event E will occur with probability x, $0 \leqslant x \leqslant 1$, what is the value of a definite and reliable message that states that E has actually occurred? If $x = 0.99$, then the event is very likely to occur, so the message has little information content. Conversely if $x = 0.01$, the information content of the message is high. Theil suggests that the information content, $h(x)$, of the message is generally agreed to take the form

$$h(x) = \log(1/x) = -\log x \quad \text{measured in bits for log base 2,}$$
$$\text{nits for log base } e.$$

The precision involved in this method is in fact more than is required here and it is best to summarise by saying that the information content

† See also Frielink [1965] pp. 48 ff, and McDonough [1963].

of a definitive message is inversely related to the surprise that the message involves.

However, all this is stated for a *definitive* message in a timeless atmosphere. The value of any message depends not only on its information content, but also on the accuracy of that information and on the time at which that information is available. The value is then the gain (or loss) that the presence of the information allows. If there is no amount to be gained then the information is valueless.

To summarise, computers produce computing power, whose use generates information. The value of that information depends on its surprise content, accuracy, relevancy, and speed of provision. Computers derive their value in use from their ability to produce computing power directly, and indirectly from the value of better information.

A practical measure of the computing power of a specific machine is the quality index constructed in the previous chapter. This index is a weighted sum of a machine's speed and power (or size) and as such has the dimensions required of a computing power measure.

The task once again is to look for indicators of fixed coefficients and scale returns. In this case the problem with scale returns is that by looking at the input of computers, or computing power, there are two possible effects; first, that as the output from an activity increases there may be scale economies in information – i.e. the amount of information required may not increase proportionately with output; secondly, there may be economies in inputs of computers or computing power in the production of information. These can only be separated in certain cases; however, as the desired result refers to how computer input varies as output varies, the reasons for the variation are not too important.

It is possible in this case to illustrate that fixed coefficients is not really applicable. There are examples which illustrate that the machine input for a specific activity can vary slightly because current labour can replace it, e.g. computer operators can be replaced by better operating software, and programmers can be replaced by the use of high level rather than low level languages.

Also data preparation staff can be replaced by optical and magnetic character readers, and some software can be replaced by hardware, e.g. the floating point arithmetic function.

The differences that are apparent across different applications of computers do not appear to justify saying that each ought to be considered a separate activity, or else there would be an infinite number of activities. The differences must thus reflect variable coefficients. However, these variations do not appear to be so large that a theoretical assumption of fixed coefficients would be too misleading.

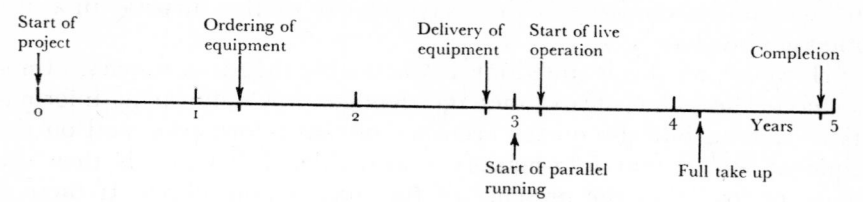

Fig. 4.1. Computer installation time profile. (SOURCE: M of L [1965].)

Turn now to scale returns. To discuss this question it is useful to first have a time profile of the life of a computer system. In fig. 4.1 the time profile of installing a computer system is presented.† This profile is based on 1964 data and illustrates that the average installation period was 59 months. The 1969 data suggests that this period had been reduced to 39 months, on average, but varied from 33 to 69 months between small and large machines. To complete the time profile some information is required on the life expectancy of a computer system. The *Computer Survey* data‡ is useful here. This data includes the vintage pattern of computer installations. Thus, for example, for machines installed in year t there is data on the numbers remaining in years $t+i$ for $i = 1, \ldots, 7$. It is this data that we use for filling the gaps in the quantity series where machines were taken out of service prior to 1961. The data shows that after seven years between 25 % and 30 % of all installations remain, and after three years 75 % remain. Half of all machines have disappeared by the fifth or sixth year of their life. The indications are that nearly all machines would have been scrapped by the tenth year.

It is useful to split our study of computer use into three stages, investigation, the provision of hardware and bundled software, and operation.§ Each stage is covered separately, to see how the inputs required to maintain computerisation, i.e. the input of both machines and current labour, vary with output.

Stage 1: Investigation

This stage took an average of 34 months in the 1964 figures but only 23 months in 1969 (M of L [1965]; D of E [1972]), although equipment would be ordered after about one year. The stage includes management education and the evaluation of hard and software as well as the taking of the computerisation decision. Not a great deal is known about this

---

† This figure is taken from M of L [1965] and the 1969 data derives from D of E [1972] Appendix 13.   ‡ The data is discussed in chapter 7.
§ For a more detailed breakdown see NCC [1971a] volume 1.

area, although in chapter 6 the same problems are studied under the heading of search and evaluation procedures. There are indications that the bigger the final installation the longer this process takes (D of E [1972] appendix 13). However, as no evidence has been found to show what level of resources is devoted at this stage there is little that can be said.

Stage 2: The provision of hardware and bundled software

Table 4.5 presents data from *Computers in Offices*, 1972, appendix 7, on the relation between the size of the user organisation and the size of the computer installation. In these figures the definition of size is related to the cost of the installation, as follows: large – over £500,000; medium – £100,000–500,000; small – £20,000–100,000. If one values

Table 4.5. *Firm size and computer usage*

No. of employees	Number of installations by computer size			All installations
	Large	Medium	Small	
Less than 1,000	1	109	352	462
1,000–3,000	4	177	248	429
3,000–6,000	14	134	113	261
6,000–10,000	23	100	57	180
10,000 plus	83	270	68	421

Table 4.6. *Average cost per installation by organisation size*

Employees	Average cost (£)
Less than 1,000	118,000
1,000–3,000	165,000
3,000–6,000	220,000
6,000–10,000	281,000
10,000 plus	349,000

large, medium and small installations at £750,000, £300,000 and £60,000 respectively, then the average cost per installation broken down by organisation size is as in table 4.6. Thus the average size of the installation increases with firm size. Taking the average cost per installation per worker, with 500 and 12,500 as the midpoints of the first and last employment groups, the pattern shown in table 4.7 results. These figures indicate that if one assumes a constant relation between total labour input and total output then the cost of providing computer services increases less than proportionately with the firm's output.

Table 4.7. *Average cost of computer installation per worker by organisation size*

Employees	Average cost per worker ($£$)
500	236
2,000	82
4,500	50
8,000	35
12,500	28

Relating firm size to the level at which an activity is run yields the result that the cost of hardware and bundled software does not increase proportionately with the level. Some comments are in order, however.

(i) The relation between a firm's labour input and the level at which an activity is run may not be constant. It is unlikely, however, that such decreasing returns to scale in labour usage would exist to negate the above conclusion.

(ii) The cost of computer hardware does not necessarily reflect the scale of the computer input. It was shown at the end of the previous section, however, that the price/characteristics regressions showed approximately constant returns to scale. The above discussion thus suggests that as the level at which an activity is run increases the input of computing power does not increase proportionately.

(iii) The very high cost per worker in the smallest employee group may not only reflect scale effects but also indivisibilities.† This would not materially affect the conclusions.

(iv) The prices of hardware often include some installation costs, and thus any results apply jointly.

(v) There is no evidence to indicate that different life spans apply to different size machines so this would not affect the results.

This section thus indicates that there are scale economies in the provision of computer hardware and bundled software in that the size of the installation does not increase proportionately with output. This also means that if in stage 3 it is possible to relate labour input to computer size then the relation between labour input and the level at which a computer using activity is run can also be established.

---

† Prior to the spread of mini computers indivisibilities were more important than now. It has been suggested, for example, that it would only be worth a firm computerising the payroll function if more than 100 employees were to be covered.

Stage 3: Implementation and running costs

In this stage unbundled software, applications software, maintenance and consumable inputs are considered. If these show increasing returns to computer size then by the above arguments they must show increasing returns to the level at which an activity is run. To study this stage of computer use, first labour inputs are studied and then consumables, but nearly all input is labour input.

Labour requirements of computer systems are studied quite extensively in chapter 8; however, at this stage it would be advantageous to see how labour requirements vary with computer size, and if possible to remove from that data any influences caused by different utilisation rates[†] and/or different uses of computers.[‡] The data we have fall short of these ideals. It is presented in table 4.8 and shows the number of employees in different categories across different sized systems. Taking

Table 4.8. *System labour requirements*

Installation value £'000s	Systems analysts	Programmers	Operators	Data processors	Total
Less than 5	0	0	1	0	1
5–19	1	1	1	2	5
20–49	2	2	2	5	11
50–119	3	5	3	10	21
120–249	4	10	6	20	40
250–499	6	12	8	30	56
500–999	10	16	12	60	98
Greater than 1,000	20	30	16	100	166

SOURCE: Humphries [1970] p. 12.

the mid-point of each category in table 4.8 for installation value (using 3 and 1,750 for the first and last categories), and regressing the log of labour requirements against the log of system value (V) one gets the following results (with standard errors in brackets):

1. log systems = -2.3710 + 0.7316 log V $R^2 = 0.9361$.
    analysts (0.1921) (0.0338)
2. log   = -2.4972 + 0.8404 log V $R^2 = 0.9469$.
    programmers (0.1998) (0.0352)

† In M of L [1965] and D of E [1972] it is indicated that larger machines work longer hours, which strengthens the conclusions drawn.
‡ In a private communication, IBM state that variations in applications cause the major variations in labour input.

3. log $= -0.9036 + 0.4930 \log V$ $R^2 = 0.9598.$
   operators (0.1013) (0.0178)
4. log data $= -2.4367 + 1.0021 \log V$ $R^2 = 0.9442.$
   processors (0.2447) (0.0431)
5. log total $= -0.5303 + 0.7775 \log V$ $R^2 = 0.9876.$
   labour (0.0875) (0.0154)

These results indicate† that the labour running costs (data processors and operators) show increasing returns to scale when scale is measured by value (although data processing staff separately show very slightly decreasing returns to scale). What we can call the investment staff (systems analysts and programmers), also show increasing returns to scale, i.e. as systems increase in value, the cost of applications software, measured solely by staff employed, does not increase proportionately.

With the comments in the discussion of stage 2 on systems value and size, the above is sufficient to allow one to say that labour requirements do not increase proportionately with computer size and thus the level at which computer using activities are run. Thus there are increasing returns to scale in the labour input for computer use.

A few comments on the other inputs are now in order. With analysts and programmers increasing returns to scale have been found, but these labour costs do not represent the whole of the cost of applications software. There are the machine costs in the testing stage, but there is little one can say about these. However, the time profiles of the labour use are also important, because if there are constant labour flows over time, but different gestation periods for different size machines, the interest element in cost will influence the conclusions about scale returns. However, the time profile of the application of software effort independent of other factors is not available. The data that is available shows that the time taken to set up installations of different sizes varies as in table 4.9. This indicates slightly decreasing returns to scale under

Table 4.9. *Installation period and system value*

System value ($£$)	Installation period (months)
Less than 100,000	48
100,000–500,000	60
More than 500,000	80

SOURCE: M of L [1965] p. 16.

† Although it must be admitted that the sample size is very small.

the assumption of a constant level of labour flow. The scarcity of data, however, prevents one from laying great stress on this result.

Other costs involved in running a system cover the consumables, i.e. stationery, magnetic tapes, etc. Although these costs may be considerable there is no reason to believe that they vary in any other manner than to yield constant returns to scale.

Finally, one should draw attention to the fact that the costs of installation are not fully covered in machine price, there has to be provided office space, special flooring, air conditioning, etc. The level of cost is again high, but we do not expect to find any considerable scale economies.

Considering all the inputs together, it would appear that the inputs of labour and consumable inputs together show increasing returns to scale with respect to installation value. Installation value on the other hand increases less than proportionately with firm size. It is thus suggested that as installation value is a fair representation of computer size (or computing power), and as firm size is a fair representation of the level at which computer using activities are run, one can conclude that increasing returns to scale exist in computer use.

4.4 CONCLUSION

This chapter has consisted of a study of the activities producing and using computers, with the intention of investigating the fixity of coefficients and scale returns. The study generates evidence to show that increasing returns to scale are available to computer users and producers. No evidence was found to contradict an assumption of fixed coefficients in computer production, but in computer use it would appear that some variation in coefficients (but only of a minor nature) can be observed.

5. TECHNOLOGICAL CHANGE

5.1 INTRODUCTION

If the growth and development of the production and use of computers is to be fully understood it is necessary to investigate the changes that have taken place in computer performance – to illustrate both what these changes were and what forces brought them about. It will be shown in this chapter that considerable changes have taken place in computer performance over time, and that these changes can be identified by the performance characteristics of new capital goods.†
It will also be argued that these changes are the result of technological change rather than substitution. To understand fully the change in computer performance it then becomes necessary to investigate those factors that influence the rate and direction of technological change, especially research and development expenditure and market structure.

The relevance of this chapter to economic theory in general concerns the determinants and characteristics of technological progress. Technological progress can be defined as a change in the basic technology matrix such that it is possible to generate a technique matrix which will produce greater output with a given set of inputs than was previously possible. A measure of technological progress is an indicator of this improvement. If one thinks in terms of a continuous flow of new activities then a continuous concept – the rate of technological progress – becomes operable. If technological progress should involve the relative saving of more of one input than another it is called biased. The questions with which economics has been most concerned are the quantification of the rate and the identification of the bias. The rate is important for it indicates the extent to which an economy can grow without increasing its long run rate of accumulation, whereas the bias

---

† The sources for the technological information used in the chapter are accredited as the discussion proceeds but the following were used extensively: Hollingdale [1970]; Rose [1969]; Freeman [1965]; OECD [1968]; OECD [1969]; Evidence to the Select Committee on Science and Technology; and *Computer Weekly*.

is important because neutrality is required if steady growth is to be feasible.† However, at the same time there is the question of embodiment – whether to change technique after technological change requires investment in new capital goods. The importance of this concept concerns the 'automaticity' of technique change. There have been two main approaches in past investigations of these questions: the first has been to measure, and the second has been to observe whether there are any consistent relations between the characteristics of technological progress and other economic indicators that can be used to predict the nature of technological progress. This study is concerned mainly with the latter approach, although to begin with a quantification of the rate of technological progress would be advantageous.

Before measurement can be attempted, however, it is necessary to clear out certain basic definitional problems. Thus in the remainder of this introduction the measurement of technological progress is discussed. In section 5.2 the problem of identifying a change in technology is investigated, and in section 5.3 the problem of separating technological change from substitution is covered. This leads into the study of the degree of technological change apparent in the computer industry in section 5.5, the nature of technological progress in section 5.6, and then the determinants of technological progress are discussed. Finally, conclusions are drawn.

There are two main genera of technological progress measures, the Hicks measure and the Harrod–Robinson–Read measure. Each has its own consequent definition of bias. Thus if attempts are to be made to quantify the rate of technological progress apparent in computer production and use (as well as any bias), a decision must be first made on which measure to use. This problem has been extensively discussed by, among others, Rymes [1971]. In essence the choice of measure centres around the decision as to what constitutes a primary input.

A primary input is any input that is non-reproducible. It is usual to define labour as non-reproducible or exogenous to the economic system. Even if it is considered partially reproducible Rymes shows that his conclusions are not affected. We will consider it as primary. Land and stocks of raw materials are non-reproducible. The main difference between the two measures is whether one considers commodity capital as reproducible or primary. The essence of the Cambridge approach to capital theory is that capital goods are produced in the economic system; commodity capital is therefore not a primary input.

Once this is realised then Read [1968] shows that the Harrod concept of technological change is the correct one. This concept considers a

† For the economy to stay on a steady growth path, technical progress must be Harrod neutral; see Hahn [1964].

continuous flow of new techniques and is thus defined in terms of rates. This measure then asks, 'Given the rate of technological advance what is the rate of change of the primary and intermediate inputs required to maintain the growth of output ... and in addition what is the rate of change of the primary and intermediate inputs required to maintain the rate of growth of the intermediate inputs?' (Rymes [1971] p. 98.) Considering an aggregate model without land and scarce raw materials we define the rate of technological progress, t_R, thus

$$t_R \equiv q - \beta(k - t_R)$$

q = rate of growth of output per head
k = rate of growth of commodity capital per head
β = share of commodity capital in total output.

Under a regime of steady growth $q = k$ thus $t_R = q$, and the rate of technical progress is equal to the rate of growth of output per head.

The problem this creates, however, is in making the definition operational, for the essence of the definition is that the improvement in the efficiency of one sector should take into account the improvements in the efficiency with which other sectors are supplying it with inputs. Thus one cannot solve for the Harrodian rate of technical progress in any sector by itself, but only by the simultaneous solution for all sectors at the same time. This means that in the present case such solutions are out of the question. However, it does not prevent one from considering qualitative rather than quantitative indicators.

Once the Harrodian measure of technical change is accepted then the appropriate definition of bias becomes operational. Turning to Joan Robinson [1972] (p. 127), considering the case without land, technical progress is unbiased if innovations are scattered evenly throughout the economy in such a way that output per head is raised at the same rate at all stages of the process of production. Bias in technological progress on either side of neutrality can then be defined as capital using when, if the rate of profit is constant, the value of capital per man required by the new technology is rising faster than output per man; and as capital saving in the contrary case.

If one wishes to consider bias in other directions one can replace the word labour with land, or labour and land, or any other factor considered to be primary.

5.2 INVENTION, INNOVATION AND TECHNOLOGICAL CHANGE

If technological change is to be discussed in a practical way it becomes necessary to define more tightly the concept of an economy's technology and changes in technology. Salter defines an economy's technology as the spectrum of 'techniques which are feasible in principle but have not (necessarily) been developed' (Salter [1969] p. 26), and he then proceeds to discuss how this spectrum might change over time. However, the observations available here are not on technology thus defined but concern the commercial application of technology. It will therefore be useful to define technological progress to cover both invention and innovation. If one is willing to accept this there is no need to go further. However, in line with Salter it is common to separate invention from innovation and consider invention alone as technological progress. However, as Schumpeter states 'As long as they are not carried into practice, inventions are economically irrelevant' (Schumpeter [1934] p. 88). Thus as far as the economy's development is concerned it is innovation which matters. If one is willing to assume that each invention automatically results in innovation then by looking at innovation we have observations on Salter's concept of technological change. This is, however, a drastic assumption. To avoid making it, one can best advance by first defining exactly what is involved in a technological advance. One can conceive of three stages in technological progress: (1) theoretical advance; (2) prototype construction; (3) commercial innovation. Salter's definition would centre on (1), and might include (2), arguing that by the time (3) is reached commercial pressures have so influenced technology reaching stage (3) that a technology observed only at level (3) does not adequately reflect what is available to the economy.

Salter's argument is that a firm can choose its technique of production from the set of theoretically available blueprints. Let us take an example. In 1947 Lyons chose the technique it wished to use for its bakery costings and it chose a technique that was theoretically feasible – the computer. Prototypes were in operation but no commercial machines. Its machine was working in 1951. The total cost of development was £129,000. When then does one say that the technological advance took place, in 1936 when the general theory of computers was first expounded (stage 1), 1941 when the first electronic computer was constructed (stage 2), 1947 when commercial usage was first considered or 1951 when it was first working (stage 3)? If a sum of many thousands of pounds was necessary for development the technique could not have been ready for use in 1947. If the first prototype was constructed in 1941 the technique could not have been available in 1936. The only logical date to say that 'then the computer was feasible as an activity for the economy to use' was 1951 when the commercial innovation had occurred.

This is in essence the conclusion that is reached by V. Ruttan: 'I suggest that we employ the term technological change in a functional sense – to designate changes in the coefficients of a function relating inputs to outputs resulting from the practical application of innovations in technology and in economic organisation' (Ruttan [1959] p. 605). In essence, therefore, technological progress is defined to occur only on innovation, for if sums have to be spent on the development of theoretical concepts, those concepts cannot represent feasible alternative activities.

5.3   Substitution versus technological progress

A common theme running through studies of the change in techniques is that one must face a basic difficulty in separating movements along a production function (substitution) and shifts of the function (technological progress). To illustrate this we again quote from Salter,

> Movements over time in best practice productivity may best be described in terms of the three measures which summarise the characteristics of technical advance and changing relative factor prices. Three effects are distinguished
> (i) the general effect of the rate of technical advance
> (ii) the bias arising out of technical advance which tends to save more of one factor than another, and
> (iii) the substitution effect reflecting changes in relative factor prices, including those arising out of technical progress in the manufacture of capital goods. Harrod's definition of labour and capital saving is inapplicable to industry analysis since it does not distinguish between the general effect and bias effect of technical advance which vary between industries, and the substitution effects arising out of cheaper capital goods which bears upon all industries.
> (Salter [1969] p. 45.)

Thus under this definition there are two substitution effects: exogenous changes in factor prices leading to changes in technique; endogenous changes in factor prices leading to changes in technique.

However, as has been shown above, once one takes into account the fact that capital goods have to be constructed, the Harrod concept of technological change is the only one that remains valid. Now, Rymes argues that once this is realised the traditional distinction between movements along a production function and shifts of the function is invalid when movements are considered to be of the endogenous type. Thus the substitution effect arising out of cheaper capital goods is not a substitution effect. The best way to show this is to use Rymes' two sector example (Rymes [1971] pp. 125–7), where no improvements are taking place in the consumption good sector but improvements are taking place neutrally in the capital good sector. The neoclassical (Hicks) measure of technical progress in the capital goods sector is

$$t_{KNC} = \alpha_K i,$$

where α_K is the share of capital in the output of capital goods and

i is the rate of growth of the output of capital goods per head), and the rate of technological progress in the consumption goods sector measured neoclassically (in the Hicks manner) is zero.

The Harrod rate of technological progress in the capital goods sector will be
$$t_{KR} = i,$$
and in the consumption goods sector
$$t_{CR} = \beta_C i < t_{KR} = i,$$
where β_C equals the share of labour in the output of consumption goods. Then to quote directly (and unfortunately at length) from Rymes

This case illustrates that because of technological improvements in the capital good sector, the consumption good sector experiences a rise in its capital/output ratio in physical units, which reflects the substitution of indirect for direct primary inputs in the production of consumption goods. The substitution permits a positive rate of increase in the output of consumption goods per unit of labour input employed in that sector, such that, when the growing commodity input in that sector is reduced to its growing 'real capital' counterpart, while the 'real capital'/labour ratio is constant, the rate of increase in output per unit of combined labour and 'real capital' input in the production of consumption goods is positive. That positive rate of increase, though less than in the capital good sector, is what the Harrod measure of the rate of technical change shows. It is clear that the efficiency with which the economic system is producing consumption goods is improving. The traditional neoclassical argument would be that a movement along the consumption goods industry's production function has occurred rather than a shift. If the production function is correctly drawn up, in terms of the relationship between output and direct and indirect primary inputs, it is clear that a 'shift' in such a 'production function' has occurred in the consumption goods sector.

If commodity capital is measured in its own units, the rate of accumulation will be equal to the Harrod rate of technical change in the capital goods sector. (Rymes [1971] p. 126.)

But if the commodity capital is measured in terms of the consumption good *as an input* in both sectors, i.e. as Read argues it should be, then the neoclassical measures show a rate of technical change in each sector the same as the Harrod measure, i.e. the substitution deduction is a fallacy as it treats inputs as outputs.

This dismissal of endogenous substitution still leaves open the possibilities of exogenous substitution – the change in technique due to externally produced changes in primary input prices.

In the general framework provided in the first chapter it was said that there may be alternative activities with a given commodity as output or one of several outputs and that these represent substitution opportunities. There are four basic questions that need answering; if it is accepted that the economy chooses that technique matrix which can yield the maximum rate of profit for a given wage rate, or the maximum real wage for a given rate of profit then

(i) Is there more than one technique on the wage–rental frontier or does one technique dominate the whole spectrum?

(ii) Are the techniques on the frontier ready to use or just theoretical possibilities?

(iii) Will an exogenous change in prices yield a change in technique if a better technique exists?

(iv) Is there any feasible reason for wage and profits rates to change exogenously?

It would really be evading the point to assume that one technique dominated the whole factor price frontier, but nor do we have any evidence that numerous techniques are represented on the frontier. However, assume that more than one technique is represented on the frontier.

What exactly is meant by a technique on the frontier? Should one define techniques in the manner that Salter defines his technology or should one consider that the frontier consists of techniques such that once it is decided to use them they are immediately available? If the frontier consists of concepts, then development will be necessary to make them usable and it has been argued that this should be defined as technological progress. Then the change in the wage–rental ratio would just lead to a different bias in technological progress if the new technique is to be adopted.

In what case then can it be said that a technique is available for use? The only definite cases are techniques which have been used in the past or in some other geographical area. Consider first techniques which have been used previously, then for them to be still available it is necessary,

(a) that knowledge once gained by an economy cannot be lost;

(b) if a technique was superseded by technological change then for it to remain a feasible alternative at a different wage–rental ratio technological change must always be of a nature that it leaves a part of the wage–rental frontier for the old technique (but to say that this is the case in general is rather drastic); and,

(c) if on the other hand a technique has been replaced because of substitution then for it to be returned to later one has to assume that technological progress has not led to it being superseded. This would also be a drastic assumption.

Thus if one is to consider development as technological progress the only real source for substitution possibilities is from techniques that are being used in alternative geographical areas which have been enjoying different wage–rental ratios.

Assume, however, that alternative techniques exist and consider whether a different wage–rental ratio will lead to their use. In fact it can be argued that there will be greater impetus to substitute than to make a change of a technological nature. If there is an exogenous change in the real wage upwards (the only feasible direction in a modern capitalist society) then on a given technique the profit rate must fall. This fall will promote the search for means to counteract it and may well lead to substitution. With technological progress, however, there is no such push for the innovator; his pressure must be profit pull (although as will be argued later there may be such pressures on the imitators).

This leads to the major question, what evidence is there that the wage–rental ratio has changed in the study period such that it might lead to a change in technique? The basic difficulty is that with the refutation of marginal productivity theory there is a void in the theory of income distribution. The prevailing viewpoint is probably best stated by Nell:

the rate of profits cannot be determined until the share of profits is given. Once relative shares are fixed, however, prices, the wage rate and the profit rate can all be determined. Relative shares can be fixed, say, by collective bargaining. Given a wage rate, prices will be determined by the competitive condition that the rate of profit must be the same in every industry. (Nell [1967] p. 19.)

There is thus a supposition that shares are institutionally determined. A change in shares must be the result of a change in institutions. Such a change is difficult to contemplate, and in the period of our study does not seem to have occurred.

Taking all these comments together (especially if development is defined as technological progress) there is very little to support any hypothesis that changes in technique have been the result of substitution. The changes in technique to be studied are thus going to be the result of technological progress.

One further point to discuss here is the relation between technological progress, substitution and diffusion. Diffusion concerns the spread of a technique across all its possible users, and may result from either technological progress or substitution. Diffusion is the process after innovation. The diffusion process is the same whether substitution or technological progress generates the new technique (although the price environment in which the diffusion occurs may be different). Substitution and technological progress are really only important in deciding the promoters of the innovators' behaviour – prices or technology. As far as the followers are concerned the choice of techniques is what matters, not why a choice is to be made. The important matter for the economy is diffusion. An innovation that is not diffused is as irrelevant to the economy as an invention that is not innovated. Thus in the next chapter a start is made on the discussion of diffusion.

The discussion in the above sections provides the basis for the following sections. First, the major innovations in the industry are discussed and then with the evidence produced the whole question of the nature and determinants of technological progress can be discussed.

5.4 THE DEGREE OF TECHNOLOGICAL CHANGE

Because the Harrod measure of technological progress stresses the interdependence of economic sectors it will not be possible in a study of one sector to quantify the rate of technological progress. What can be done is to generate qualitative indicators, but at the same time to look at three sectors – computer use, computer production and component production. If new products or new processes can be found then these shall be defined as indicators of technological progress and be dated by the time of the first application, i.e. by the date of innovation.

Electronic components

The electronics components industry has grown from a base of one product (the thermionic valve), through to transistors, integrated circuits and large scale integration.

However, as OECD state, 'Measuring the importance of technological change in the components industry is difficult largely for the reasons that the decrease in cost has been matched by a corresponding increase in performance. In the late fifties and early sixties the average price of semi-conductor devices has been falling at an annual rate of approximately 30 %.' (OECD [1969] p. 72.) The newer devices have lower power usage, higher reliability, less heat loss and are physically smaller.

The vacuum tube existed long before computers, the transistor although invented in 1947 was only commercialised in 1954 and integrated circuits (ICs) were commercialised in 1964–5. The point contactor transistor was invented in 1947 but was not suitable for use in computers, the junction transistor was the first to be used (in proximity fuses) in 1951, but not until the planar silicon transistor in 1957 overcame unreliability and slow speed relative to latter day valves were transistors used in computers. As Professor Shockley, the inventor of the transistor, said, inventing a device was one thing, making a useful repeatable transistor was another (Aldous [1973]). The basic problems were in the area of production processes.

Similar things happened with integrated circuits. IBM constructed and developed its own components, and in the early years of their development IBM decided to use hybrid integrated circuits made from two types of material rather than the monolithic integrated circuits made from one chip of silicon. They had such problems with the production of these circuits that they were abandoned and replaced by the monolithic circuits where production methods had advanced faster. ICT could then boast in 1968 that in 1965 they had found that ICs with the right tolerances were not available but that by 1967 technical problems had been overcome (ICT [1968]).

Similar developments continue. *The Times* (Owen [1971a]) gives an account of the price history of an integrated circuit known as the quad gate. This sold in 1967 at £3, and improved production technology reduced the price to 75p by 1968–9. In the early days of microcircuit production it proved difficult to achieve efficiency in the diffusion process. Wafers were being produced with a proportion of satisfactory circuits of only 2, 4 or 8 %. In a short period this rose to an 80 % yield.

Thus as far as these basic components are concerned there has been a continuous process of improvements of products and production methods. Freeman [1965] (p. 65) states that there have also been revolutionary improvements in the design and performance of most other components, including the so-called 'passive' components (capacitors and resistors).

The components sector also supplies the mainframe manufacturers with store devices. A store has three main characteristics, size, volatility (ability to retain data once stored), and access time. The first electronic computer, ENIAC, could only store twenty words of data. In 1948 the Williams Cathode Ray Tube store was first demonstrated, and in 1949 the mercury delay line store was built into EDSAC. However, both stores were volatile and small. The slower magnetic drum was invented at the same time but slow access time made it unsuitable as a main store.

The delay line store is still used in some computers but the major breakthrough in the main memory market was the ferrite core store which has dominated the market since 1956. Over time the production processes for these memories have improved and the size of the store that can be made to work has increased dramatically. In the late sixties and early seventies the semiconductor stores, newly developed, have begun to supersede the core store. The past, however, has again been one of continuous invention, development, and innovation of new products and processes.

Computer manufacture

The computer system has been defined as made up of the hardware (the CPU and peripherals) and software. In this section most can be said about the hardware, mainly the CPU, but some comments on the other elements are possible.

The first indicator to be analysed is the price series constructed in chapter 3. This series falls over time by a factor of five. However, more significant is the way this fall is achieved. The series may be characterised by a pattern of the following form. The series appears to fluctuate around 180 for the period to 1959, and then falls to 100 in 1960. It remains at about this level and then falls in 1964–5 to 45, around which it fluctuates for the remainder of the period. If we are to investigate the causes of the falls in this series it is first necessary to see which machines were being installed in different time periods, since the series is constructed to reflect the prices of the machines with the largest market share in each year.

If one considers first the period up to 1959, there appears to be a two way split in the types of machines installed. Prior to 1956/7 the machines being installed were Ferranti Mark I and Mark I*, Leo I and the Elliott 401 up to 1954, to be supplemented by the 402 and 3 and the English Electric Deuce and Deuce Mark I in 1955. All these machines were based on university or research institution prototypes, Leo on a Cambridge University machine, the Ferrantis on a Manchester University design and Deuce on a National Physical Laboratory machine. However, around 1956–7 these machines began to be ousted from the market by a new wave of machines, really the first independently commercially designed machines. This set included the Ferranti Pegasus first installed in 1956, the ICT 1201 (1956), the Elliott 405 (1956), the Stantec Zebra (1958), the Ferranti Mercury (1957) and Leo II (1957). A few of these machines were installed in 1956 but only in 1957 did they begin to appear in quantity. Using *Computer Survey* data (Summary Table, July 1962), not including machines taken out of service prior to 1961, 29 out of 40 of the machines installed in 1957 were of this type and all but 7 of those installed in 1958.

The next major change in the model installation pattern began in 1960. In that year 22 of the 88 machines installed (*Computer Survey* data, July 1963) were of one model, the Elliott 803, of which one had been installed in 1959. The IBM 1401 was first installed in 1960, the ICT 1301 in 1961, the ICT 1500 in 1962, the IBM 7000 series in 1961 and Leo III in 1962. These new machines accounted for 30 of the 88 machines installed during 1960, 84 of 122 during 1961 and all but 20 of the 222 machines installed during 1962.

The third new wave of machines started with the Honeywell 200 in 1964, the IBM 360 series in the same year, the ICT 1900 series in 1965 and the System 4 which soon followed. The data (*Computer Survey*, July 1965) shows only six of these machines installed during 1964, but the data used for weighting the price series includes orders from 1963 and there were 135 machines of the 360 series alone on order in

1964. In the following year some of these had been reflected in installations and large numbers of both 360s and 1900s were also on order.

It is therefore argued that there were four different groups of machines each of which dominated certain time periods. These can be labelled the zeroth generation (up to and including 1956), the first generation (1957–9), the second generation (1960–3) and the third generation (1964–70).

Returning to the price series, the manner in which it has been characterised shows that it falls at exactly the time that the generations changed from the first to second and second to third. If this is to be attributed to technological change it is necessary to show what the changes in technology were.

It has already been stated that the zeroth generation were not much more than university prototypes and were soon replaced by the first commercial machines of the first generation. The price series shows up little difference in price between these two sets of machines although the latter type soon dominated the market. The technology of the two sets, however, was very similar. The machines used thermionic valves, capacitors, resistors and soldered joints. The store was either delay lines, Williams tubes and/or magnetic drums. It may be that certain aspects of the later machines, e.g. less heat generation, easier programming, etc. are not reflected in the price series as they are not really hardware characteristics.

The second generation of machines differed considerably in technology. They were all transistorised, the Elliott 803 being the first transistorised British machine, and they all had the new ferrite core stores. The third generation cannot, however, be so neatly divided in terms of technology. The earlier 360 machines used hybrid circuits but the 1900 series were built with transistors. Soon all third generation machines had settled down to the use of monolithic integrated circuits. However, the 360s were designed initially to use monolithic integrated circuits when they became available, and ICT had also designed their 1900 machines around these circuits: 'ICT design teams developed plans for an integrated circuit central processor...Once the designs were completed in 1965 it was found that circuits with the right tolerances were not available. By 1967 technical problems...had been solved.' (ICT [1968].)† The third generation machines still used core stores but their performance was greatly improved in relation to those used in second generation machines. The third generation also saw the development of the computer family concept and great expansions in the maximum size of computers.

† The evidence to support the statement about IBM can be found in Harman [1971] p. 12, footnote 10.

Given the dates at which components were becoming available from the components industry and the time profile of the computer development effort it would appear that there was very little lag between the dates at which new machines appeared in the installations data and the date at which those machines became available. One can therefore state that the time profile of generations produced above is a good reflection of the time at which the technology of different generations was available to the user.

It is therefore suggested that the major falls in the price series are attributable to the design and production of new machines around the new components that were coming from the components industry, and can thus be attributed to technological progress.

To support this conclusion it is necessary to show that the relation apparent between falls in machine price and technological change is not in fact the result of other factors. There are a number of influences that could cause falls in a price series:

(i) Changes in input prices could reduce costs and thus prices. There is no evidence to show that changes in component costs (independent of technology) caused the pattern of computer prices, but the study of components showed that the major technological change in components was apparent in the performance of the new products. This would support our conclusion.

(ii) Changes in production processes independent of changes in components could cause a fall in price. In the previous chapter no such changes were found, although there is some evidence that a change in components requires slight changes in manufacturing processes.

The new technology required new methods for mounting and connecting circuit modules. (ICT [1968].)

The nature of the industry's manufacturing organisation has changed from one of high labour intensity with plants of up to a million square feet and employing 5,000 people...to one of even higher design engineering intensity with a much greater number of small plants typically covering 100,000 sq. ft. and employing 500 people.†

It seems to be of little use to try to separate out the effects of changes in component technology and changes in the production processes resulting. The only independent change in production technology that has been isolated is the application of computers to computer design and manufacture (CW [1972b]). This was happening in the 1970–1 period and is not reflected in the price series.

(iii) It has been shown that increasing returns to scale exist in computer production; thus it may be that the falls in price are the result of increasing scale rather than technological change. As technology has developed, the sales of each generation have increased enormously

† R. Macdonald, president of Burroughs Corporation, reported in CW [1972f].

Table 5.1. *Improvements in the performance of computer system components: regression results. Estimated parameters of log $E/C = a + bt$*

Component	Size of sample	R^2	a	b	t statistic
CPU/memory	117	0.631	−0.918	0.0575	(14.01)
Card reader	44	0.499	−2.064	0.0155	(6.47)
Tape drives	54	0.614	−4.389	0.0128	(9.10)
Line printer	46	0.375	−2.160	0.0105	(5.13)
Card punch	42	0.415	−2.567	0.0103	(5.32)

relative to the previous generation and at the same time the number of firms in the industry has reduced. If the price charged for a machine depends on expected sales (i.e. the number over which R & D can be spread) then one would expect price to fall as sales and expectations of sales increase. However, I do not feel that this can explain the whole price fall since the computer in its present form could not have been produced at an earlier date. The scale effect could have some influence, however, on the price series, but not of a nature to affect our qualitative conclusions.

Thus the conclusions can be maintained. However, at the same time, as it has been said before, the price series concentrates on the CPU aspects of hardware to the disadvantage of other elements in the computer system. These must therefore be looked at separately. First peripherals are studied and then software.

Some useful results have been derived by Skattum.† Cost (C) is measured by monthly rental, and different measures of effectiveness per unit of cost are related to a time variable (T) the first delivery date measured as the number of months since December 1950. The effectiveness measures were:

(i) for the CPU, $E_{\text{cpu}}^s = M \cdot N_c$,
where M is the high speed memory storage capacity and N_c is cycles per second;

(ii) for magnetic tape, E_{tape}, the maximum transfer rate;

(iii) for printers, E_{print}, the maximum no. of lines printed per minute;

(iv) for card readers, E_{cr}, the maximum no. of cards read per minute.

Fitting an equation of the form

$$\log E/C = a + bT$$

he achieved the results in table 5.1.

† S. Skattum, 'Changes in Performance of Components for Computer Systems' (unpublished), reported in Sharpe [1969] pp. 297–8.

It has already been argued that the coefficient on T should not be taken as an estimate of the rate of technological progress, but what these results can show is that different elements in the computer system have advanced at different rates. This conclusion holds because all hardware was produced in similar price and component environments. There are three points to be considered: why this should be, what form the technological change has taken, and what other changes have occurred that are not reflected in these figures? To answer, we shall consider separately input devices, output devices, backing store and the development of man–machine interaction.

A 1972 estimate suggests that over 50 % of all data input is via punched cards, around 25 % by paper tape, some 20 % by magnetic tape devices and the rest by other means, e.g. optical character readers, terminals, etc. (Noakes [1973]). In early computers punched cards and paper tape were the basic input media. These existed prior to computers. The original methods used for sensing cards were electro-mechanical but after 1956 photoelectric sensing was developed although mechanical aspects have still not been banished completely. By 1964 there had been an increase in the number of cards read from 200 to 1600 per minute. Paper tape readers by that date could read about 1,000 characters per second. These speeds were, however, still slow in relation to the CPU, the main problem being the residual mechanical element which has not been replaced by electronic advance. New products have thus been developed, e.g. optical and magnetic character readers, key to tape encoders, key to disc systems, buffered card punches, and remote job entry terminals.

The early devices used for output were cards or paper tape and these had to be interpreted on a separate machine. A major advance was the on-line 'line at a time printer' which allowed direct hard copy. This has been improved over time in speed and quality of print although mechanical limits exist. The Xeronic printers developed are not thus constrained. In addition to these popular devices, output on plotters, VDUs, microfilm and terminals is now feasible.

A computer's backing store can consist of a number of devices all dependent on magnetism. The magnetic drum was invented in 1947, but magnetic tape was not used, although existing prior to computers, until it was possible to improve the recording performance to a level suitable for computers. Disc stores were developed around 1962, and magnetic cards have also been used.

With tapes the developments over time have involved increasing the packing density, reducing tape wear, and improving passing speeds. The most radical design change seems to have been the cluster tape unit in which feed and take up spools share a common spindle, common electronics and common hardware, thus reducing cost. The main improvements in discs and drums have been in increased bit and tracking densities and reducing access time.

Over the last few years there have been developments in the use of one central computer from a number of remote locations, by means of terminals. These terminals were developed from teleprinters, and the data is transferred by Post Office lines that have exhibited increasing performance rates over time.

The conclusions that we can draw with regard to peripherals are that there have been technological improvements over time in the form of improved versions of existing products and the production of new products. However, the improvements in the original products have been limited by their mechanical aspects, and this in turn has led to the new products. Even so, it has not been possible to match the improvements in the performance of the CPU. This in turn has led to the development of multi-access and real time systems and simultaneity, so that the CPU can use its potential speed by running more than one job at a time without being limited by the peripherals.

Finally in this section, the improvements in manufacturers' software can be considered, with emphasis on operating systems, executives and compilers. For the user, software is a joint capital input and if the full advantages of the CPU developments are to be enjoyed then improved software is required. However, a government report can make the following two statements:

The inefficiency of compilers and the object code they produce is of continuing concern. (CSD [1971] p. 133.)

Operating software is an area in which there have been many setbacks and much work remains to be done before it will be possible to exploit to the full effect the great power and processing capability of the large computer. (CSD [1971] p. 136.)

and ICL can say that on very large machines operating software makes the overheads of managing the system too great for it to be economic.

However, advances have been made over time. The compilers were produced and have been continually improved over time, especially by the introduction of optimising compilers. Operating systems have been developed to allow for simultaneity and multiprogramming to offset slow peripheral speeds. Huge investments have been made in the construction of software for on-line systems.

The product has thus improved over time even though not at a rate to keep up with the hardware advances. There is no reason to believe that production methods have changed considerably – the software writing function is still very labour intensive. Perhaps the major changes will have been improvements in the quality of the labour input over time as it learns from previous experience.

Computer usage

There are two main themes to be considered in this section: the new improved products coming from the computer producers reducing costs and changing production relations in the user sector, and the innovations that are attributable to the user sector, i.e. the extension of applications and the development of applications software.

Consider first the inputs into the sector from the manufacturers. The collection of data and conversion to machine readable form has for long been one of the weakest links in the computer chain. The main technological changes have been in the development of data capture from source and the use of faster traditional methods of data preparation. The use of the different input mediums discussed above allows benefits in speed and accuracy and a slight reduction in staffing. Also the improvements in operating systems have saved operating staff. The improvements in the CPU have enabled reductions in cost and improvements in reliability, power consumption and, by the miniaturisation process, reductions in office space and land use.

However, some major advances in the user sector have been in the area of applications – the discovery of new areas and new tasks to which computers can be applied. With the development of the computer in line with the generation concept there have been three conceived generations of computer applications: (i) the electronic clerk – the glorified adding machine concept; (ii) the integrated data processing approach; (iii) the total or management information system. These concepts have been promoted by the computer manufacturers as their equipment improved. However, the discovery of a new application is only part of the technological process; the applications software has to be available to make the hardware perform the tasks set it.

Once again there are two sides to look at, the methods of producing the software and the nature of the product produced. In total, Sharpe [1969] estimates that the costs of developing software have fallen at only a quarter of the rate at which the CPU has advanced. However, the efficiency of producing applications software has improved over time with the development of high level languages, better compilers and diagnostic aides, modular programming and subroutines. Perhaps one of the major contributing factors to lower software costs was the introduction of compatibility in machines either via a high level language, the family concept, or just machine software compatible with IBM, for this increases the length of life of software thus making it cheaper.

There have also been other influences that increased software costs. The extension of applications has led to the need for ever more sophisticated software, and the art of software production has not always been up to the challenge. This has been the case especially when attempting to develop complex management information systems.†

One reaction to this has been the growth of the specialised software houses where either one-off jobs are written or application packages are made available to the user. Alongside this the bureaux industry, time sharing and hiring, and turnkey companies have all grown to take the burden of some or all the computer work from the user.‡ As was shown in chapter 2, this sector represents a large proportion of the computer market.

All the above comments can be neatly summarised by referring to the evidence of ICL to the Select Committee (SCST [1970a] pp. 9–10). In their evidence they show that in the period 1963–70 the proportion of system value attributable to different elements of the computer system has changed considerably over time, and that the cost breakdown of running a computer system is likely to continue a past trend and reflect the predictions of table 5.2.

Finally reference can be made to a summary table produced by OECD [1969] (table 1, p. 61) that details the major advances in the computer industry with dates, inventors and commercial innovators. This table is reproduced below as table 5.4.

Table 5.2. *Expected changes in market shares of*
computer elements

Element	User expenditure (%)	
	1968	1975
CPU	14	10
File peripherals	14	12
I/O peripherals	7	5
Communication terminals	1	3
Total hardware	36	30
Data transmission	2	4
Supplies	9	9
Maintenance	6	5
Operators	17	16
Software	23	26
Consultancy	1	1
Bureaux	6	9
Total others	64	70

† See, for example, *Economist* [1971b].
‡ The function of turnkey companies is to provide an installation service for computer users. If the user specifies his data requirements such a company will determine what hardware and software are required, purchase them, supervise installation, and once the system is running satisfactorily hand over to the user, who has just to 'turn a key' to have a complete, usable computer system.

5.5   THE NATURE OF TECHNOLOGICAL PROGRESS

The discussion in the previous section has shown that considerable technological progress has taken place; in this section the questions of embodiment and bias are studied.

We define product innovation as the production of a new product, and process innovation as a change in the method of production. Embodiment is concerned with the changes in productive methods consequent upon technological change. Technological progress is disembodied if the old method of producing a good can be costlessly transformed into the new method of producing that good or the method of producing the new good, i.e. if the old technique can be costlessly transformed into the new technique. The degree of embodiment concerns the proportion of the cost of the new technique (at the ruling profit rate) that it is necessary to outlay to transform the old technique to the new.

It has been shown that the major advances in the computer manufacturing sector have taken the form of product innovations with the development of new and improved hardware and software. In the user sector the main advances have been in the expansion of the areas of computer applications, which in turn were dependent on the use of new hardware. It would appear therefore that if the user sector is to reap the benefits of the technological advances in the industry it can only do so by the use of new products. It would thus seem that for the user sector technological advance has a high degree of embodiment. There are however three modifying factors.

(i) Because hardware is modular, if plug compatibility exists then it is possible to use old peripherals with a new CPU and vice versa; however, it would be unlikely that this would allow full advantage to be taken of the new product(s).

(ii) If the new hardware is program compatible with the existing software then once again the degree of embodiment may be less than unity. However, it would again be the case that the old software would probably not allow full advantage to be taken of the new hardware. New software on old hardware would not be subject to this criticism.

(iii) There is one further influence that is interesting, for it suggests that it may be possible to change just one part of a single hardware piece. The following quote shows both the existing degree of embodiment and a possible pattern for the future.

With certain limitations those 'A' series processors with corresponding 'S' series processors can be enhanced on site. In this original way the major part of the customers hardware investment is preserved – in sharp contrast with some recent hardware developments for which the customer is asked to pay more than the cost of the system being replaced. (ICL [1971].)

There is a built-in advantage for the computer manufacturers if a high degree of embodiment exists in computer use, e.g. it is argued that IBM limit the maximum sizes of store on their machines so that the customer will have to upgrade more often, thus giving IBM more sales of whole rather than part systems (Enticknap [1972]). However, the development of the computer family led to a considerable fall in the degree of embodiment.

In the components sector there has been both product innovation and process innovation although little has been said of the nature of the process innovation. The incorporation of the new components has led to the product innovation in the computer producing sector with only slight apparent change in processes. It would appear therefore that the innovations in the computer producing sector have had little effects on processes and thus a low degree of embodiment, whereas sufficient has been said of component manufacture to indicate that their product innovations have also meant process innovations and thus a high degree of embodiment.

Thus the pattern of embodiment varies between sectors and the only generalisation possible is to say that it would appear that a product innovation often means a process innovation for the producers of that product but to differing degrees. Product innovation in one sector implies also at least some process innovation in the using sector but to differing degrees. Only if the innovation means a complete change in process at some stage can it be called totally embodied, but as product innovation has characterised the history of computer *production* a generally high degree of embodiment in computer *use* is implied. This leads us into the discussion of bias. In the first section of this chapter bias was defined, but a more useful definition also provided by Joan Robinson is:

When output per head is raised by more in the investment sector than in the commodity sector the progress is said to have a capital-saving bias, and when it is more in the commodity sector, a capital-using bias. An even development throughout the system which raises output per head equally for all workers is described as neutral technical progress. (Robinson [1962] p. 70.)

Within this definition one can classify the broad lines of technological change. Consider the economy as split into two sectors, computer producers and computer users. The first computer was for use in clerical applications where very few machines were in use. Its effect was to create an investment good sector and to raise output per head in the user sector. We may judge this to be capital using. As time proceeded computers improved greatly in terms of quality per unit of cost but their manning requirements in the user sector only changed slightly. We may thus term this capital saving. The third development was the

4

extension of computer usage into areas that again were labour intensive. This again may be classed as capital using.

The conclusion to be derived is that there is no reason to believe that the technological progress has been biased in any particular direction. As it is often argued that technological progess is capital using, the important point is that the improvements in capital goods that tend to be a characteristic of most new capital goods industries in their developing years (Chow [1967]), may, by being classified as capital saving, negate this conclusion. The computer example thus shows that technical progress should not be presumed to be biased in any particular direction, or for that matter assumed to be neutral. (Harrod argues, however, that this is as one would expect, but that the capital and labour saving biases will cancel out across the whole economy to generate neutral progress overall (Harrod [1948] p. 83).)

However, although this conclusion is relevant for growth theories the interesting point is why it should be so. As it will not be possible to classify every innovation as capital using or saving the study will concentrate on another indicator of bias that has been observed, the changes over time in the relative proportions of the different elements of the computer system in total computer costs. As these proportions are the result of differing rates of advance of different computer system products and processes and these products and processes and their rates of development are the determinants of capital or labour saving bias, if one can explain why some products and processes have advanced faster than others one can also gain indications why biases have gone the way they have. This question can only be answered, however, within a general discussion on the wider questions on the sources and determinants of technological progress. Thus the rest of this chapter is devoted to the study of the sources of technological progress in the computer industry.

5.6 THE SOURCES OF TECHNOLOGICAL PROGRESS

The first question to be answered is why technological change took place at all once the first generation computers were in use. The OECD report isolates four main influences.

(i) The first computers were so primitive that the need for change was obvious.

(ii) There is a competitive effect concerned with IBM building up and maintaining its market position.

(iii) It can be argued that the practice of leasing in the industry makes the market amenable to technological change and thus more conducive to it.

(iv) Finally, it is argued that changes in component technology have promoted technological change in computer manufacture.

The problem with the leasing argument is that it ignores the fact that software is not leased but can represent a large share of computer using costs. Not much stress is therefore laid on this argument. The first reason just indicates that improvements could yield benefits. The main forces promoting technological change must therefore centre around reasons (ii) and (iv). If one generalises, they say that technological change in computers was the result of the existence of technological possibilities and the pressure of competition bringing these possibilities to innovations and technological progress.

The industry has certainly been faced with improved technological possibilities over time, but whether these were presented to the industry or generated by the industry in response to the continuing innovative pressure is a matter to be considered below. Considering, however, that these possibilities were available why did the industry proceed to spend money either developing or generating technology? Of the four reasons above all that is left is the competitive pressure argument.

It can be argued that the structure of the industry and the nature of its technology are such that a natural result is technological progress. The first point to consider is the background of the manufacturers who entered computer production (with examples from the UK, but the US pattern is little different). There are three groups: (i) the manufacturers of office machinery, e.g. IBM and The British Tabulating Machine Company (later ICT); (ii) the manufacturers of electronic equipment or components, e.g. English Electric, Ferranti, Elliott, Marconi, etc.; (iii) new firms to electronics, e.g. LEO (Lyons) and completely new firms, e.g. Computer Technology.

The firms that came to computers via office machinery had a distinct advantage over the other entrants – they had a customer base. The existence of this customer base provided these companies, especially IBM, with a ready made market for their products. Moreover, IBM was receiving huge rentals on their office machines to finance their computer section.

The main characteristic of computer production technology was found to be the existence of increasing returns to scale. The firm with the largest market share can reap these benefits. IBM captured this share with the benefit of the customer base. As 10% of the world market has been specified as the minimum for long run profitability and IBM soon had 60%, if the other companies were to survive they must capture some of this share. However, price competition would be out of the question for they would not be able to offset the advantages of a large market share. With backgrounds in electronics it would seem

4-2

to be a logical tactic to compete technologically. However, the resources made available from a large market share can finance the expenditure necessary for the preservation of market share by the major company. The competition in the industry thus becomes of a technological nature. The industry advances technologically because that is the way it competes, and the uneven spread of market shares combined with scale returns ensures that competition is necessary.

This suggestion that technological progress is the main competitive mechanism because of market structure and the nature of computer technology leads into a discussion of bias in technological progress. It has been shown that certain sectors of the computer system have advanced faster than other sectors, e.g. the CPU has advanced in cost effectiveness terms much faster than the peripherals and software. This has tended to mean that the pattern in computer use has been for the labour input to remain relatively constant but the share of hardware in total costs to fall, i.e. capital saving bias. At the same time there have been developments of new input media. It has also been suggested that the latest developments in computer technology are aimed in a different direction to past improvements, e.g.

One of the most significant developments in the data processing industry over the past few years has been the elevation of the user to the master not slave of the system. Description of computers always started with technical details. According to the enlightened ones, the new machine was concerned with binary arithmetic, core stores, punched cards, magnetic tape and highly complicated programs which could be written only by specially trained programmers.
It is a sign of the increasing maturity of the industry as well as the realities of a more sophisticated and competitive market, that most of the new developments are aimed at providing, simpler, more effective user services. The move towards remote terminal applications and modular software designed for easy tailoring to user requirements are two of the most significant trends towards satisfying customer needs. (CW [1972c].)

Hardly a week now passes without the announcement of a new product which does not emphasise the particular marketing need that the product fulfils...in the past computer products often came first followed by a search to find the relevant user function. (CW [1972d].)

The pattern of development can be explained in the following manner. As competition is to take place through technological change, and because as time passed new components were appearing from the components industries, it was a logical progression that these components should be incorporated in new machines. However, the use of these components yielded greater benefits to the CPU than to the peripherals, and software also tended to lag behind. This meant that the pattern of the computer users' costs had changed. As the user would be interested in the total costs of using his system, technological change can be most effective if directed at the elements constituting the major

Table 5.3. *Patent registering activity 1951–62*

1951–4	No. of patents	1955–8	No. of patents	1959–62	No. of patents
NCR	76	IBM	177	IBM	246
NRDC	76	NCR	111	STC	93
BTM	72	NRDC	103	ICT	77
Powers Samas	36	STC	97	NCR	69
STC	32	BTM	45	NRDC	51
IBM	29	Landis & Gyr	31	Sperry Rand	48
BTH	28	Burroughs	30	Philips	43
Landis & Gyr	24	Bendix Aviation	26	AEI	37
Bell Punch	22	Powers Samas	24	Western Electric	36
Bendix Aviation	18	Western Electric	23	Burroughs	34
Machines Bull	18				

proportion of costs. Thus we see the shift away from technological sophistication towards user costs, the reduction of data preparation costs through new machines, easier programming ability, etc. The technological change will take the directions that are either directed by component improvements or where user costs can be reduced most drastically by a technological advance, i.e. possibilities and potential are both important.

There is, however, one further interesting observation. The reaction to the user sector's demands has been to develop new hardware rather than to concentrate on user processes. This may be the only way that technology could have advanced, but there are definite benefits for the mainframe manufacturers in this tendency. If hardware improvement is to be the means of effecting technological improvement then the hardware manufacturers' market is preserved. As the costs of entry to the industry are high (research and development expenditure, need for a market base, and scale returns make it so), there can be little for the industry to fear from outsiders, so they have the ability to impose such development. Unfortunately no evidence is available to support these assertions.

From this discussion on the forces promoting technological advance in general and its direction in particular the next step is to attempt to discover the origins of technological change. As invention is prior to innovation, it is necessary to track down the origins of both inventions and innovations. A start can be made on this by looking at the register of patents. Freeman [1965] has performed this exercise, and the ten main registrants of patents for computing, calculating and registering machinery in three different periods, were as shown in table 5.3. The most interesting aspect of this table is the emergence of IBM as the

Table 5.4. *The main inventions and innovations in the computer industry*

(A = theoretical advance, B = first application, C = first commercial application)

Description	Type, country and year			Responsible firm or individual	Remarks
1. General theory of computers	A.	France	1936	L. Couffignal	Unknown outside France
		Germany	1936	K. Zuse	No publications. Totally unknown
		United Kingdom	1937	A. M. Turing	Relatively important influence
2. First electronic computer	B.	Germany	1941	K. Zuse	Z3 computer. Little known outside Germany
		United States	1946	J. P. Eckert and J. W. Mauchley	ENIAC. Important work was also done by G. Stibitz at Bell Telephone (1940), H. Aiken and IBM at Harvard (1944) and V. Bush at MIT (late 1930s and early 1940s)
	C.	United States	1951	Remington Rand	UNIVAC I
3. Internally stored program	A.	United Kingdom	1937	A. M. Turing	
	A.	United States	1946	J. von Neumann (University of Pennsylvania)	MADM ⎫
	B.	United Kingdom	1948	University of Manchester	EDSAC ⎬ Close scientific interchange between the United States and the United Kingdom
	C.	United States	1949	University of Cambridge	UNIVAC I ⎭
4. Subroutine concept	A.	United Kingdom	1951	Remington Rand	
	A.	United States	1937	A. M. Turing	
			(1946)	J. von Neumann	
5. Read-only memory	A.	—		—	The read-only memory has been used in automatic telephone exchanges
	B.	United States	1946	J. P. Eckert and J. W. Mauchley	ENIAC computer. Limited storage
		United Kingdom	1949	University of Cambridge	EDSAC II computer. Storage of the entire control information
6. Associative memory concept	C.	Several countries		Most manufacturers	
	A.	United States	1946	V. Bush	
	B.	United Kingdom	1952	Ferranti	ATLAS ⎱ The full possibilities of associative
	C.	United States	1965	IBM	360-67 ⎰ memories have not yet been exploited
7. Microprogramming	A.	United Kingdom	1948	University of Manchester	
	B.	United Kingdom	1948	University of Cambridge	⎱ Close interchange
		United States		IBM (J. Backus), US Navy (G. Hopper)	⎰
8. First compiler (A2)	B.	United States	1951	US Navy (G. Hopper)	In the late 1940s Grace Hopper worked in the UK
	C.	United States	1951	Remington Rand	UNIVAC I: first computer to have a compiler

Description	Type, country and year	Responsible firm or individual	Remarks
9. FORTRAN language	B. United States 1953-4	IBM Users Association (SHARE) and IBM	First FORTRAN compiler written by J. Backus of IBM
10. High speed drum printer	C. United States 1954	IBM	First application of the 'on the fly' principle for printing
11. Ferrite core memory	C. France 1954	Bull	
	A. ⎫ B. ⎬ United States 1955	MIT (Lincoln Laboratory)	Important work was also done at Harvard
12. Transistorised computers	C. ⎭ United States 1956	Remington Rand, then IBM	UNIVAC 1103A, IBM 704 and 705
	A. United States 1947	Bell Telephone	Discovery of the transistor effect in 1947
	B. United States 1956	Bell Telephone	Leprechaun computer
	C. United States 1958	Philco, IBM, GE	Philco 2000, IBM 7090, ERMR system
	United Kingdom 1959	Elliott	Elliott 803
	Germany 1959	SEL	ER56 computer (SEL is a subsidiary of the American ITT)
13. ALGOL language	B. Several countries 1958	ACM (US) and GAMM (Germany)	ALGOL was jointly developed by American and European specialists convened in Zurich, Switzerland. The first ALGOL compiler was written by Dijkstra of the Netherlands. ALGOL was subsequently adopted by most manufacturers, and is presently more widely used in Europe than in the US
	C. All countries after 1958	Several manufacturers	
14. Multiprogramming	C. United States 1960	Honeywell	H800 computer ⎫
15. COBOL language	B. United Kingdom 1962	Ferranti	Orion I computer ⎬ No interchange, independent developments
	C. United States 1960	US Department of Defense	
	C. Several countries after 1960	Most manufacturers	
16. Family of compatible computers	B. United States 1955	US Army	FIELDATA plan.
	C. United States 1963-4	IBM, Honeywell, RCA, GE, CDC	IBM 360 series, CDC 3000 and 6000 series, Honeywell H 200 series, RCA Spectra 70 series
17. Time-sharing	B. United States 1964	MIT, Dartmouth College, GE	Civilian application (Project MAC)
	C. United States 1966	GE, then several large US manufacturers (IBM, CDC, etc.)	

SOURCE: OECD [1969] table 11, p. 61.

main registrant and its lead in the final period relative to the middle period. The performance of NCR can probably be attributed to its interests in cash registers rather than computers. The high placing of the National Research and Development Corporation is due to the fact that it provided finance for a number of UK computer projects and held the results in a common patents pool.

There are two main problems with using patent data to indicate the sources of invention. There is no way of telling which patents are important and which are of a minor nature, and moreover software cannot be patented. To illustrate this point, ICL can say that 'we have been able for many years successively to renew our patent agreement with IBM on a basis of no payment. We have been able to persuade them that we have sufficient value in patents to justify them making available to us all their patents without money being exchanged.' But the statement goes on: 'That is almost a unique situation in regard to IBM and its other competitors who seek licences' (SCST [1971b] para. 874, p. 157).

The second main problem is that universities do not patent the results of their research, thus the importance of their contribution is not reflected in patent data.

To get around these problems it is necessary to return to the discussion of the degree of technological progress and especially the OECD summary table (table 5.4). In this table the first thing that is apparent is that the major theoretical advances are either attributable to individuals or universities, and the first applications are commonly attributable to universities or the US Defence Department. First commercial applications are not attributable to any one company more than any other, although the importance of UK manufacturers as innovators declined markedly over time in comparison to US manufacturers. This means that the commercial companies are not in fact generators of inventions but are mainly concerned in the development of university or defence department inventions to the stage of commercial application. This is also the conclusion that Freeman reaches.

If the question of the sources of technological advance is to be fully understood we must now trace out the link between R & D and innovative activity. It has been shown that IBM spend as much on R & D as their next six competitors put together, but the OECD data does not show that they innovate faster than other companies. The question that has to be answered is, does this discrepancy indicate that there is no relation between R & D expenditure and the rate of innovation or does it mean that the data gives a poor indicator of innovative activity? At the same time it may be possible to trace out a relation between R & D expenditure and innovative activity that would help to explain the relatively poor performance of the UK industry.

The major question must centre around the performance of IBM, for as OECD state, 'there is not much correlation between the market position of a particular company and its technological contribution to the (computer) industry. In the semi-conductor industry on the contrary the firms with a leading share of the market are precisely those who have been at the origin of the most important innovations.' (OECD [1969].)

The nature of R & D is such that a company has first to decide the direction that its R & D will take and then find the resources to finance it. A high level of R & D expenditure may just mean that a large number of areas are being investigated simultaneously, and a low level may mean a more selective approach. It is argued for example that IBM carry out protective R & D, and IBM do not deny this,† whereas other companies are limited to defensive and offensive R & D. However, in general one would expect that if all companies were working in the same direction the one with the major resources would get there first. If there is no strong correlation between the level of R & D expenditure and innovative activity it may well be that some companies are more successful than others in the selection of targets – i.e. in their forecasting activity. It is within this context that one can understand ICL's plea to the government for directions in R & D expenditure, 'it is very important with these very complex applications that we have development contracts in order to make sure that we are going to do the right thing the right way before it is ordered' (SCST [1970a] para. 2070, p. 417). We can extend the argument about the direction of R & D by reference to two major successes in the computer industry:

(i) CDC, although a relatively small company, was a major innovator in the technology of very large computers. It concentrated its efforts in an area where no other companies were seriously competing.

(ii) The peripheral manufacturers have been able to develop machines with better cost-effectiveness ratings than the giants of the computer industry (Enticknap [1972]). Once again the tactic has been to concentrate resources in a small area.

However, the major mainframe manufacturers cannot all go their own way, for the position of IBM in the market is so strong that if IBM announce a new product the other companies have to divert resources to match it.‡ This would again limit any direct relationship between R & D expenditure and innovation.

---

† See SCST [1970a] paras. 334–5, p. 70. Protective R & D is research undertaken to combat possible innovations by other companies, but without necessarily any intention to innovate.   ‡ SCST [1970a] para. 51, p. 29. This is known as defensive R & D.

These arguments can be used to support the implications drawn from the OECD table. However, in contradiction Harman finds that

the implementation of innovations in computers was studied measuring innovative achievement of firms by their maximum achievement in computer performance up to a given date. It was firmly established by this analysis that, although the elasticities of response in computer performance from research expenditure may vary across firms, all firms get increasing returns in potential improvement of computer performance from their research expenditure. However, through caution in implementing innovation, the effective response in actual computer performance may be inelastic. (Harman [1971] pp. 145–6.)

There are thus two points to consider here; first that innovative activity should not necessarily be measured by being the first to market a new product because many introduce that product in a short period of time; and second, innovations are not necessarily marketed (protective innovation). Support for both these hypotheses can be found. Consider the first, that many firms tend to market a similar new product at the same or nearly the same time. For example, many third generation computers were announced at a similar point in time. Given that it can take from two to four years to produce a new range of computers, it means that the first to launch the new product was only a little more successful than the others. (It may also mean that the innovator is willing to launch a product of a less than attainable quality – with, for example poor software.)† This means that the Harman approach of looking at the cost effectiveness of a company's products may be a better indicator of the relation between R & D and innovative activity. Then a relation between R & D and technological progress of the expected direction can be justified. The differences between companies that he notes could then be attributed to some extent to forecasting effects and the need for defensive R & D.

The other point to take up is the failure of marketed innovations to reflect innovative activity as Harman noticed. This is mainly relevant to IBM, for the showing of IBM in the OECD table relative to its expenditure is poor. Dr H. R. J. Grosch gives some insight to IBM's innovative activity.‡

They have an enormous R & D expenditure each year and, believe me, it is well spent. I have many friends and many sources of information about what goes on in IBM other than the things they announce in the market place. Enormous reservoirs of knowledge are available there. I do not think it is necessary to have that much to be reasonably competitive... If you could have a Western European union... I would think a reasonable amount of expenditure on the part of the three or four major companies that would be involved could add up to a viable amount of research and

† There is some evidence that IBM did this with their 360 series, see *Sunday Times* [1973].
‡ SCST [1971b] para. 1369, p. 249. This quote illustrates another aspect of IBM's involvement in protective R & D.

development vis-a-vis IBM's use of its R & D at the present time. If they dug deeper into their enormous shelf full of fancy items you might have to put more into the pot, but at least for one generation you would have the chance.

A reasonable summary of our findings is thus that in terms of computer performance achieved to date there is a relation between R & D expenditure and innovative activity showing increasing returns to scale. Differences between firms may reflect their skill in forecasting and the extent to which they have to undertake defensive R & D; at the same time IBM undertake protective R & D, which may be used to explain their poor performance as innovators, and the tendency that IBM have to spread their R & D over a very wide range of products allows other firms who concentrate to innovate faster in certain areas.

With the above findings on the progenitors of technological change and the role of R & D expenditure we can analyse two important questions. First, why was the US pre-eminent in technological advances; and second, would more equal market shares have increased or decreased the rate of technological progress? Freeman suggests that the US lead in computer technology was the result first, of the US success in component technology, in that all important component inventions and innovations came 1–4 years earlier in the US than Europe, and that geographical proximity promoted their earlier use in computers, and second, as Freeman discovered, that there are shorter lead times between the designation of a new product and its commercial launch in the US than the UK. This latter result he attributes partly to better component technology, and partly to what we can call better management and stronger 'animal spirits'.

It is very difficult to quantify 'animal spirits' and better management, although the components argument appears reasonable. As it has been shown that there is a connection between R & D expenditure and innovation, if the animal spirits argument is to hold it must be shown that US companies have been more willing to finance R & D than British companies, whereas if the better management argument is to be used it must be shown that the R & D expenditure has been better directed in the US than the UK.

When one looks at the data both of these points are difficult to substantiate, especially when it is realised that during the first generation and including Atlas there was no US lead. One would not expect animal spirits and management quality to change drastically over time. The crucial factor, according to the British computing industry was the US government, military and space projects. Using Freeman's data the leading US firms in electronics ventured $4,206m of their own capital on R & D but this was supported by $4,242m of government money during 1951–9. The major government support in the

British market was £10m distributed by the NRDC. Between 1949 and 1959 IBM spent $254m of government money on R & D, and Sperry Rand after 1955 about double. The figures for 1969 and 1970 are as in table 5.5.

Table 5.5. *Government support for R & D in US computer companies* (£m)

| Company | 1969 | | 1970 | | |
	Co. exp.	Govt. exp.	Co. exp.	Govt. exp.	Turnover
IBM	167	121	175	125	3,127
Burroughs	15	43	19	24	372
NCR	17	34	20	11	592
CDC	18	n.a.	13	n.a.	225
Honeywell/GE	42	201	n.a.	n.a.	n.a.

SOURCE: SCST [1971c] p. 82.

It would seem that the expenditure of US government money has been as great as private capital in the US industry. In the British industry it has not been so. The other main point to consider is that with government expenditure the direction is contracted in. This means that the direction of R & D is dictated – it need not be the result of better management. The effect has been, for example, that nearly all CDC processors have been funded by government contracts and Burroughs large commercial computers are a direct development from military processors.

It would seem, therefore, that although animal spirits and better management may have some role to play, the effect would be swamped by the huge differences in R & D expenditure and government influence. Moreover, with scale economies, the US home market allows the production of surpluses of a size that the UK market cannot. This means that the resources are not available for research in the UK. It also means that a greater proportion of the resources that are available must be devoted to defensive research, which leaves little over for offensive research and innovation. When the component lag argument is included the loss of the UK lead is not surprising.

Next, we must try to answer whether a more equal distribution of market shares would have affected the rate of technological progress in the industry. There are a number of separate factors to consider.

(i) As R & D is the generator of technological change (theoretical advances coming from outside the commercial sphere), the first point to consider is whether more equal market shares would have affected the industry's total expenditure on R & D. There are two influences, one on resources the other on motivation. First, if market shares were more equal would the same resources be available to finance R & D? In the US, where most R & D has been undertaken, it has been shown that about half was financed by government money, and it can be assumed that this would not have changed. This leaves private sources to consider. It has been argued that much of IBM R & D expenditure came from its revenue from office machinery, where it held a monopoly position. This it can be assumed would remain the same. In later years its finance came through surpluses on computer business, and in the same way most firms attempt to finance R & D out of current surplus. More equal market shares would reduce the surplus through the loss of increasing returns to scale in computer production. More equal shares may also lead to price competition, further reducing the surplus. Less resources may therefore be available.

With more equal market shares would the motivation for R & D be any less strong? We suggested that competition arose because of the fight for market shares to get the benefits of scale returns. This motivation would still have existed. However, with more equal market shares price competition may have become feasible whereas in fact no company had the resources to produce the cuts in prices that IBM could have done with its large market share. However, the cuts in price that could have been generated by reducing profit per machine could not have matched the price reductions to be generated from technological innovation. For the competitor, therefore, technological change would still appear to have been the way to larger market shares.

(ii) If the same resources were devoted to R & D would they have been more or less effective? The results that Harman generated indicate that there are increasing returns to scale in R & D expenditure, which would mean that a more even share would have reduced the effectiveness. Moreover, a more even distribution of research funds may also have meant more duplication of effort. To offset this there would probably have been less funds devoted to financing wasteful protective R & D. However, a major influence of having more equal market shares could have been that the industry would not have had a leader. As it was, IBM acted as leader, in that to attack its large market share other companies have developed compatible machines and software, and also matched its innovations. This effect of standardisation has meant that a reduction has been effected in wasteful user expenditure. There is no way of telling, however, whether these standards are the best that the industry could have produced, or whether without a leader some defensive R & D would have been replaced by socially more productive offensive R & D.

(iii) The third point to consider is whether more equal market shares would have meant more marketed innovations. It has been shown that IBM do not necessarily market all innovations. With more evenly distributed research funds these innovations would probably have been more evenly spread between companies. It would seem to be of little use for all firms in an industry to store innovations, although for one there may be advantages. The IBM store can be used to combat innovations by any competitor, whereas to market them independently has little benefit for the company, since with a large market share it would only be attacking its own market, to increase its market share may involve it even further with the US anti-trust laws, and to market an innovation means replacing mainly its own products, and with fixed development costs the longer the marketable life of a product, with fixed prices, the greater the profit. With more equal market shares and a more even distribution of innovations, the pressures to gain more market share through innovation may have been stronger and the loss to a company from replacing its own products less important. It is suggested that it is here that the major effect of more equal market shares would lie.

We suggest therefore that resources devoted to R & D may well have fallen under a regime of more equal market shares and that the effectiveness of these resources in generating technological change may also have been reduced. However, the results of the expenditure may well have been marketed more quickly.

Related to the link between technological change and market structure as analysed above is the link in the opposite direction, i.e. what effect has the continuous technological change had on the market structure?

The two salient features of the industry that we have isolated are increasing returns to scale through fixed R & D expenditures and the technological nature of competition promoting these R & D expenditures. A market share equal to 10 % of the world market has been estimated as the minimum scale for long run profitability. The fact that the industry has experienced heavy merger activity is, one can hypothesise, the result of these factors. It is perhaps significant that having captured a large market share very early IBM never had to engage in merger activity.

However, at the same time as the mainframe manufacturers have reduced in numbers there has been a conflicting trend, i.e. the growing influence of the peripheral manufacturers (Owen [1971a]) and service companies. The peripheral manufacturers are more important in the US than the UK. Their strategy has been to develop peripherals to compete with IBM products but which are cheaper and more efficient. Their success is most probably the result of concentrating R & D resources on a very small section of the market.

In the UK the service sector is more important (see chapter 2). The services provided vary from time hire, program running, program writing and systems development, to turnkey operations and installation management. We suggest that there are three main reasons for the existence of this sector: indivisibilities, scale returns and expertise. The small user can thus get computer time without owning a machine too big for him to utilise fully, and in multi-access systems the user can have available the capacity of a large machine for a short time without having the burden of owning one for the whole time. This is the indivisibilities argument.

The scale returns argument is that if a large machine is utilised by many users it is cheaper than each user having a small machine. Moreover the use of one piece of software by many users reduces the cost to each.

The expertise argument refers mainly to turnkey companies and software houses. They enable the user to buy in expertise rather than developing his own. As expertise is not required at all stages of computer installation and use, the presence of a service sector allows a more efficient usage of manpower than if each user had his own expert.

The rapid technological change in the industry promotes the existence of the service sector which takes some burden off the final user. Thus one may say that technology is changing the market structure.

Before proceeding to our conclusions, some comments ought to be made on the stresses that have been laid in this chapter. First, innovation has been taken as the production of a technologically more advanced machine. However, this machine has to be installed and very little has been said about the innovators in the user sector who install the machine, Moreover very little has been said about the first users to apply computers to new areas. The reason for this is that there is not really any data. When the data on installations by industry is investigated no one industry appears to install a new machine before any other. The first machine was installed in the UK by Lyons, and this case has been discussed, although no significant points arise. Because of this neglect, some observations on user innovation will be made in the next chapter.

Second, this chapter has concentrated on improvements over time in the activities in which computers are used or produced and has largely ignored the appearance of the first computer in the commercial sphere. It has been shown that all early machines were developments of university built prototypes, so the question of why the first commercial machine appeared is only a matter of application and not really basic development. It has also been shown that in the first commercial UK application Lyons had to build their own machine as no computer manufacturing sector existed – they did not however start to become machine suppliers until 1958. Thus computers as a technique for users only appeared when ICT (as HEC), Ferranti, English Electric and Elliott started to produce them. Profit potential must have influenced the decision to enter computer manufacturing in some manner (although few firms had managed to make profits out of computers before the middle and late sixties – the R & D demands were so great), but it is of use to consider again the market backgrounds of the participants. The manufacturers of office equipment would be threatened by computers for they were replacements for punched card machines, especially in their original applications as electronic clerks (although the manufacturers may have seen possibilities of market expansion through computers). The manufacturers of electronic components and electronic products would not have a threatened market but could have seen market potentials for their products and had the expertise to enter the market. Moreover in the UK as well as in the US there were certain government and defense pressures pushing companies into developing computers – the Elliott 401, Ferranti Pegasus, and EMI 2400 computers were all developed with NRDC financial support. It is interesting that the computer industry really developed with few new companies (more so in the UK than in the US although it is true there at a later stage). Nearly all participants were diversifying – this may, however, have been the problems of barriers to entry caused by the required large R & D expenditure. It would seem reasonable to assume that computers appeared in the commercial sphere because the basic technology was available and profit potential, in the form of market preservation and/or market expansion, drew participants to computer manufacturing.

The third point that has been largely ignored is why the technological change in the components industry occurred. It has been shown that the improvements in components have been a major force influencing technological change. However, to attempt to explain the forces behind the change in components is a major task, and a matter to which one cannot do justice in the present context. The reader is therefore referred to the OECD [1969] publication.

5.7 CONCLUSION

It has been shown that the computer user has been able to reduce his costs over time by the input of technologically improved products coming from the computer manufacturing sector. At the same time these products have promoted the applications of computers to new areas. These new products were the results of R & D expenditure in the production sector developing new machines (both completely new and improved versions of old products) based on improved components coming from the components sector and basic research outside the industry. The major improvements in products, it has been shown, occurred when generations changed.

The nature of the industry is such, it has been argued, that technological advance was the only feasible competitive mechanism because of scale returns, IBM's market share, and the advances made available by new components. This process, however, has led to uneven development in different aspects of the computer system and also affected market structure. It has been argued that the major effect of the market structure on technological advance has been through the reluctance of IBM to market all its innovations, but there were compensations through standardisation.

6. THE CHOICE OF TECHNIQUES

6.1 INTRODUCTION

Up to this point this study has provided information on the nature and development of computer using and producing activities in general, and in particular has indicated what opportunities are available for, and what costs are involved in, computer use, and what the characteristics of the computer using activity are. With this background it is now possible to advance with the explanation of the spread of computer usage. There are two possible ways to approach this subject. The first is to assume some behaviour patterns on the part of potential computer users working within the technological framework already discussed and to see if they can explain cross-section and time series data on the level of computer usage. The second approach is to go to direct data on the computerisation decision. In this study the computerisation decision is approached directly in this chapter, then on the basis of the results a theory is constructed that can be used in the next chapter to explain the data on patterns of computer usage.

The decision to computerise is one example of the firm's decision on the choice of technique. In a dynamic economy technique choice has three dimensions. The first dimension is time – at what moment in time is the decision made to change or maintain the present technology? The second dimension is level – at what scale is a technique to be operated? The third is composition – what technique is actually chosen? The three dimensions combine to yield determinants of the level and composition of the desired gross investment and capital stock at a moment in time. In this chapter the time and composition dimensions are studied, and the level at which a technique is run is discussed in the next chapter.

By looking at the decision to computerise it is hoped to be possible to draw conclusions that are not only applicable to the decision to computerise but can also be applied to the technique choice decision in general.

The state of existing theory on the technique choice decision (when it is not assumed away by homogeneous capital goods) can be characterised by two simple statements:†

(i) the technique chosen is that which maximises an objective function in which profit usually enters;

(ii) gross investment occurs in the technique resulting from choice procedures either when expansion is desired, or when the net present value of the existing technique is less than the net present value expected from the activity resulting from choice procedures.

This would suggest that the firm continually has in mind that technique which can maximise its objective function and, if production is to occur, will shift to that technique as soon as the net present value of the benefits from that technique exceed the present value of the benefits resulting from its existing technique.

The outline of this chapter is that in section 6.2 the activities that are alternatives to computers are discussed and in section 6.3 data is presented to show that existing theory cannot be accepted and further data is provided, an explanation of which supports an alternative theory. In section 6.4 conclusions are drawn.

6.2 THE ALTERNATIVE TECHNIQUES

One way to discover the alternative techniques is to see what computers have replaced. Two surveys have asked for details of methods superseded by Automatic Data Processing (ADP) (M of L [1965]; D of E [1972]). In table 6.1 the results for 1964 are presented. These show that of 328 installations, 270 said that some clerical work had been taken over, 249 reported some transfer from punched card processing and 229 had replaced keyboard accounting machines to some extent. The 1969 study showed that methods superseded were similar in both type and extent except that the proportion of installations taking over from punched cards had dropped from 76% to 56%. About 80% replaced some clerical labour and 67% replaced some keyboard accounting machines.

The main problem with this data is that only office or administrative functions are considered. It is shown in chapter 8 that this covers the largest proportion of computer usage. In scientific and process control applications both labour and special purpose logging and control equipment are being replaced.

The other comment that ought to be made is that the data only covers activities actually replaced, and not those that are competing but not

† These statements characterise the technique choice decision as discussed by Salter [1969] pp. 48–65.

Table 6.1. *Methods superseded by ADP 1964*

Methods	No. of affected installations
Clerical, punched card and keyboard machines	148
Clerical and punched cards	57
Clerical and keyboard accounting machines	51
Punched cards only	24
Punched cards and keyboard accounting machines	20
Clerical only	14
Keyboard accounting machines only	10
New work only	4
New work and any of the above	25
Others (addressing machines and calculators)	43

replaced. There is no obvious way around this problem, except to say that in the search for information for this study no such techniques were found by the author.

6.3 THE DECISION TO COMPUTERISE

As the major propositions in this section rely heavily on direct observation in the form of survey data, the first task is to present this data. The majority of the observations refer to the firm's decision to computerise, although it will be possible to add some comments from data on the decision to change computer model.

The *Computers in Offices* surveys supply the first set of data. In 1964 all computer users were asked 'to state why you decided to obtain the

Table 6.2. *Reasons for installing computers 1964 and 1969*

Reason	No. of affected installations	
	1964	1969
Quicker processing	144	659
Savings in data processing costs	137	347
Better service to management	115	747
Better quality results	110	—
Replacement of worn out equipment	66	415
Savings in office space	62	—
Savings in manpower	40	220
Better service to customers	29	437
Other	42	208
Total no. of installations	344	806

NOTES: see tables **6.3** and **6.4**.

Table 6.3. *Prime reasons for installing computers 1964*

Reason	No. of installations
Replacement of worn-out equipment	26
Better service to management	25
Savings in data processing costs	23
Savings in manpower	9
Savings in office space	6
Quicker processing	5
Better service to customers	3
Better quality results	—
Other	7

NOTES: About a third of the sample specified a prime reason or only gave one reason. Savings in manpower relate only to those cases where there were indications of difficulty in recruiting staff. Savings in manpower in order to save expenditure on salaries were classified as savings in costs. Similarly, saving in space relates only to cases in which there had been difficulty in finding office accommodation. The study also finds that there had been no significant difference in the years up to 1964 in the reasons given for computerising.

Table 6.4. *Prime reasons for installing computers 1969*

Reasons	Installations
Difficulty in recruiting staff	22
To replace worn out equipment	197
To reduce cost of processing data	83
To speed processing of data	97
To provide better service to management	325
To provide better service to customers	75
Other	27
Total number of installations	806

NOTES: Over 80% of the newer installations who replied gave only one reason or specified their main reason for installing ADP. A small number gave two reasons of equal importance. There was a slight variation in the replies over different sized installations, notably some 40% of larger installations gave reduction of processing cost as their prime reason compared with 10% of all installations.

A.D.P. equipment'. In 1969, those users who had computerised in the previous two years were asked 'why are you installing the A.D.P. equipment?', and had to select from a number of possible replies. The pattern of replies was as shown in table 6.2.

It was possible to separate out the prime reasons for installing computers in the two samples. In tables 6.3 and 6.4, the pattern of prime reasons is presented.

The major difference in the replies for the two years is the growth in the importance of providing a better service to management, although replacing worn out equipment and reducing the cost of processing data

Table 6.5. *Reasons for installing a computer.*
Miles Roman Ltd 1970

Reason suggested	No. of installations agreeing
To improve manpower utilisation	246
To improve service to customers	245
To improve general administration	242
To improve financial planning and control	234
To improve departmental planning and control	189
To improve corporate planning and control	102
To improve capital equipment utilisation	71
Total no. of installations	340

Table 6.6. *Reasons for rejecting computers (1)*

Reason	Number
Insufficient work	11
Too expensive	8
No technical staff	2
Delivery of results reputed to be too late	1
Computer not thought suitable	3
Other/don't know	2
Sample size	19

have maintained a relative importance. However, saving manpower has fallen from 9 % to less than 3 % of the prime reasons, and the quicker processing of data has increased in importance from 5 % to 12 %.

An independent survey carried out by Miles Roman Ltd (NCC [1972]) also considered the motives behind computerisation. The question asked was 'Please indicate...which of the following objectives have played a role in influencing your organisation to invest in a computer installation'. The results were as in table 6.5. These results, however, are not as useful as those above for they do not isolate prime reasons nor do they have anything to say about costs.

This data can be supplemented by some observations on why certain firms have not computerised. In a survey of computers in textiles (NCC [1968a]) it was found that of the non-users sampled, 19 % had considered but rejected computerisation. The reasons given for rejection are tabulated in table 6.6.

In a study of the hotel and catering industry (NCC [1968b]) a similar question was asked concerning the reason why certain tasks had not been computerised. The results are detailed in table 6.7.

Table 6.7. *Reasons for rejecting computers (2)*

	All	Computers Used	Computers Not used
Numbers sampled	95	24	71
Computerisation not considered	62	8	54
Computerisation considered but:	33	16	17
Insufficient work	13	3	10
Too expensive	11	3	8
No technical staff	1	—	1
Intend to; no time yet	4	4	—
Other	11	2	9

NOTES: Of the 'Other' category, only two of the sample preferred their present arrangement; the other reasons were speed, wait for own machine, or firm not large enough.

The final set of survey data is taken from a British Institute of Management survey of the current practice of technique evaluation when computers are installed (NCC [1971a] Vol. i). Two samples of 360 and 270 were asked what evaluation method was used to justify their investment in computers. Table 6.8 details the results from the completed returns although the response rate was very low.

Table 6.8. *Current practice with respect to evaluation methods*

	Number using Sample no. 1	Number using Sample no. 2
Evaluation method		
Discounted cash flow	24	12
Payback	14	4
Book return	2	5
Other	16	26
Total	72	56

The totals do not equal the sum of the replies for in some cases two methods were used.

A few comments on the above data are in order. The data on the textile industry was collected from a random sample of 140 firms from a population of 3,600 firms with thirty-nine known computer users added. In the industry only 4% of the companies own computers and 12% make some use of them, although most users are in the consumer or growth areas of the industry. The Hotel and Catering study used a sample of 127 with 95 replies. Neither of these industries are considered as in any way typical of other industries but it is felt that if one can find any data on why a task has not been performed one is very fortunate, for it enables one to overcome some of the bias that results from studies including only those members of the population who have performed the task.

The study of current practice with regard to evaluation methods had a very low response rate as detailed. The first sample was taken from the National Computing Centre list of users, the second from its membership list. The first sample was biased towards the engineering industry (twenty-three replies) with thirteen from coal, petroleum and chemicals and ten from other manufacturing. Thirty replicants had their first machine, twenty-eight their second and ten their fourth. The average data processing costs of this first sample were £252,000 per annum. The main bias that could come from this sample relates to the degree to which managers should attempt to imply rationality in their replies (see below). The low response rate may be because those who do not evaluate their computer systems felt unable to reply to the questionnaire. Both biases would strengthen the conclusions drawn below.

It is therefore suggested that if we could have unbiased data then the evidence for the conclusions drawn below would be stronger.

With the data we have it is possible to start to draw some conclusions about the choice of techniques. The first matter to consider is the costs and benefits of computer use. In chapter 4 the costs were considered at some length, so at this point only benefits need be covered. However, to discuss technique choice one really needs information about expected benefits, not realised benefits. *Ex post* realised benefits can only provide *ex post* justification for an investment decision and cannot play an *ex ante* role in choice. Thus whether benefits have been realised or not is irrelevant at this stage – all that matters is that certain benefits were expected to be realised. The use of survey data to investigate expectations obviously has difficulties when that data is collected after the investment decision has been made for it may be in the subject's personal interest to attribute *ex ante* expectation to *ex post* realisation. This can only be borne in mind but not eliminated. Tables 6.2, 6.3, 6.4 and 6.5 indicate what users were seeking from their computer systems. These expectations can be summarised as savings in costs in general, or manpower and office space in particular; improvement in service to customers; and/or improvements in the quality and quantity of management information to improve planning, control and efficiency in the organisation.

Given the nature of the costs and benefits, the next problem is evaluation. Table 6.8 gives indications of current practice with regard to evaluation, but a few relevant comments are in order. The discounted cash flow (DCF) rates when quoted varied from 10 % net to 30 % gross although no indication is given of net or gross of what, or what prices are used in the evaluation. The payback rates varied between 10 % and 100 %. We interpret 'payback' as meaning some measure of the average annual net or gross return on the historic cost. It is not to be taken as the payoff period criterion. The companies in sample 1 who used other methods nearly all used adaptations of the payback method. Ten companies in this sample used two or more methods.

Consider then the data in sample 1. It would seem, if the effects of double counting are removed, that forty-six out of the sample of seventy-one use some evaluation method. This implies that 25 % of the sample do not evaluate their systems. In the second sample a similar statement is not possible as we do not have data on double counting. However, in another question in the survey companies were asked whether they evaluated their computer systems with the same criteria used for other investments. The positive replies totalled thirty-eight in the first sample and twenty-five in the second. It seems implausible that 47 % in the first and 49 % in the second sample should use different evaluation techniques for this one investment, thus in the 47 % or 49 % there must be an element of users who never evaluated their systems and thus could not answer positively.

If one incorporates the 'others' into the payback criterion the pattern of evaluation becomes (for sample 1): DCF, 42 %; payback, 53 %; book return, 1 %; no evaluation, 25 %, realising that more than one method is used in certain cases. The most relevant point that we can draw at this stage is simple but basic. The DCF and payback criteria imply the principle of meeting targets, not of obtaining a maximum return. If one considers the above data and also realises that government and nationalised industries use the DCF methods,† then one can conclude that the majority of computerisation projects that are evaluated use satisficing rather than optimising techniques.

Thus a point has been reached where one can reject any theory of technique choice that depends upon maximisation, for it has been shown that in many cases no evaluation takes place, and in the cases where it does take place the methods used are of a satisficing and not optimising (or maximising) nature.

Even if maximisation is rejected is it still possible to maintain the hypothesis that firms have in mind a certain technique that they will use as soon as the time is right? Thus one must ask can a concept of the continuous re-evaluation of technology be supported such that the costs and benefits of the existing technique are continuously being compared to those of a 'preferred' activity?

Consider the replies tabulated in table 6.7. As one can see, from a

† See below.

sample of 95, 71 did not use computers (although 24 did use them) and of this 71, 54 had never even considered computer usage. In the study of computers in textiles, 12 % of the firms made some use of computers and of the other 88 % only 19 % had considered and rejected them. This leaves approximately two-thirds of the sample that had never considered computer usage. Realising that 20 % of the sample considered them the technique to use, if two-thirds of the sample have never considered their use, then a theory that relies solely on the continual comparison of techniques cannot be supported. There must therefore be other forces at work leading to the re-evaluation of the firm's technique. This does not mean, however, that continuous comparisons of techniques never occur, for in fact the Civil Service Department insist that this is how they operate:

The aim of the Civil Service Department has been to encourage Departments to have computers constantly in mind when considering how to do their work. Management service units (including O & M and Operational Research sections) both in the Civil Service Department and in other departments are always on the alert for new ways of exploiting the computer in the interests of efficiency and economy, in all fields of government activity. O & M and ADP assignment officers are trained to look for and bring to notice possible areas of computer application. (SCST [1970a] p. 427.)

Enough evidence has been presented to show that this cannot be the case in all applications. It has become obvious that a different theoretical framework is required if the above data is to be interpreted consistently. This framework must be able to predict that techniques will not be reconsidered continuously but will only at times be re-evaluated. It must also allow for the evaluation procedures to depend on satisficing rather than maximising, with different evaluation methods in different firms, and no evaluation at all in others. The framework which, it is felt, can best accommodate these influences is 'behavioural'. The version of the theory presented by Cyert and March will be used below.†

The theory argues that decision making in the firm can be analysed in terms of the variables that affect an organisation's goals, expectations, and choice. The firm has certain goals to be achieved in a period. These goals could refer, for example, to level of production, sales, profit and market share. The level at which goals are set depends on the past performance of the organisation and the performance of comparable institutions. If the organisation cannot meet its goals there is a stimulus to change. Such a stimulus may also come from a member of the organisation seeking a problem for which a pet project is a solu-

† Cyert [1963]. A summary of the theory is provided in pages 114–27. It is interesting that a similar view to technical change has been quite independently developed by two other writers; see Nelson [1973] and [1974].

Table 6.9. *Reasons for installing computers as % of*
all installations

Reason	1964 (%)	1969 (%)
Replacement of worn-out equipment	19	51
Difficulty in recruiting staff (savings in manpower)	11	27
Savings in office space	18	—

tion. The problem stimulates search behaviour for a solution, this search being initially localised and only spreading if no local solution is available. The results of the search behaviour are evaluated in a simple manner, the evaluation also being biased by the aspirations of the evaluator. Uncertainty is avoided by working in terms of the short run; feasibility in terms of finance being available is a major consideration. The choice of solution is in terms of satisficing rather than optimising, with non-marketed benefits being considered as constraints so as to avoid uncertainty.

Thus, with a bias towards the present context, the theory says that prior to a change in technique a problem is required, or an expected problem or a pet solution seeking a problem. The problem stimulates a search for a solution which to be accepted must satisfy certain standard rules and if it does not search will continue. Once the decision is made to implement the solution a further problem must arise before another solution will be considered.

The application of this framework to the data on the computerisation decision must begin with some discussion of the nature of the problem stimuli that have been apparent. Turn to tables 6.2 to 6.4. An initial important observation is that among the reasons given for installing computers certain categories can be identified that imply that computerisation resulted from the inoperability of the existing technique. These reasons are listed as the replacement of worn out equipment, savings in office space and savings in manpower and difficulty in recruiting staff. It may well be that office and staff considerations are just indicators that the firm is not willing to operate its old technique at higher prices, but they still indicate that the firm is being forced to reconsider its technique. The proportional importance of these reasons among all reasons in 1964 and 1969 were as in table 6.9.

Thus, depending on the degree of overlap, anything between 51 % and 78 % in 1969, or 19 % and 48 % in 1964, of installations were the result of the inability of the old method to continue to operate. Turning to prime reasons the pattern in table 6.10 emerges.

Table 6.10. *Prime reasons for installing computers as % of all installations*

Reason	1964 (%)	1969 (%)
Replacement of worn-out equipment	8.0	24
Difficulty in recruiting staff	2.5	3
Savings in office space	1.5	—

In 1964 the replacement of worn out equipment is the largest single category of reasons given, only one-third of the sample giving a prime reason (it was not asked for specifically in the questionnaire). When one considers that in many cases the change was from clerical labour the relative importance of replacement increases. Taking the two totals, in 1964 12 % and in 1969 27 % of machines were installed primarily because the old technique was no longer operable. If one considers prime reasons as a percentage of all prime reasons given then this sector increases to 40 %. It is interesting to note that similar forces are at work in forming the decision to change computers to the latest type. The following statement illustrates this point.

There is a market force that is illogical in the extreme and uncommercial. The market force is the desires and wishes of those very scarce people, the programmers. If a new, up to date, modern machine which requires a vast investment in new programmes, new techniques, and so on, is brought out it will be very difficult to recruit and retain programmers to work on older style machines. We have already seen this problem in the move from second to third generation in investment and retraining and having to move up to the more modern machines because of the programmers desires. (SCST [1970a] para. 1410, p. 263.)

These problems of obsolescence and obtaining inputs are obviously indicators on the non-achievement of the production goal. However, there is little evidence that the other goals with which the firms have been attributed have any influence. If one looks again at tables 6.3 to 6.5, the fact that firms list a number of benefits that they wish to obtain from computers indicates that different firms value different benefits differently. One way to explain this is to say that the different valuations depend on the need that the firms have for improvements in specific areas, i.e. the problems that are being met in the achievement of different goals. Thus, for example, if a firm installs a computer and expects benefits of reduced cost and a better service to customers, the fact that they list the better service as the prime reason for the installation suggests that the organisation was in need of sales improvement rather than cost reduction. Another firm might also generate cost reductions and better service but list the cost reduction as the prime reason. It would seem that this firm would be seeking profit increases. In other words it would appear that nearly all firms can gain the same benefits from computers, but the fact that they order the relative importance of the benefits differently suggests that they are trying to find solutions to different goal achievement problems.

It is not possible, however, except in the production goal category to identify any specific benefit as solely attributable to the need for improvement in the achievement of any specific goal. Take, for example, a firm having problems achieving its profit goal. To generate greater profits the firm may either reduce data processing costs, provide better service to customers, or improve efficiency by a better service to management by installing a computer. However, another firm installing a machine to increase sales could quote exactly the same desired benefits. Thus one-to-one links do not exist.

Some further evidence† that can be brought to bear consists of a list of often quoted reasons given to justify a computer installation. This list begins,

> because our accounting machines are falling apart
> because of clerical labour problems
> because more information is needed
> because of decimilisation or metrication,

where in each case a problem is stimulating the change of technique. However, the list also contains,

> because it is a sign of a progressive organisation
> because our competition has started using one
> because of the persistence of the computer salesman
> because training courses are always recommending their use.

These last four can be considered as examples of the 'solution looking for a problem' category. The prestige and outside pressure put the firm in the position where a technique is held in mind while a problem is sought. However, the second set of reasons might also be considered as influences changing the organisation's goals and promoting technique change that way.

So far, however, we have not taken account of any influence that the growth of the firm may have on the decision to computerise. The influence of growth may be reflected as revisions of the level of production goal and the search for means of effecting a change. It has been shown, however, that there are indivisibilities in computer use, which would suggest that if a firm's size increases over a certain threshold, not only the increases but all production may be computerised. On the

† The statements are taken from NCC [1971b] p. 15.

other hand, with indivisibilities the appearance of new firms, if they are only small, may not have any influence on computer usage. There is one category in which this growth effect may be included in the data, however, and that is under the desire for better management information. The reason for this is that the faster firms grow, the more problems they may have with control. These problems may be solved by computerisation but be labelled as the desire for management information.

To draw some conclusions from this section, it would seem that once one removes the concept of the continuous re-evaluation of techniques it becomes necessary to provide a rationalisation of why techniques are re-evaluated. This theory indicates that stimuli come through the problems that the organisation meets, or is expected to meet, in the attainment of its goals. Some evidence has been provided to illustrate that the production goal can be reflected in the data, although the evidence to support the other goal achievement problems is circumstantial.

The next stage in the theory states that a problem stimulates search and evaluation. Enough evidence has already been provided to suggest that satisficing rather than optimising takes place but one may be able to find that the evidence and the theory correspond in more cases.

In those cases where search behaviour is necessary the theory states that search is initially localised and also limited. The fact that satisficing rather than optimising takes place supports the limitation contention. To support the localised nature of search one can argue that the more of an organisation's competitors that are using computers the more it is likely to use them itself. This is definitely reflected in the study contained in the next chapter. However, there is some further data that can be used. In the hotel and catering study (data in table 6.7) the sample were asked why they had not applied computers to specific tasks, and of the users 33 % said they had not considered it but 75 % of non-users had not considered computer usage. This would tend to indicate that the contact with the computer promoted consideration of it, i.e. search is localised.

What is it possible to say on evaluation procedures? Earlier discussion has already supported the satisficing proposition, but table 6.8 also implies that simple standard operating rules are used for evaluation, e.g. mainly payback rates and discounted cash flow. The importance of the use of payback rates is that it is a procedure that implies dependence on current prices and thus avoids prediction of the future as the theory would suggest. The theory also suggests that non-marketed benefits are treated as constraints. The data on technique selection gives no indication of how intangibles such as better service are valued,

Table 6.11. *Computer evaluators*

	Sample	
Group	1	2
Financial staff	32	15
DP staff	52	39
Consultants	8	3
Others	7	18

or even if they are valued. However, in its evidence to the Select Committee, the Civil Service Department state that,

Currently, ADP projects are appraised by the discounted cash flow technique using a test discount rate of 10% (formerly 8%). They are normally required to show a substantial surplus, but cost is not the only criterion. Projects which do not show a positive present value are approved if it can be shown that sufficient additional direct savings or operating advantage can be achieved or if there will be unquantifiable benefits which justify the cost. (SCST [1970a] p. 428.)

This suggests that unquantifiable benefits are considered separately and treated as parameters. It may well be the case that private organisations behave in the same way.

Some support for the theory can be gained from tables 6.6 and 6.7 on why computers are rejected. The two main reasons for rejection are indivisibilities and expense. The interpretation of 'too expensive' can be twofold, either the computer would not pass evaluation procedures, or what appears more likely, the cost of computerisation is too great to be met from the organisation's resources – what the theory calls feasibility. It is significant that Mansfield [1968] (p. 153) finds that the probability that a firm will introduce a new technique is a decreasing function of the size of the investment required.

The final point of the theory on which some comments can be made is the bias in evaluation procedures. These biases can arise from the views of the evaluators. The BIM survey (NCC [1971a] Vol. i) tabulates the distribution of responsibility for computer evaluation, and the results are reproduced in table 6.11, although of the financial staff category in Sample 1, twenty-two were helped by data processing (DP) staff. The first indication that bias occurs in evaluation is provided by the results of the McKinsey Report (McKinsey [1968]), where it was found that of the eighteen less successful applications of computers only three involved operating managers in the specification of benefits whereas of the eighteen more successful users eleven did so. However, some more direct evidence of the influence of personalities can be found. In table 6.12 the use and planned use of advanced techniques

Table 6.12. *The use of advanced techniques*
(*% applying*)

	Computer department status							
	Autonomous		In accounts dept		In manage-ment services		Other	
	1971	1974	1971	1974	1971	1974	1971	1974
Mathematical models	18	53	11	48	35	73	46	43
Management information systems	21	39	18	20	30	65	14	50
Teletype terminals	13	33	8	35	27	56	25	46
On line	10	36	6	25	15	51	25	46
Graphics	7	35	4	19	16	47	25	21
Other terminals	8	27	4	15	10	36	6	21
VDUs	5	22	2	7	7	31	3	36
Real time	3	14	1	7	7	27	11	32
Microfilm	2	11	2	7	2	21	3	7

SOURCE: NCC [1972] p. 42.

in computers relative to the status of the computer department is detailed.

The relevant point about these figures is that the machines that are under the control of the accounting department are being used much less adventurously than those controlled by other departments. This impression is also carried over into the plans for 1974. It would therefore seem that the concept of organisational bias is reflected in computer use.

The conclusions of this section thus state that the *timing* of the technique choice decision is determined for the firm by the interaction of its goal formation and goal achievement characteristics, leading to problems and the search for solution. The actual *composition* of the technique choice decision depends on the nature of the search and evaluation procedures, which have been shown to be simple minded and biased. The search procedures are influenced by the number of machines installed in comparable organisations, and if new tasks are being considered, whether a machine is already installed. The evaluation procedures are also simple minded, satisficing rather than optimising is the rule, non-quantifiable benefits are considered as parameters, feasibility is important, and short run considerations dominate. Moreover it has been illustrated that the conception of the costs and benefits is biased by the views of the evaluator.

If one wishes to extend the above propositions to the choice of techniques in general it would appear to be advantageous to illustrate that the behavioural theory could also be applied to technological change (characterised by product innovation) in the computer producing sector. Unfortunately the data on producers' behaviour is not available and it is not, therefore, a practicable exercise.

6.4 Conclusion

The aim of this chapter has been to investigate the decision to computerise in order to find out about the choice of techniques in general and to provide a base upon which to build an explanation of cross-sectional and time series data on the spread of computer usage in the UK. It has been argued that one cannot accept a theory of technique choice that relies on maximisation and the continuous re-evaluation of technology. A theoretical structure was thus provided which would rationalise both the timing of the technique choice decision and the composition of the decision. This theory has been termed behavioural.†

It is interesting to ask why the theory that has been accepted, based on real world data, differs so markedly from the more traditional construct. The traditional concept of the firm is of an institution that is owner controlled in an environment without uncertainty, with free information and perfect competition. The owner–controller makes all decisions and thus there is no bias, the lack of uncertainty does not reduce all decisions to the short run, the free information precludes the need for search procedures and perfect competition is assumed to mean the maximisation of profits. In these conditions the rational producer must operate in the way of traditional theory. It is therefore suggested that our results differ as the environment is uncertain and not perfectly competitive, information is costly and firms on the whole are not owner controlled.

To terminate this chapter two further comments can be made on matters left over from previous chapters.

(a) In chapter 4 the costs involved in computer installation at stage 1 (evaluation) were left open. This chapter has now filled in that gap.

(b) At the end of the previous chapter it was stated that it may be possible to talk of user innovation in this chapter. The above discussion now makes this possible. It was found that there were no seemingly special characteristics of industries that installed a new machine first. This can be explained as the result of the means by which the timing of the computerisation decision is determined. There are no special characteristics of the firm that should make it time its decision to computerise at any special date, and thus if it is timed when a new machine appears it will innovate with that machine. Nothing special is required of the firm.

† For further statements of a similar view on technique choice see Nelson [1973] and [1974].

However, there is the matter of innovation in the sense of the first firm to use a totally new technique. Here we can argue that if a firm is to be an innovator in this sense it first requires a problem to be solved and then will undertake search procedures. The characteristics of a firm that determine whether it will innovate in this sense must refer to those influences that determine its search procedures and those influences that affect its evaluation procedures. Size may be important because then its members would have a wide ranging outlook and its resources would make practically any new technique feasible. In general, however, it would appear that one can argue that innovation can be covered in a general theory of technique choice. On that point it is time to turn to look at the data.

7. THE SPREAD OF COMPUTER USAGE IN THE UK, 1954–1970

7.1 INTRODUCTION

In chapter 6 a start was made on the explanation of the spread of computer usage in the UK with a study of the decision to computerise. No such study would be complete, however, without an investigation into the data that summarises the inter-temporal and inter-industry spread of computer usage. That branch of economic theory concerned with the penetration of new goods into an existing market is termed the theory of diffusion. In the appendix it is shown that the patterns of the diffusion process can determine the time path of an economy changing techniques. The importance of the subject to economic theory is thus illustrated.

The explanation of the diffusion process must rely on three main concepts:

a theory of supply to determine the number of new-type capital goods produced in a specific period – the maximum number that can be produced in a period limits the addition to the stock in that period;

a theory of demand – the demand for new-type capital goods will, without supply difficulties, determine the maximum number installed in a period, and the relative demands of different industries must determine the inter-industry spread;

a theory of market adjustment to balance the forces of supply and demand.

The present explanation of the spread of computer usage is thus based on the following principles:

(i) the desired supply of new capital goods depends on the demand expectations of the capital goods industry;

(ii) the demand for new capital goods is based on the principles expounded in the study of the decision to computerise;

(iii) capital goods are distributed between industries in relation to their demands;

(iv) excess or deficient demand causes changes in orders or inventories.

The present attempt to use this structure to explain the data proceeds as follows. In section 7.2 the general approach is discussed more fully, and in section 7.3 the data is presented. In section 7.4 the relevant literature is surveyed. Section 7.5 contains the major part of the study, an analysis of the demand for computers. This is followed in section 7.6 by a study of supply and disequilibrium, to be followed in section 7.7 by the conclusions.

7.2 THREE PRELIMINARY DIFFICULTIES

It has been shown at great length above that during its relatively short life the technique characterised by computers has undergone considerable technological change. However, the theory of diffusion is concerned with the spread of the use of one technique and not a number of different techniques. Although it is necessary to hold in mind the nature of the technical change that has taken place, one side steps this problem by assuming that all computers can be grouped into one commodity, and thus one technique. In chapter 3 the method of effecting this reduction was illustrated and involved the identification of certain basic characteristics common to all machines. Using the results of that chapter, the level at which a technique is run is represented by the machine input's quality multiple and all technological change is reflected in the price index for machines.

The next matter to consider is whether when one looks at the spread of computer usage it is in fact a case of diffusion. Casual empiricism indicates that over the last twenty years there has been a continuous spread of computer usage which would suggest that a diffusion has been under way. Computer usage has increased at 30–40 % p.a. at the expense of technologically older techniques, with the economy growing at 2–3 %. This is sufficient to indicate that it is a diffusion process.

Finally in this section some comments on the statistical methods used are in order. The technique used in this study is ordinary least squares (OLS) regression analysis. However, in studies of simultaneous equation systems the use of OLS can lead to bias in the coefficient estimates. There are two types of simultaneity in our models. The first is in supply and demand relations. The reason for using OLS here is explained in section 7.6. The second type is more complex. In the appendix it will be argued that, in the type of models used there, performance in one sector of the economy can affect the macroeconomic variables such as Gross National Product, which are treated in this context as independent variables. If this is the case it will cause bias in estimates. However, this simultaneity has been ignored because to reflect this effect one would need to build a whole transition model and try to fit that to the data. The objections to this are that the data and resources are just not available to perform such an exercise, and the coefficient estimates resulting from the application of simultaneous equation estimation methods to such a model, e.g. two stage least squares and indirect least squares, would still be biased but would be consistent (Johnston [1963] pp. 231–7). The advantage of consistency given the present small sample sizes is very limited. Thus the possible simultaneity that might arise in this area has been ignored.

7.3 THE DATA

There are two sets of data, one on the total number of computers installed and one on their distribution between user industries. In chapter 3 the sources of the data were discussed and a number of price series and a set of quality multiples were produced. In this chapter price series (e) generated in chapter 3 will be used.

To construct the quality adjusted quantity series every computer installed is represented by its quality multiple and the sum of these calculated for each time period. One then has a series of the stock of computers installed, measured in estimated 1963 introduction prices. For further comment it is useful to treat the aggregate and industry data separately.

The only problem left to overcome with regard to the aggregate data is the correction of the quantity series for machines that were taken out of service prior to 1961 and thus not included in the source estimates. The data available lists machines installed at the end of each year from 1961 to 1970 and the year in which they were installed. One can thus look at either the death pattern of computers added to the stock in a given year or the death pattern of all computers existing in a given year.

The first approach to solving the probelm was to attempt to estimate death curves for the computer investment of a given year in the hope of backward prediction. The results were not satisfactory. Thus what we have done is best illustrated in terms of the data in table 7.1. In this table all data below the horizontal line were taken directly from *Computer Survey*. Working on this data on the cumulative stock of computers and its life profile we calculated the entries for years prior to 1961 by assuming that the relationship between the size of a stock of ages V and $V+1$ will be equal to that apparent in the earliest year

Table 7.1. *Cumulative computer stock, not adjusted for quality*

Stock remaining at end of	Stock installed at end of																
	1954	1955	1956	1957	1958	1959	1960	1961	1962	1963	1964	1965	1966	1967	1968	1969	1970
1954	12																
1955	12	23															
1956	11	22	40														
1957	10	21	38	87													
1958	10	19	35	83	161												
1959	9	18	33	78	154	220											
1960	8	17	32	74	146	209	306										
1961	8	16	30	70	138	198	292	417									
1962		14	26	65	130	188	276	398	620								
1963		8	19	56	116	168	244	362	585	875							
1964		4	11	33	66	93	138	229	407	636	982						
1965				19	38	54	96	178	349	556	949	1424					
1966					33	47	80	151	293	490	847	1331	1956				
1967						35	61	115	222	373	679	1136	1734	2595			
1968							40	80	162	291	542	926	1493	2396	3522		
1969								46	99	204	393	704	1193	1928	3058	4319	
1970									63	146	286	551	961	1699	2697	3959	5470

Table 7.2. *Quality adjusted quantity series of the computer stock and orders measured in predicted 1963 introduction prices (£)*

Year	Installed at end of year	On order mid year
1954	139,425	—
1955	305,462	—
1956	614,870	—
1957	2,253,330	—
1958	4,086,162	—
1959	6,283,237	—
1960	13,027,441	—
1961	23,283,770	—
1962	39,721,240	—
1963	63,050,703	26,193,745
1964	92,831,480	70,022,707
1965	156,521,759	121,504,629
1966	283,821,673	125,071,476
1967	427,932,118	140,552,436
1968	603,230,391	152,078,397
1969	830,642,967	141,078,208
1970	990,405,300	129,166,897

for which we have data, i.e. if we let S^{V+1}/S^V be the proportion of the stock of age V still existing in age $V+1$, we assume that

$$S^1/S^0 = S^1_{1961}/S^0_{1961}$$
$$S^2/S^1 = S^2_{1960}/S^1_{1960}$$
$$S^3/S^2 = S^3_{1959}/S^2_{1959}$$
$$S^4/S^3 = S^4_{1958}/S^3_{1958}$$
$$S^5/S^4 = S^5_{1957}/S^4_{1957}$$
$$S^6/S^5 = S^6_{1956}/S^5_{1956}$$
$$S^7/S^6 = S^7_{1955}/S^6_{1955}.$$

With these multipliers one can find S^{V+i}/S^V for all i, which enables us to generate the required data. This is then rounded to the nearest integer for obvious reasons. With the data on stocks, the figures for annual additions to the stock were easily calculated. It is assumed that all machines, of whatever quality, have the same life pattern and one can thus generate the quality adjusted stock existing in a given year. To allow for any variations in a machine's share of the stock of a particular vintage as that vintage ages would require a very large data coding and handling problem for little reward. It is because of this assumption of constant shares as ages increase that the price series in chapter 3 were not based on the corrected data.

After the adjustments for machines taken out of service the resulting quality adjusted indices of the total stock of computers at the end of each year, and orders based mid-year, are as presented in table 7.2.

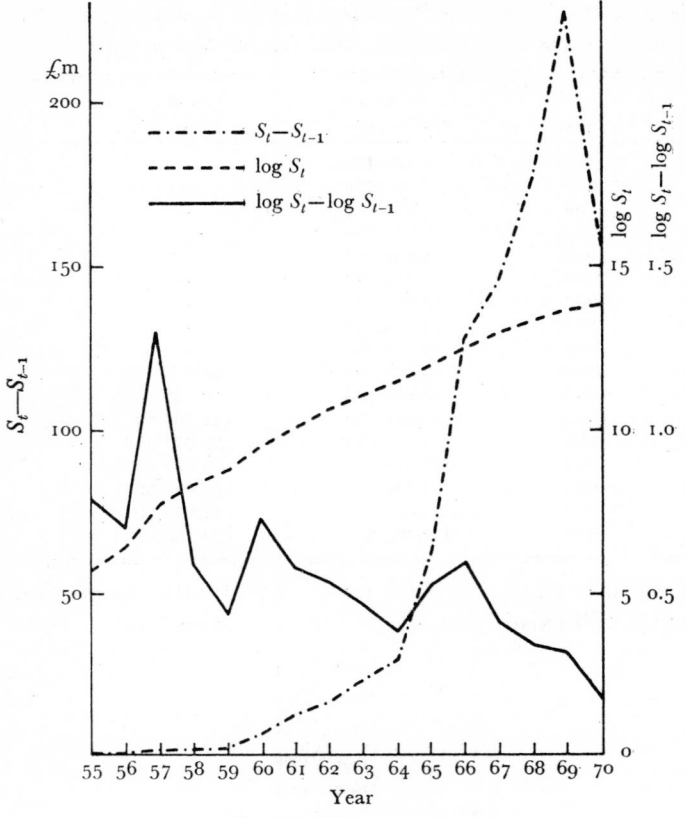

Fig. 7.1. The computer stock.

In fig. 7.1 a number of series that arise from this data are plotted; they are the log of the stock, $\log S_t$, the growth of the stock, $\log S_t - \log S_{t-1}$ and the change in the stock, $S_t - S_{t-1}$. These curves indicate what has been happening in the computer market since 1954. The curve of the total stock shows, as expected, a continuous increase over time, and correlates very well to a curve which shows a constant growth rate. However, the curve of the growth in the stock shows that the growth rate has in fact declined over time but has been kept high by boosts in 1960 and 1965/6, i.e. around the introduction date of the second and third generations. Thus a fair view of the industry seems to be one of a continually increasing stock, but increasing at a declining rate, and the whole growth curve being periodically shifted upwards.

If one now looks at the change in the stock each year, the positive growth in the industry with the discontinuity occurring in 1960 and

Table 7.3. Computer Survey *industry groups and SIC (1968)*
MLH classification

Group no.	*Computer Survey* classification	SIC MLH
1	Aircraft manufacturers and guided weapons	383
2	Armed services	901 (1–5)
3	Atomic energy	part 876
4	Chemicals, rubber, glass, plastics, paints, cosmetics	V, 463, 491, 496
5	Computer manufacturers and service bureaux	366 plus
6	Electrical engineering	361–5, 367–9
7	Ferrous and non ferrous metals, mining and quarrying	VI, 102, 103, 109 (1, 2)
8	Financial: banks, building societies, etc.	861, 862
9	Food, drink and tobacco manufacturers	III
10	Retail, wholesale, mail order, merchants	810, 812–32
11	General and constructional engineering	VII, VIII, X, XII, XX
12	Government departments	901 (6)
13	Government and other research establishments	part 876
14	Insurance and assurance	860
15	Local government	906 (3)
16	Motor	380–2
17	Oil	104, 262,263
18	Public bodies (mainly Post Office)	N/A
19	Public utilities (coal, electricity, gas, water)	101, XXI
20	Transport	701–7, 709
21	Universities and other educational establishments	872 (3, 4, 5)
22	Textiles, clothing, furniture and toys	472–3, 494, XII, XIV, XV
23	Publishing, printing, paper, bookclubs	XVIII
24	Sports, leisure, TV, films, hotels	881–7

1965/6 is apparent, but also one can see the extent of the slump that the industry suffered in 1970.

If we turn now to the industry data, it was stated in chapter 3 that the data was broken down from machine groups into individual machines by assuming that each industry had the same mix of machines in a group as was evident at the aggregate level. Data exists on numbers installed and on order for a number of years split into twenty-six different industry groups. The industry grouping of *Computer Survey* has been translated into SIC (1968) MLH classifications, with the result shown in table 7.3.†

The data is available for the period 1962 to 1970 on numbers installed, and 1962–9 for orders (all end year figures), except for groups 22 23 and 24, which start in 1963, 1964 and 1966 respectively. Industry 9 is defined as including industry 10 until 1968, when industry 10 has

† I wish to thank Mr Peddar, the compiler of *Computer Survey*, for his advice in this reclassification. Table 7.3 contains twenty-four categories, industries numbers 25 and 26 cover unknown and miscellaneous machines respectively.

Table 7.4. *Computer ownership by industry* (£ *thousands*)

Industry				Installed					
	1962	1963	1964	1965	1966	1967	1968	1969	1970
1	1,793.081	2,133.508	3,114.802	5,262.842	8,134.332	11,606.862	14,237.317	20,709.405	19,192.895
2	1,210.828	1,793.309	2,865.613	4,705.515	6,198.088	9,706.314	18,236.794	20,373.510	26,140.776
3	1,770.980	1,775.515	3,244.552	2,620.875	4,017.029	6,478.271	6,757.991	8,618.804	7,823.257
4	1,836.164	4,553.171	6,468.243	9,919.916	22,739.975	31,096.186	47,740.821	59,588.650	70,037.665
5	4,819.033	8,456.677	13,203.087	16,123.987	29,195.687	46,761.941	65,876.730	86,585.795	101,492.918
6	1,874.611	4,076.038	8,716.493	15,877.099	25,049.907	28,419.964	30,519.540	39,850.152	49,675.878
7	1,158.965	2,484.904	4,874.417	9,608.766	16,546.867	24,109.814	24,485.278	30,519.540	36,724.892
8	1,549.697	2,719.003	5,197.434	9,971.511	16,433.000	27,725.029	40,845.078	61,324.300	75,557.406
9	1,395.337	4,092.626	7,893.752	13,941.999	22,116.756	29,078.626	35,939.978	46,186.132	55,086.041
10	1,336.677	2,577.713	6,452.136	13,773.075	31,740.310	47,990.212	66,071.543	84,680.833	113,757.379
11	1,581.188	3,461.133	6,460.568	5,331.882	7,042.536	13,742.755	15,519.179	15,136.010	21,753.970
12	1,654.150	2,877.677	4,173.157	6,409.153	12,008.125	11,650.993	17,458.064	25,029.669	34,581.814
13	1,150.603	3,135.949	5,594.587	10,462.504	14,337.440	17,387.381	28,136.819	30,362.891	35,703.636
14	1,079.474	2,444.984	4,486.499	11,381.782	18,639.628	33,387.381	46,379.443	55,934.591	69,155.983
15	1,112.835	1,909.362	2,687.614	6,514.016	9,229.377	11,532.220	17,458.208	24,485.278	21,742.525
16	1,450.680	2,333.672	3,228.160	9,229.377	11,532.220	12,151.664	15,525.468	15,591.720	15,591.720
17	434.174	465.099	2,505.062	5,858.657	6,731.575	6,732.838	7,285.588	18,217.208	28,571.359
18	1,646.149	2,658.912	2,786.741	7,233.377	10,389.805	18,055.892	23,571.755	30,650.121	31,438.606
19	671.027	1,853.268	3,952.397	3,280.672	4,932.035	9,605.199	15,682.289	20,038.349	24,406.333
20	2,883.397	6,971.008	11,026.530	20,521.229	28,613.717	37,494.454	50,286.277	57,292.872	57,292.872
21	*	*	4,326.564	5,519.597	9,286.674	15,728.937	22,879.426	32,387.273	35,292.872
22	*	1,580.372	2,829.834	2,194.024	5,002.889	10,752.084	15,627.087	24,785.771	30,315.984
23	*	*	1,015.813	2,887.424	2,294.263	4,486.753	6,155.025	7,612.195	10,057.895
24	*	*	*	*	2,215.658	10,464.329	10,258.082	16,021.616	20,745.504
25	1,328.446	1,641.675	2,563.065	6,232.617	2,185.058	*	*	*	*
26	89.594	1,239.982	1,809.829	*	*	*	*	*	*
Total	33,827.089	68,083.033	115,101.223	175,848.268	296,736.079	461,544.018	647,860.470	850,603.510	1,022,862.146

On order

Industry	1962	1963	1964	1965	1966	1967	1968	1969	1970
1	1,440.828	1,527.156	1,269.690	2,617.545	2,380.860	1,725.296	1,527.821	1,943.937	*
2	259.877	371.109	316.407	2,525.443	1,791.807	7,470.164	14,512.423	15,601.515	*
3	977.819	2,370.248	2,492.035	1,139.637	901.890	429.607	1,490.424	414.486	*
4	1,014.492	1,515.361	6,436.274	12,687.993	11,020.052	5,940.834	9,103.718	6,089.153	*
5	445.855	1,807.389	2,094.935	6,853.077	6,417.170	10,019.582	8,809.385	9,827.335	*
6	549.250	729.519	3,501.468	6,696.483	6,996.464	4,696.334	5,171.814	4,556.310	*
7	340.112	1,479.758	3,004.075	4,101.820	4,461.383	4,348.809	3,253.145	2,343.465	*
8	775.016	922.335	7,339.771	8,444.920	13,679.133	11,711.596	11,670.657	13,587.168	*
9	2,171.727	2,332.100	4,048.390	11,278.581	11,876.677	9,023.289	6,322.810	10,272.524	*
10	*	*	*	*	*	*	8,189.351	4,713.511	*
11	856.038	1,401.285	5,789.744	14,990.645	17,023.851	15,356.910	11,812.899	17,028.471	*
12	695.122	2,249.401	2,755.271	2,422.562	6,868.236	8,954.094	6,374.025	8,917.055	*
13	341.102	1,066.216	174.866	1,576.289	2,034.115	3,717.201	3,717.201	861.473	*
14	617.860	1,965.444	4,561.576	3,705.966	3,697.834	2,761.704	2,951.588	4,278.566	*
15	893.085	1,264.427	7,635.652	12,293.219	15,697.200	7,786.189	6,534.467	8,467.671	*
16	409.785	544.885	2,107.783	2,983.518	2,787.735	1,263.680	2,041.561	1,152.334	*
17	827.436	777.060	538.472	1,013.669	2,297.084	2,072.237	231.062	173.586	*
18	124.109	130.795	1,053.570	2,660.756	5,540.613	2,326.191	4,851.508	5,564.402	*
19	1,305.934	1,680.644	5,017.730	5,147.225	1,465.660	5,463.975	4,077.765	2,323.639	*
20	0.000	2,119.161	2,317.526	5,299.490	3,941.616	3,941.616	2,181.748	2,356.277	*
21	3,289.950	1,327.153	1,142.112	6,352.703	6,724.375	5,337.777	4,369.688	3,972.989	*
22	*	781.749	2,595.121	5,271.644	10,773.074	3,109.201	5,564.034	3,582.978	*
23	*	*	626.945	1,212.635	4,749.185	3,417.380	2,521.132	3,405.186	*
24	*	*	*	*	1,765.342	2,421.677	3,464.102	870.441	*
25	982.523	1,012.844	1,443.610	2,491.250	1,165.455	*	5,648.924	5,214.665	*
26	1,244.110	266.113	12,597.177	6,203.252	3,751.469	4,383.650	*	*	*
Total	19,562.080	32,042.152	80,860.199	127,415.056	150,708.330	136,393.251	137,519.135	137,519.135	*

* Indicates no data available.

a separate category. To quality adjust the series one represents every computer by its quality multiple. The data that result are listed in table 7.4.

There is one problem with the data listed above; an attempt is being made to identify the total usage of computers, but certain firms do not own machines, they use the service sector. The aggregate data includes machines in the service sector but the industry breakdown includes a separate service sector category. In 1968 the service and computer manufacturing sector controlled 10 % of the total computer stock. This cannot be broken down into the present existing industry categories and thus has had to be ignored. It is hoped that not too great an error will result.

7.4 LITERATURE SURVEY

The literature on the spread of innovations is usually split into a study of innovators and a study of the imitation process once an innovation has been adopted. The work in this chapter is concerned solely with the spread of an innovation, the subject of the characteristics of those firms and industries that adopt first has been considered above. As all the data available starts some time after the innovation it is not really of any concern at this stage.

The literature on the diffusion process has been studied elsewhere,† so in this study it is only necessary to present results and not to go into the matter too deeply. There is, however, a definite two way split in the approaches that have been taken to explain diffusion processes, the *ad hoc* models and the stock adjustment models. The stock adjustment models are usually used for the analysis of time series data and the *ad hoc* models are used for analysing inter-firm, intra-industry or intra-firm examples of diffusion. These *ad hoc* models will be looked at first and then comments will be made on the stock adjustment models.

The results quoted by Kennedy and Thirlwall are mainly derived from the work of Mansfield [1968] (chapters 7–10). The relevant conclusions are that:

(i) As the number of firms in an industry using an innovation increases, the probability of its adoption by a non-user increases.

(ii) The rate of diffusion tends to be higher for more profitable innovations and for those requiring small investments. There is some

---

† Kennedy [1972]. It is of interest that it is found in this study that there have been very few attempts to explain diffusion processes in the UK although US data has been studied more extensively. This conclusion is supported by Phelps Brown [1972]. Quoting from Lord Roberthall he states, 'In this period Britain seems to have learnt nothing at all about the motivation of entrepreneurs in what seems a most elementary requirement for growth models – the rate at which technical innovations already understood will be adopted.' It is hoped that the study in this and the previous chapter will help to fill that gap.

indication that less concentrated industries diffuse innovations quicker.

(iii) Differences between firms in rates of intra-firm diffusion can be attributed to the profit they derive from the new technique, differences in size, liquidity, and the date when they first used the new technique.

(iv) There are indications that the rate of imitation is higher if not very durable equipment is being replaced and if output is growing rapidly.

(v) Mansfield has found, as have most studies in the diffusion field, that as a function of time the percentage of the total potential usage of a new technique actually converted can be best approximated by an S-shaped curve.

These results are supported to a large extent by the work of Ray [1969] in his study of international differences in diffusion rates, but he adds the rider that pioneers tend to innovate slower. Williamson [1965] disputes Mansfield's findings as regards market concentration and diffusion.

The *ad hoc* studies have been outnumbered by the applications of stock adjustment models. The authors include Chow [1967], Wigley [1966], and Stone and Rowe (Stone [1957]), also a survey of the stock adjustment approach to investment is available by Jorgenson [1971]. This genus of models is characterised by saying that the investment in a process in a given period is some function of the difference between the actual and the equilibrium stock, and the equilibrium stock is some function of price and output, e.g.

$$S_t - S_{t-1} = \lambda(S_t^* - S_{t-1}) \quad 0 < \lambda < 1$$
$$S_t^* = F(P_t, Y_t) \tag{1}$$

where S_t^* is the equilibrium stock in time t, S_t the actual stock, P_t the price of the good under consideration in time t, and Y_t output in time t. The main characteristics of these models is that the rate of adjustment (λ) is usually taken as either a constant or some function of S_t and S_t^*.†

There has been one rather successful attempt to combine the *ad hoc* and stock adjustment hypotheses. Griliches [1957] fitted a logistic curve to data on the spread of hybrid corn in different geographical areas of the US and attempted to discover the influences causing the

---

† Although it is shown by Stone and Rowe in Stone [1957] that it can be related to other variables. I wish to thank one of the King's College Fellowship referees for this point and for also pointing out that one stock adjustment hypothesis utilised in an earlier draft of this study had no claim to be labelled a Stone and Rowe hypothesis.

differences in parameters between areas. Thus to the data for each area he fitted the curve

$$R = \frac{K}{1 + e^{-(a+bt)}} \qquad (2)$$

in the form

$$\log_e \left(\frac{R}{K-R} \right) = a + bt,$$

where

$R = \%$ of acreage planted with hybrid seed
$K = $ ceiling value of R
$t = $ time
$b = $ rate of growth coefficient
$a = $ constant of integration which positions the curve on the time scale.

Thus a determines the date of first innovation, b the rate at which usage spreads and K the level at which satiation exists. By investigating the differences between the estimates of a, b and K for different areas, Griliches finds that:

1. a is related to market density and the cost of entry.
2. b can be explained by the profitability of the innovation.
3. K is explained by the average profitability of the innovation in an area.

This study of the results achieved by other writers will be left at this point, but at the end of the next section some of the major propositions will be investigated once again.

7.5 THE DEMAND FOR COMPUTERS IN THE UK, 1954–70

The above studies of diffusion concentrate practically exclusively on the demand aspects of the diffusion process, and it is therefore considered advantageous to begin in the same way here. It has been stated that the demand for new type capital goods should be based on the principles derived in chapter 6, where the choice of techniques was pursued at length. In that chapter we covered both the timing of the technique choice decision and the search and evaluation procedures that lead to the composition of the technique choice decision.

It was also stated that there is a dimension of levels that has yet to be covered. The crucial point about this three dimensional approach is that the composition and level aspects determine the scale at which a new technique will be run, and the time dimension will yield results on the time path of computer usage, which is in fact the diffusion path.

The scale at which the problem solution technique is run must be determined by the scale that it is necessary to operate the technique to overcome the problem that stimulates its use. It can be hypothesised, however, that the bigger is the organisation the greater will be the scale at which the technique is run, for if, for example, the firm wishes to computerise to reduce its data processing costs, then the larger the firm the larger is its data processing function and thus the greater is the required computer input. To take another example, if the firm requires a management information system the larger the firm the more information required and the more areas from which it has to be derived and so the greater input of computers required. As firm size can usually be represented by its output level, it would be expected that if two firms met the same problem the one with the greater output would require a greater input of computers to solve that problem. If one therefore hypothesises that there is a satiation number of applications of computers in an organisation then the satiation level of computer input would vary with the output of the organisation. The proportion of that satiation level installed at a moment in time would depend on the problems the firm has met or has expected to meet and its search and evaluation procedures. If one aggregates across all firms then the total satiation level of computer usage (S_t^* in the stock adjustment models) should vary with GNP. However, as it has been shown that increasing returns to scale exist in computer usage such a relation should also reflect this.

The basic problem with the use of the behavioural approach to explain aggregate (economy-wide and industry-wide) data is that it is essentially concerned with firm behaviour and does not aggregate well. To illustrate this, consider data on an industry; the theory would then suggest, for example, that if a firm's profit goal is not being attained then one might expect some move towards computerisation as a solution to that problem. Thus it might be argued that if an industry suffers a fall in profits relative to the previous year they are not attaining objectives and computerisation might be extensive. However, the theory also states that a firm's goals are not only determined by its past performance but also by the present performance of comparable institutions, so the industry-wide poor profit performance may just mean a reconsideration of goals and not an increase in computer input. If, however, one could identify one firm in which profits fell in an industry where profits in general were rising and that firm was seen to computerise then the theory would be verified.

There is yet another aspect to the theory that can be illustrated with this profit example. If it is assumed that a firm's profit goals do not change but it fails to meet those goals, then before computerisation can take place the problem solution must pass 'feasibility' tests. Feasibility has been considered as the ability of the firm to fund the solution from its resources. If a firm is suffering a profit fall then the resources available to it are less. There are thus conflicting influences on the firm. Now, it would be possible to take this all into account by setting up goal-formation functions based on the relevant variables, constructing feasibility variables, etc. and trying to fit the theory to data. In the present context that is not practicable since the test must really be carried out on data at the firm level, and even if one can get around aggregation difficulties and fit it at the industry or economy level the number of variables would be far too large for the small data sets available.†

Because of these difficulties it has been decided to attempt to explain the data on the spread of computer usage by the use of stock adjustment models and to take the results of chapter 6 into account in two ways.

(i) The stock adjustment hypothesis will be fitted without modification and the results of the previous chapter will be taken into account in the interpretation of the results.

(ii) Because it has been argued that the concept of the equilibrium or satiation level of computer usage is relevant in both the stock adjustment and behavioural approaches to diffusion, an attempt will be made to investigate whether the adjustment coefficient can be shown to vary systematically with the variables which the behavioural theory predicts are relevant. However, because of the above comments not very much is expected of this approach.

These studies will be carried out in two distinct halves, one on the aggregate data, the other on the industry data.

The basis of the stock adjustment approach is that

First the quantity of existing stock asserts a positive influence [on the rate of growth], partly rationalised by the idea that the more the product has been accepted, the more prospective buyers have come into contact with and learned about the product. Second, the difference or ratio between the equilibrium level, ultimately to be reached and the existing level also asserts a positive influence. Although the existing stock has a positive effect on the rate of growth, as it shows the extent of the awareness of the product, the closer it comes to the equilibrium level the smaller will be the number of prospective buyers remaining. (Chow [1967] p. 1118.)

Chow details two forms of stock adjustment hypotheses which he

---

† An alternative approach to the one taken here would be to use simulation methods as in Nelson [1973] and [1974], but even for that approach data is required on firms at a much lower level of aggregation.

labels Gompertz and Logistic. The Gompertz hypothesis he states can be represented as

$$\frac{\mathrm{d}\log S_t}{\mathrm{d}t} = \lambda(\log S_t^* - \log S_t).\tag{3}$$

The Logistic hypothesis he states as

$$\frac{\mathrm{d}\log S_t}{\mathrm{d}t} = \lambda(S_t^* - S_t).\tag{4}$$

However, Pyatt [1971] states the Logistic curve in a slightly different form – the form used by Griliches [1957]:

$$\frac{\mathrm{d}S_t}{\mathrm{d}t} = g(t)S_t\left(1 - \frac{S_t}{S_t^*}\right)\tag{5}$$

which yields,

$$\frac{\mathrm{d}\log S_t}{\mathrm{d}t} = g(t)\left(\frac{S_t^* - S_t}{S_t^*}\right).\tag{6}$$

Only if one considers

$$g(t) = \lambda S_t^*\tag{7}$$

does the Chow version result. However, in the present study the Chow version is used – mainly so that the results should be comparable.† Thus attempts have been made to fit the two Chow formulations to the aggregate data. In addition the Stone and Rowe approach has also been investigated, which although using the Gompertz adjustment function redefines the dependent variable. The data used in applying these hypotheses was,

(a) for S_t, the stock installed in time t, the quality adjusted stock from table 7.2 is used,

(b) the computer price series is series (e) from chapter 3 (p_t^c),

(c) for output, the GNP at constant 1963 prices is used (Y_t),

(d) the general price level is represented by an index of prices for all final goods and services sold on the home market (π_t).‡

Looking at the Logistic hypothesis first, this is most conveniently combined with a function for the equilibrium stock of the form

$$S_t^* = a + bY_t + c\frac{p_t^c}{\pi_t}\quad b > 0,\ c < 0\tag{8}$$

---

† In the sense that Chow also studies the spread of computer usage, for it should be noted that we use a different functional form than Chow to represent the satiation stock.

‡ The output and price series data are taken from *National Income and Expenditure 1971*, HMSO 1972.

which yields an estimable function†

$$\log S_t - \log S_{t-1} = \lambda a + \lambda b Y_t + \lambda c \frac{p_t^c}{\pi_t} + \lambda S_{t-1} + U_t \qquad (9)$$

in which $\log S_t - \log S_{t-1}$ is a proxy for $d \log S_t/dt$ and S_{t-1} approximates S_t (an inelegance caused by working in discrete rather than continuous time). Using the data specified, the results shown in table 7.5 were produced.‡

Table 7.5. *The logistic hypothesis*

Coefficient	Coefficient estimate	t statistic
λ	−0.0000	−0.0574
λa	2.36	0.92
λb	−0.00006	−0.744
λc	−0.079	−0.0267

$R^2 = 0.478$ $\qquad$ $\bar{R}^2 = 0.289$

The adjustment coefficient is of the correct sign but much too small and it is not significant at the 95% level. In fact not one of the variables is significant at the 95% level, and thus the hypothesis cannot be accepted as it stands.

Better results were expected from the Gompertz hypothesis for Chow was happy with its fit to the US data, which has a similar time profile to the UK data. In this case the equilibrium stock is represented by

$$\log S_t^* = a + b \log Y_t + c \log \frac{p_t^c}{\pi_t} \qquad b > 0, c < 0 \qquad (10)$$

and this yields the estimable function

$$\log S_t - \log S_{t-1} = \lambda a + \lambda b \log Y_t + \lambda c \log \frac{p_t^c}{\pi_t}$$
$$+ \lambda \log S_{t-1} + U_t. \qquad (11)$$

Using the same data as above the results in table 7.6 were generated. In the estimated equation the coefficient on $\log S_{t-1}$ is negative and thus the adjustment rate is positive and the estimates of b and c are of the correct sign. However, the lagged stock is the only significant variable at the 95% level and the explanatory power of the hypothesis is low.

Because of these relatively poor results it was decided to try to reproduce Chow's results more closely by restricting the time period

---

† All logarithms used in this chapter are to the base e.
‡ In equation (9) the lagged stock is entered with a positive coefficient but (4) and (8) imply a negative coefficient; thus one would expect the coefficient estimated to be negative and thus the estimate of λ positive.

Table 7.6. *The Gompertz hypothesis*

Coefficient	Coefficient estimate	t statistic
λ	-0.208	-2.19
λa	-1.699	-0.070
λb	0.421	0.172
λc	-0.400	-1.477

$R^2 = 0.686$ $\bar{R}^2 = 0.573$

Table 7.7. *Gompertz hypothesis 1957–64*

Coefficient	Coefficient estimate	t statistic
λ	$-0.464\ (-0.474)$	$-4.05\ (-4.64)$
λa	$-52.39\ (-63.28)$	$-1.55\ (-3.26)$
λb	$5.648\quad(6.73)$	$1.66\quad(3.37)$
λc	-0.169	-0.42

$R^2 = 0.882\ (0.877)$ $\bar{R}^2 = 0.764\ (0.803)$

to one equivalent to the time span of his study, i.e. from the first generation peak (1957) to the trough of the second generation (1964). It is
interesting to note that Chow's results do not predict the second
generation peak at all well. When the Gompertz curve is fitted to the
1957–64 period the results shown in table 7.7 are generated. The results
in brackets are derived by running the regression without the price
variable. (If one drops variables that are insignificant at the 95 % level
from the regression over the whole time period, one is left with an
equation in the log of the stock and log Y, and an estimate for λ of
0.084.) In general then, the shorter time period yields better results
and would imply a much higher adjustment coefficient. It was not
possible, however, to generate results in which all variables were
significant at the 95 % level. The question to be answered is why the
results should be better for the shorter time period. All one can really
say is that there might be structural influences that in this formulation
only show up in the longer period but can be successfully ignored in
a shorter time period.

Finally the Stone and Rowe hypothesis was applied to the data.
To derive the estimating equation, let

v equal net investment,
u equal current consumption, and
q equal total purchases in a time period.

Then

$$q \equiv v + u. \tag{12}$$

Let the stock used up in a period equal $1/n$th of the stock at the beginning of the period and $1/m$th of the stock installed during the period $(m \geqslant n \geqslant 1)$, then

$$u_t = \frac{S_t}{n} + \frac{q_t}{m}. \tag{13}$$

Stone and Rowe show that

$$\frac{1}{m} = 1 - \frac{1}{n \log_e \left(\dfrac{n}{n-1} \right)}. \tag{14}$$

From (12) and (13) one can derive

$$u_t \equiv \frac{m}{n(m-1)} S_t + \frac{1}{m-1} v_t. \tag{15}$$

But

$$v_t \equiv S_{t+1} - S_t.$$

Therefore,

$$u_t \equiv \frac{m}{n(m-1)} S_t + \frac{1}{m-1} (S_{t+1} - S_t). \tag{16}$$

Therefore,

$$u_t \equiv \frac{(m-n) S_t + n S_{t+1}}{n(m-1)}. \tag{17}$$

From *Computer Survey* data (see table 7.1) it is possible to calculate n, with which m can be estimated from equation (14). With these, u can be estimated from equation (17).

It is hypothesised that net investment is based on the stock adjustment principle

$$v_t = \frac{mS_t}{n} \left[\left(\frac{S_t^*}{S_t} \right)^{\lambda} - 1 \right] \tag{18}$$

and the equilibrium stock is represented by

$$S_t^* = \frac{an(m-1)}{m} Y_t^b \cdot \left(\frac{p_t^c}{\pi_t} \right)^c \cdot e^{gt} \tag{19}$$

in which g is a growth rate. Combining (15), (18) and (19), taking logs and first differences yields the estimable function,

$$\Delta \log u_t = b\lambda \Delta \log Y_t + c\lambda \Delta \log \frac{p_t^c}{\pi_t} + g\lambda + (1-\lambda)\Delta \log S_t + u_t. \tag{20}$$

The data used for fitting this equation was derived from (17) using *Computer Survey* data and the same series for S_t as used above. The values of n calculated for different years (only for those years with full data) were

1961	1962	1963	1964	1965	1966	1967	1968	1969
1.047	1.060	1.376	1.035	1.070	1.129	1.083	1.152	1.091

The equation was fitted using the minimum, maximum and average value for n, i.e.

$$\text{min:} \quad u_1 = 0.72S_t + 1.68S_{t+1}$$
$$\text{average:} \quad u_2 = 0.88S_t + 2.46S_{t+1}$$
$$\text{max:} \quad u_3 = 0.508S_t + 0.80S_{t+1}.$$

The results achieved, however, were not very satisfactory. They are presented in table 7.8 with the t statistics in brackets.

Table 7.8. *The Stone and Rowe hypothesis*

	Coefficient estimates		
Coefficient	u_1	u_2	u_3
$g\lambda$	0.145 (0.24)	0.147 (0.25)	0.138 (0.23)
$1-\lambda$	0.095 (5.13)	0.099 (5.26)	0.084 (4.79)
$b\lambda$	0.610 (0.27)	0.602 (0.27)	0.633 (0.25)
$c\lambda$	−0.349 (0.30)	−0.361 (0.31)	−0.321 (0.28)
$\bar{R}^2$	0.128	0.106	0.191
DW statistic	2.180	2.180	2.180

These results indicate that the hypothesis is yielding little explanation of the data, and that $\Delta \log S_t$ is the only significant variable, its coefficient also being of the correct sign. Its size, however, suggests an adjustment rate of 0.9, which seems rather high.

Because of the generally unsatisfactory performance of these hypotheses it was decided to try and improve them by modification. In the above hypotheses the demand for computers is represented by the change in the stocks. The first improvement made is to replace this by the change in the sum of stocks and orders because orders will take up any surplus of demand over supply so that the new variable will reflect the level of demand more closely, and the inclusion of orders, by removing the time lag between ordering and delivery, will locate the computerisation decision at the moment in time that it is made. Thus a new variable Z_t is defined as

$$Z_t \equiv S_t + O_t, \tag{21}$$

where O_t is the quality adjusted level of orders in time t. This improvement involves two problems.

(i) To include orders may involve some double counting if a machine is being replaced, for the original machine may be included in the stock data and the replacement in the order data. This is accepted but assumed away.

(ii) To include orders some data is required. In table 7.4 a series of order data is presented for the period 1963–70. However, that data is mid-year based and the stock data is end-year based. The order data is therefore taken from the industry data which is end-year based. This data is only available for the period 1962–9. To complete the series to 1970, it is assumed that 1970 orders have the same machine mix as 1969 orders. This means that full data is available for 1962–70 and partial data for 1954–61. Thus the new dependent variable is defined as

$$\log S_t - \log S_{t-1} \quad \text{for the period 1954–62}$$

and $\qquad \log Z_t - \log Z_{t-1} \quad$ for the period 1963–70.

This series is plotted in fig. 7.2 and labelled $\Delta \log Z_t$. The major differences between the series with and without orders centre around the period 1964–6. In the original series the second generation growth rate is at its lowest in 1964, and the third generation takes two periods to reach its peak in 1966. The new series has the second generation minimum in 1963 and the third generation peak appearing in 1964, which is the year that the price series and the technological change chapter indicate that the third generation appears. It is this 1964 peak relative to the previous 1964 trough that makes one feel that the new series is an improvement, for if one believes that computer generations are to have any effect on computer usage one would not expect a trough when the new generation appears. It is significant that during 1964 346 machines were installed but 474 machines were on order at the end of the year, of which 193 were for the new third generation 360s and 1900s.[†]

The introduction of the order data considerably complicates the dependent variable in the Stone and Rowe approach, and considering the poor performance at the cruder level, it was decided not to proceed with this hypothesis any further. The Logistic hypothesis, on the other hand, does not involve this complication, but now the time shape of the growth rate series is such that it always peaks early after the price falls which occur when generations change, which suggests that the Logistic hypothesis is not as appropriate as the Gompertz.[‡] It was therefore decided to proceed with the Gompertz hypothesis. This was fitted to the new data with one further change – the price variable was redefined as the price of computers relative to all input costs, for it was felt that

[†] The data is from CS [1965], summary tables March and July.
[‡] For a discussion of the time profiles implied by the two hypotheses see Chow [1967].

computers are a productive input and thus their price ought to be compared to the price of other productive inputs not the prices of outputs. The new variable is represented by p_t^c/TC_t.[†] The resulting estimated equation was

$$\Delta \log Z_t = 8.565 - 0.668 \log Y_t - 0.124 \log S_{t-1} - 0.318 \log \frac{p_t^c}{TC_t} \quad (22)$$
$$(0.377)(-0.292) \quad (-1.389) \quad (-1.065)$$

$$R^2 = 0.656; \quad \bar{R}^2 = 0.541; \quad DW = 2.132.$$

Dropping the non-significant variables at the 95 % level,

$$\Delta \log Z_t = 1.298 \quad -0.075 \log S_{t-1} \quad (23)$$
$$(7.807)(-4.772)$$

$$R^2 = 0.619; \quad \bar{R}^2 = 0.565; \quad DW = 2.28.$$

Correcting for autocorrelation,[‡] an adjustment factor of -0.181 is required, but the pattern of the results is not significantly affected.

These results are not very satisfactory. The failure of the price and output variables would suggest that the equilibrium stock is not affected by either price or output. However, just a visual inspection of the series on Z_t would indicate that something is affecting the equilibrium stock when generations change. It is therefore hypothesised that price will influence the equilibrium stock, but a change in generations by itself also affects the equilibrium stock. We thus define four new variables in line with the generation concept discussed in section 5.4. This discussion indicates that the generations were available according to a time pattern reflected in the following dummies,

D_0, the zero generation dummy, equals 1 for the period 1954–6 and 0 elsewhere,

D_1, the first generation dummy, equals 1 for the period 1957–9 and 0 elsewhere,

D_2, the second generation dummy, equals 1 for the period 1960–3 and 0 elsewhere,

D_3, the third generation dummy, equals 1 for the period 1964–70 and 0 elsewhere.

Using these dummies two hypotheses were tested. If one lets

$$S_t^* = e^a Y_t^b (p_t^c/TC_t)^c$$

then the dummies can be incorporated as influences on a or b. The latter approach would suggest that the degree of scale returns varied

---

† The total cost series (TC_t) is taken from the same source as the other data, i.e. the Blue Book. Attempts were made to use a series to reflect the price of clerical labour relative to computers but they were not very successful.

‡ Assuming a first order autoregressive scheme. Rex uses a method for calculating the serial correlation adjustment coefficient detailed in Malinvaud [1966] pp. 442–3.

across generations. The former approach yielded

$$\log Z_t = -45.66 + 4.95 \log Y_t - 0.423 \log Z_{t-1} + 0.027 \log p_t^c / TC_t$$
$$ (-2.22)\ (2.37) (-4.69) (0.26)$$
$$-1.012 D_0 \quad -0.261 D_1 + 0.229 D_3 \quad (24)$$
$$(-4.99) \quad (-2.09) \quad (1.45)$$
$$R^2 = 0.905; \quad \bar{R}^2 = 0.831; \quad DW = 0.901.$$

The Durbin–Watson statistic implies the presence of autocorrelation. However, the main feature of this regression is that the price variable is not significant at the 95 % level and has a coefficient of the wrong sign. The dummies do not perform particularly well.

The second approach did not perform a great deal better, the coefficient on price is again of the wrong sign and the variable not significant at the 95 % level. The dummies, however, were significant and this implies a significant difference in scale returns between generations. If the price variable is disregarded the alternative approaches yield

$$\Delta \log Z_t = -43.94 + 4.81 \log Y_t - 0.42 \log Z_{t-1} - 1.246 D_0$$
$$ (-2.36)\ (2.50) (-4.89) (-4.51)$$
$$-0.49 D_1 - 0.235 D_2 \quad (25)$$
$$(-2.10)\ (-1.62)$$
$$R^2 = 0.904; \quad \bar{R}^2 = 0.846; \quad DW = 1.29,$$

$$\Delta \log Z_t = -43.90 + 4.68 \log Y_t - 0.42 \log Z_{t-1} - 0.12 D_0 \log Y_t$$
$$ (-2.33)\ (2.43) (-4.90) (-4.48)$$
$$-0.048 D_1 \log Y_t - 0.022 D_2 \log Y_t \quad (26)$$
$$(-2.13) (-1.55)$$
$$R^2 = 0.903; \quad \bar{R}^2 = 0.845; \quad DW = 1.34.$$

Attempts to correct for autocorrelation in the first regression using a first order autoregressive scheme required an adjustment factor of 0.538, and drove D_0 and D_1 into insignificance.

The position now is that the dummies perform reasonably but the price variable does not appear to gain significance at any stage. However, behind these regressions there is one basic difficulty and that is that the correlation between $\log Y_t$ and $\log Z_{t-1}$, measured by the correlation coefficient, is 0.9827. This would indicate the possibility of multicollinearity. The effect of this would be to generate large variances and covariances for the coefficient estimates, making them very imprecise (Kmenta [1971] pp. 384–9). If one considers the estimate of the coefficient on $\log Y_t$ it is usually estimated at about 4.7, and combines with a coefficient on $\log Z_{t-1}$ of 0.4. This implies that with

$$S_t^* = e^a Y_t^b \left(\frac{p_t^c}{TC_t}\right)^c \quad (27)$$

Table 7.9. *The Gompertz hypothesis modified to show scale returns*

				Coefficient estimates					
b	λa_0	λa_1	λa_2	λa_3	λ	λc	R^2	$\bar{R}^2$	DW
0.6	1.880	−1.261	−0.73	−0.415	0.237	−0.040	0.847	0.756	1.85
	(6.08)	(−2.68)	(−1.84)	(−1.778)	(4.313)	(−0.135)			
	1.887	−1.304	−0.773	−0.439	0.233		0.847	0.778	1.88
	(6.48)	(−3.92)	(−3.21)	(−2.955)	(5.37)				
	1.082				0.144	−0.261	0.652	0.572	2.05
	(4.758)				(2.323)	(−1.111)			
0.7	1.641	−1.262	−0.730	−0.415	0.239	−0.041	0.848	0.757	1.85
	(6.03)	(−2.692)	(−1.842)	(−1.778)	(4.326)	(−0.13)			
	1.652	−1.304	−0.772	−0.438	0.234		0.847	0.778	1.88
	(6.676)	(−3.93)	(−3.22)	(−2.96)	(5.386)				
	0.144				0.144	−0.259	0.652	0.572	2.05
	(2.322)				(5.629)	(−1.107)			
0.8	1.399	−1.263	−0.729	−0.414	0.240	−0.041	0.848	0.758	1.84
	(5.79)	(−2.69)	(−1.84)	(−1.779)	(4.339)	(−0.137)			
	1.414	−1.306	−0.771	−0.438	0.236		0.848	0.780	1.88
	(6.94)	(−3.94)	(−3.228)	(−2.96)	(5.400)				
	0.789				0.145	−0.258	0.652	0.572	2.06
	(7.39)				(2.32)	(−1.104)			
0.9	1.155	−1.264	−0.728	−0.413	0.241	−0.041	0.849	0.759	1.84
	(5.20)	(−2.70)	(−1.845)	(−1.779)	(4.352)	(−0.137)			
	1.174	−1.306	−0.771	−0.437	0.237		0.849	0.780	1.88
	(7.315)	(−3.952)	(−3.235)	(−2.97)	(5.415)				
	0.642				0.145	−0.257	0.652	0.572	2.05
	(11.49)				(2.319)	(−1.100)			

the coefficient b is being estimated as $4.7/0.4 = 12.0$. The coefficient b is equivalent to the degree of scale returns in computer use. This coefficient implies very large decreasing returns to scale. It has been shown, however, that in terms of computer hardware input there are increasing returns to scale in computer use. It has therefore been decided to introduce b as a parameter into the regressions. To prevent multi-collinearity appearing in dummy variables the dummies are introduced as influencing a and not b. The coefficient b was allowed to take values between 0.6 and 1.5 in intervals of 0.1. In table 7.9 the results for the lower values are presented. Three types of equation were fitted, one with a price variable and no dummies, one with dummies and no price variable and one with dummies and prices, i.e. variations on

$$\Delta \log Z_t = \lambda a_0 + \lambda a_1 D_0 + \lambda a_2 D_1 + \lambda a_3 D_2$$
$$+ \lambda (b \log Y_t - \log Z_{t-1}) + \lambda c \log (p_t^c / TC_t) + U_t. \quad (28)$$

The results for higher values of b were similar in all respects to these results. The conclusions that can be drawn are that a role cannot be found for the price variable in this formulation judging by significance at the 95 % probability level. In these equations, however, the dummies were always significant at the 95 % level. It was therefore decided to concentrate on the version including dummies but no price variable. In all these results the R^2s were reasonable and in each case the DW statistic was in the indecisive area at a 99 % significance level. Calculated F statistics were also significant, i.e. the hypothesis of all $\beta_i = 0$ was not accepted. The R^2 varies from 0.847 for b equal to 0.6 to 0.852 for b equal 1.5 (hardly a difference worth bothering about), which compares with 0.904 in the unrestricted version. The DW statistic has improved relative to the non-restricted equations.

The main difference between these equations and the unrestricted form is the estimate of the coefficient λ. In the version for b equal to 0.6, λ is estimated as 0.233 with a standard error 0.043, whereas on the non-restricted form the estimate is 0.424 with a standard error 0.086. Using a test for the difference between two means,[†] these estimates are, at the 95 % level, significantly different but the null hypothesis that they come from the same distribution cannot be rejected at the 99 % level. This is as one would expect if all the present procedure has done is to remove multicollinearity, for multicollinearity only affects the variance and not the mean of the coefficient estimates.

To judge between the estimates achieved for different values of b requires some external information because the results are not significantly improved or worsened when b varies in the region of unity. The study of the industry data below indicates that a coefficient around 0.7 is appropriate. This corresponds sufficiently to what had been expected from the scale returns analysis to justify our proceeding by concentrating on the results for b equal to 0.7.

In fig. 7.2 the resulting estimate of Z_t^* is plotted and the predictions on $\Delta \log Z_t$ are also provided to be compared to the actual figures. Consider first the period 1967–70. Here the predictions are not very good. One problem to consider is whether it is possible that the actual 1967 growth rate is an underestimate or the 1968 and 1969 stock estimates are too high. An investigation of the basic data shows that comparing the industry data to the aggregate data, the aggregate data on machines installed exceeded the industry total by £34m in 1966 and only £13m in 1967. The apparent fall in the growth rate in 1967 may therefore be the result of bad data. However, it can be argued that there is no error in the data estimates. During the period 1966 to 1970 computers were singled out for special investment incentive treatment

† Hoel [1966] pp. 172–6. This test is primarily intended for large samples, and thus the 99 % level may be considered the appropriate level at which to judge.

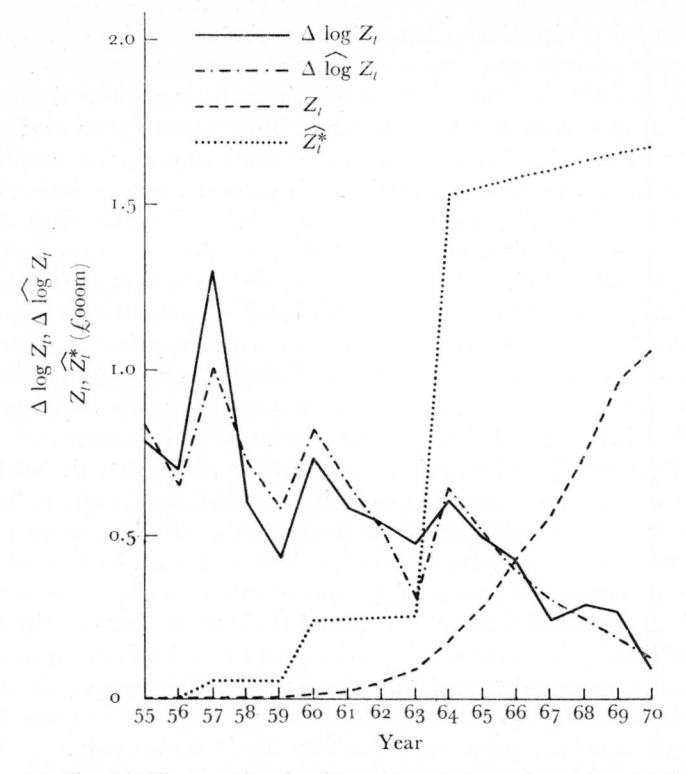

Fig. 7.2. The actual and estimated computer stock and its rate of growth.

by the government (although there were incentives before this date the machines were grouped with all other investment). A grant towards the cost of the machine was available at the rate of 20% in 1966, 1969 and 1970 and 25% in 1967 and 1968. If this was combined with a one year lag it might explain the movement around the period 1966–70. It was also considered, however, that the boost in the 1968–9 period may have been the result of the introduction of the 1900 A series. To test these hypotheses a number of different dummy variables were tried but the results did not improve materially. The grants were also considered by reflecting them in the price series with an overall one year lag on that series but the resulting variable was not significant at the 95% level.

One interesting point that arises out of the results is that the diffusion study would predict a further fall in the growth rate after 1970, a year in which our figures show that the net additions to the stock were in absolute terms less than in the year before. Thus the depression that the industry suffered in 1971 and 1972 could be a natural result of this diffusion process. The analysis would also suggest that to raise the growth rate a new generation would be required. By the beginning of 1973 the industry was picking up again, but the new machines being installed, the 1900 S series, Burroughs 1700s and the IBM 370s, etc., were only introduced in the previous eighteen months, and may constitute this new generation. Unfortunately our intention to pursue this line of enquiry was frustrated by a lack of compatible data.

Moving back through time the estimated curve does not predict too well for the 1955–63 period. It has not been possible to reflect adequately the peak of 1957, and 1963 has yielded a bad underestimate. The former deficiency may be the result of the fact that with very few machines installed in 1956 a small error in the data for 1957 could reflect in a large error in the growth rate. The 1963 result cannot be explained, however, unless it is argued that the functional form is incorrect.

Assuming that this functional form adequately represents the diffusion process, then one must consider exactly what the results mean. The first question concerns what exactly the calculated Z_t^* represents. It would seem that the best interpretation is that for a given level of output, Z_t^* represents that stock of computers that would have been installed had all potential users re-evaluated their technology in time t. This does not imply, necessarily, any concept of equilibrium for some machines may be installed mistakenly and others not installed when it might have been better to have installed them. It is in essence the saturation stock however users may evaluate their technology.

The second question is more important: why has it not been possible to relate the saturation stock to price although the dummies are significant? The significance of the dummies could be taken to imply two things.

(a) When generations change, the nature of computer applications change, e.g. electronic clerk, integrated systems, management information systems, and these changes are reflected in increases in the satiation stock.

(b) The dummies could also reflect price changes, either by arguing that the price series, by concentrating on hardware characteristics, does not adequately reflect prices to the user, whereas the dummies by changing with generations do reflect such prices which must change most when generations change; or one can argue that prices change most when generations change and minor price changes do not matter, so the dummies perform well and the price variable does not.

What then are the *a priori* arguments for price to influence the saturation stock? One may argue that as price falls more firms may be able to achieve their evaluation targets, and for more firms the machine is a 'feasible' alternative. The problem with relying on price relative to targets is that the evaluation procedures also depend on expectations of returns, and minor variations in these returns may swamp minor changes in price. The feasibility argument is again weak with regard to minor changes in price. However, it could be argued that both arguments are realistic for major changes in price, i.e. those reflected in the generation concept.

It can also be argued that as the price falls the application of computers to different tasks may pass evaluation and feasibility tests. Once again it would seem more likely with major changes in prices, but in this case there is another element to consider. To apply computers to more tasks more software is needed and it has already been stated that the price series does not adequately reflect this (although the generation concept may).

In total therefore it would seem reasonable to assume that prices should affect the saturation stock, but it would require major changes for this influence to be reflected. It is therefore argued that the importance of the dummy variables is that they reflect different price levels for computers of different generations and also reflect the extensions of the application area as technology has proceeded.

The economic meaning that one can read into the results so far is that the number of machines that it is desired to install during a period is related to the difference between the actual and the saturation stock. The existing stock also exerts influence by acting as a proxy for an information variable. The saturation stock varies with the level of output and has changed as generations have changed. This generation change reflects both increases in the area of computer applications and major changes in the price of computers. This is the only means by which it has been possible to introduce the price variable, and at the same time it has only been possible to generate the scale returns that are apparent in computer use by entering them through a predetermined parameter.

In spite of this interpretation one still has to face the problem stated by Phelps Brown, 'how any statistical procedure can enable us to distinguish casual from merely contingent relations' (Phelps Brown [1972] p. 6). By the use of dummies, the above regressions have attributed all peaks in the expansion of computer usage to the expansion of the saturation stock and this stock has been estimated on the basis that a constant proportion of the difference between it and the actual stock has to be cleared in each period subject only to the level of the previous stock. However, it was argued above that there are specific forces that influence the rate of adjustment. The failure to take account of these may have provided results that are merely contingent relations.

Thus it is now necessary to attempt to include a variable adjustment coefficient.

Before attempting this one ought to discuss the error term in the equations fitted so far. These regressions have centred on the functional form (11). The error term U_t in this equation has implicitly been assumed to have the properties required for regression analysis, i.e.

$$U_t \text{ is } N(0, \sigma^2),$$
$$E(U_i, U_j) = 0,$$
$$E(X_i, U_j) = 0.$$

That is, the error term is normally distributed with mean zero and constant variance σ^2, the error terms are not autocorrelated, and the error term is independent of observations on the independent variables (Kmenta [1971] p. 348). Now the regression equation (11) includes the expression for the saturation stock (10). If equation (10) were stochastic then (11) would have an error term which was a mix of the error term from the adjustment function (U_1) and the error term from the saturation stock equation (U_2), such that

$$U_t = U_{1t} + \lambda \log U_{2t}. \tag{29}$$

We must therefore consider (10) to be non-stochastic.†

For reasons stated below the adjustment rate is considered to be a multiplicative function of a number of variables. Thus to separate out the influence of these variables on the adjustment rate the most appropriate form to estimate‡ would be

$$\log (\Delta \log Z_t) = \log \lambda + \log (\log Z_t^* - \log Z_{t-1}) + U_t. \tag{30}$$

However, if this were to be an estimable form then the error term would have to enter (11) multiplicatively, which would suggest that all the above work is based on mistaken assumptions about the error term. We are not willing to accept this. This means that the adjustment rate must enter as a direct function.§

The reason for believing that the adjustment rate is a multiplicative function relates to the way the behavioural theory works. At a moment in time there is a potential additional stock of computers that would be installed if all conditions were right $(Z_t^* - Z_t)$. The proportion of this stock coming up for replacement depends on the goal achievement pressures. Consider that at the aggregate level these pressures can be represented by the growth in profits, (g_{PROF_t}), costs (g_{TC_t}) and outputs (g_{Y_t}) and a constant to represent obscolescence. The proportion of the

† This appears to be commonly assumed, cf. Chow [1967].
‡ Because it would then be linear in the variables that influence λ.
§ This is also recommended in Stone [1957].

resulting numbers coming up for re-evaluation that will be actually converted to computers depends on feasibility, evaluation and search. Consider that these can be represented by the variables, level of profits ($PROF_t$) price of computers and total installed to date. This suggests that *in toto* the determinants of the additions to the stock in the period can be summarised as,

$$Z_t - Z_{t-1} = (Z_t^* - Z_{t-1}) \ [F(g_{Y_t}, g_{TC_t}, g_{PROF_t})] \ [G(Z_{t-1}, PROF_t, p_t^c)]. \tag{31}$$

However, the stock adjustment model already takes into account the influence of the existing stock as an information variable; thus it was considered that one way to put this theory to the test was to consider λ as

$$\lambda = e^{\mu_0} \cdot g_{Y_t}^{\mu_1} \cdot g_{TC_t}^{\mu_2} \cdot g_{PROF_t}^{\mu_3} \cdot PROF_t^{\mu_4} \cdot \left(\frac{p_t^c}{TC_t}\right)^{\mu_5}. \tag{32}$$

Attempts were made to introduce this into the Gompertz hypothesis assuming that all coefficients were unity, but in every case the explanatory power of the hypothesis was reduced.

It was therefore decided to consider a hypothesis closer to the above propositions. This stated that

$$\frac{dZ_t}{dt} = \lambda(Z_t^* - Z_t) \cdot U_t, \tag{33}$$

where the log of the error term is assumed to have the desired properties, and λ is represented as in (32), but with the lagged stock introduced, so that

$$\log (Z_t - Z_{t-1}) = \mu_0 + \mu_1 \log g_{Y_t} + \mu_2 \log g_{TC_t} + \mu_3 \log g_{PROF_t}$$
$$+ \mu_4 \log PROF_t + \mu_5 \log \left(\frac{p_t^c}{TC_t}\right) + \mu_6 \log Z_{t-1}$$
$$+ \log (Z_t^* - Z_{t-1}) + \log U_t. \tag{34}$$

The problem in this case is the estimation of the saturation stock. There are two possible approaches. One would be to undertake a detailed market survey, which is infeasible. The other is to assume a function as in the above stock adjustment models. However, the saturation stock in the Gompertz hypothesis in its final form applied above has four parameters. As equation (34) does not allow one to estimate these parameters directly it is necessary to derive them from external sources. To make 'trial and error' assumptions about parameters is not practicable because there are four of them. Thus in an attempt to fit equation (34) it was assumed that the estimates of Z_t^* derived from the applications of the straight Gompertz hypothesis should be used.

Attempts were made to fit the function for values of b varying from 0.6 to 1.0. This is in fact not a very satisfactory approach for if this version of the diffusion process is correct then the Gompertz hypothesis is not, and therefore the estimates of the saturation stock are spurious.

The actual function estimated, in order to constrain the coefficient on $\log (Z_t^* - Z_{t-1})$ to unity, was

$$\log (Z_t - Z_{t-1}) - \log (Z_t^* - Z_{t-1}) = \mu_0 + \mu_1 \log g_{Y_t} + \mu_2 \log g_{TC_t}$$
$$+ \mu_3 \log g_{PROF_t} + \mu_4 \log PROF_t + \mu_5 \log \left(\frac{p_t^c}{TC_t}\right) + \mu_6 \log Z_{t-1} + \log U_t$$
$$(35)$$

and the growth rates were replaced by ratios to prevent attempts to take the logarithm of negative numbers. As an example of the results the case for b equal to 0.7 can be discussed. Significance at the 95 % level could be achieved for either the profit rate and the log of the stock of the previous period, or a constant and (introduced at a later stage) the log of the general price level. As the profit variable was supposed to represent feasibility a positive coefficient was expected, but it was negative. As changes in the general price level were supposed to represent an alternative to a change in technique a negative coefficient was expected, but it was positive. The coefficient on the lagged stock was of the expected sign – positive. The highest corrected R^2 achieved was 0.620.

These results thus extend the explanation of the data on computer usage no further than had been achieved with the fitting of the Gompertz curve. However, at this stage the failure to reflect the behavioural theory in the results should not be taken as an indication of the fact that it cannot explain computer usage. The above discussions of the difficulties of applying the theory to the data probably best explain why it is not performing well.

Before proceeding to the industry data a summary of the present position is desirable. The study of the decision to computerise led us to expect to find an adjustment coefficient that varies systematically with certain economic variables. When this approach was applied in very crude form to the data on computer usage it did not perform well, but an approach that does not include systematic variation in the adjustment coefficient does perform well. However, in this case it may be that this is more the result of contingent relations, for the study of the decision to computerise indicated that this adjustment coefficient would vary.

A basic problem in the use of functions including variable adjustment coefficients is the estimation of Z_t^*. Griliches manages this by looking at different geographical areas. It was initially hoped to per-

Table 7.10. *Data on industries*

Indus-try	Y (£m) 1963	Y (£m) 1968	Cl ('000) 1963	Cl ('000) 1968	W (£m) 1963	W (£m) 1968	C (£m) 1963	C (£m) 1968	S (£m) 1963	S (£m) 1968
1	324.7	478.1	107.9	106.9	217.3	280.1	187.0	259.6	550.3	861.9
4	1,324.7	1,959.4	233.9	269.8	541.8	785.9	1,281.7	1,982.4	2,640.6	3,933.4
6	912.7	1,357.4	234.0	248.4	522.3	697.6	755.8	1,161.2	1,681.2	2,483.9
7	932.0	1,259.4	128.0	142.2	513.0	672.6	1,649.6	2,379.0	2,627.8	3,629.3
11	4,160.3	6,464.5	689.6	809.8	2,593.6	2,733.7	3,147.2	4,876.6	8,204.6	12,733.0
16	807.6	1,092.9	103.1	114.8	434.1	631.9	1,269.6	1,779.4	2,073.4	2,839.9
17	107.8	171.1	10.7	9.8	32.8	38.9	479.8	825.3	592.1	1,001.4
19	1,636.4	2,114.3	178.4	188.8	781.3	834.2	842.2	987.0	2,475.5	3,116.6
22	1,399.3	1,953.8	206.0	206.4	790.0	1,052.1	1,911.1	2,353.6	3,343.4	4,368.6
23	846.5	1,252.5	157.0	178.0	457.4	674.1	675.4	965.1	1,629.0	2,352.6

All prices are current. Y = output, Cl = total number of clerical, technical and administrative workers, W = total wage bill, C = total costs of fuel and materials, S = sales of goods produced and work done.

form a similar exercise on computers by looking across industries. However, because of the industry groupings of the data it was only possible to obtain data on independent variables from the Census of Production,† which meant that data was only available for the years 1963 and 1968 and then only on groups 1, 4, 6, 7, 11, 16, 17, 19, 22 and 23. This meant that a combined cross-section–time-series analysis was not possible.

Several approaches have been tried in attempts to explain the inter-industry pattern of computer ownership. The data used in these studies is contained in table 7.10.

The first hypothesis tested was that one could explain inter-industry differences in the demand for computers by means of the Gompertz hypothesis. This hypothesis was fitted to 1968 data but the results were not encouraging. In an attempt to improve the performance of the hypothesis a new variable was introduced as a proxy for the equilibrium stock. This variable was based on $(Cl_{63}/Y_{63})Y_{68}$, i.e. the number of clerical workers that an industry would have required in 1968 if the ratio of clerical workers to output was as in 1963. This was rationalised on the grounds that as few industries used computers extensively in 1963 the variable would reflect inter-industry differences in potential applications of computers. However, the performance of the hypothesis did not improve markedly. A second approach was made to the use of the Gompertz hypothesis; this time instead of letting Z_{t-1} be represented by 1967 data it was represented by 1964 data, so the hypothesis is applied to the 1964–8 stretch. 1964 was chosen for it is the first year

† *Census of Production 1963*, HMSO 1965; *Census of Production 1968*, HMSO 1970.

STD

in which data is available on computer stock for the whole sample used. The result achieved was

$$\log \left(\frac{Z^i_{68}}{Z^i_{64}} \right) = 4.013 + 0.364 \log Y^i_{68} - 0.586 \log Z^i_{64}, \tag{36}$$
$$\phantom{\log \left(\frac{Z^i_{68}}{Z^i_{64}} \right) = } (4.147) \; (4.213) \phantom{\log Y^i_{68}} (-4.417)$$
$$R^2 = 0.775; \quad \bar{R}^2 = 0.678;$$

or when the clerical labour term replaces the output variable,

$$\log \left(\frac{Z^i_{68}}{Z^i_{64}} \right) = 4.5119 + 0.313 \log \left(\frac{Cl^i_{63}}{Y^i_{63}} \right) Y^i_{68} - 0.537 \log Z^i_{64}, \tag{37}$$
$$\phantom{\log \left(\frac{Z^i_{68}}{Z^i_{64}} \right) = } (4.395) \; (3.929) \phantom{\log \left(\frac{Cl^i_{63}}{Y^i_{63}} \right)} (-4.016)$$
$$R^2 = 0.751; \quad \bar{R}^2 = 0.645.$$

These results are reasonable but the long time stretch makes one wonder whether it is still a true Gompertz hypothesis in which the lagged term really only appears because of working in discrete time.

The next stage was to attempt to reflect inter-industry differences in computer usage in line with behavioural theory. The first approach was to consider that when a diffusion process is complete, the share of industry i in the total stock of computers $(Z^i/\bar{Z})$ must equal the share of industry i in the satiation stock $(Z^{i*}/\bar{Z}^*)$. Thus the ratio

$$\frac{Z^i/\bar{Z}}{Z^{i*}/\bar{Z}^*} = J^i \tag{38}$$

must reflect the distance into the transition that an industry has proceeded. It was hypothesised that inter-industry differences in J may be related to those variables that were considered above as influencing the adjustment rate. If one assumes that

$$Z^{i*} = aY^{ib}$$

and that

$$\bar{Z}^* = aY^b, \tag{39}$$

then

$$Z^{i*}/\bar{Z}^* = \left(\frac{Y^i}{Y} \right)^b.$$

This implied a form to be estimated, as an example,†

$$\log \left(\frac{Z^i}{\bar{Z}} \right)_{68} = \mu_0 + \mu_1 \log \left(\frac{PROF^i_{68}}{PROF^i_{63}} \right) + \mu_2 \log \left(\frac{Y^i_{68}}{Y^i_{63}} \right)$$
$$+ \mu_3 \log \left(\frac{SALES^i_{68}}{SALES^i_{63}} \right) + b \log \left(\frac{Y^i_{68}}{\bar{Y}_{68}} \right) + U_i. \tag{40}$$

† Profit was calculated as total sales minus total wages and raw material and fuel costs.

Table 7.11. *Cross-section Gompertz hypothesis with variable adjustment coefficient*

Adjustment coefficient	Constant	Coefficient on		R^2	$\bar{R}^2$	F
		$\log Y^i$	$\log Z^i_{64}$			
λ	4.013	0.364	-0.586	0.774	0.678	12.03
	(4.148)	(4.213)	(-4.417)			
$\lambda \left(\dfrac{Y^i_{68}}{Y^i_{63}}\right)$	2.675	0.257	-0.398	0.918	0.882	500.03
	(6.803)	(7.578)	(-7.323)			
$\lambda \left(\dfrac{SALES^i_{68}}{SALES^i_{63}}\right)$	2.714	0.290	-0.429	0.907	0.867	447.39
	(6.438)	(8.224)	(-7.309)			
$\lambda \left(\dfrac{PROF^i_{68}}{PROF^i_{63}}\right)$	3.0909	0.257	-0.459	0.356	0.081	62.45
	(2.895)	(3.029)	(-2.961)			
$\lambda \left(\dfrac{Y^i_{68}}{Y^i_{63}}\dfrac{SALES^i_{68}}{SALES^i_{63}}\right)$	1.8401	0.203	-0.295	0.915	0.879	491.05
	(6.785)	(9.241)	(7.759)			

The best result achieved was

$$\log\left(\frac{Z^i}{\bar{\bar{Z}}}\right)_{68} = -2.207 + 2.4198 \log\left(\frac{SALES^i_{68}}{SALES^i_{63}}\right) + 0.6195 \log\left(\frac{Y^i_{68}}{\bar{\bar{Y}}_{68}}\right), \quad (41)$$
$$\phantom{\log\left(\frac{Z^i}{\bar{\bar{Z}}}\right)_{68} =} (-6.155) \ (2.400) \phantom{\log\left(\frac{SALES^i_{68}}{SALES^i_{63}}\right) + 0.} (6.028)$$

$$R^2 = 0.864; \quad \bar{R}^2 = 0.805,$$

which only gives the growth in sales any role to play.

In a further attempt to improve on this, it was hypothesised that the relevant variables show their influence by affecting the change in the share, i.e. the industry with the greatest change in profits, saturation stock, sales, etc. would have the greatest change in the share of total demand. The results were not very satisfactory as it was not possible in general to achieve even a 10 % significance for the relevant variables.

Finally, it was decided to return to the Gompertz form based on the 1964–8 stretch, and attempt to introduce a variable adjustment function. The output form for the saturation stock was used and the results are presented in table 7.11. The estimating equation was, using the second one presented as an example,

$$\log\left(\frac{Z^i_{68}}{Z^i_{64}}\right) = \alpha\lambda\left(\frac{Y^i_{68}}{Y^i_{63}}\right) + b\lambda\left(\frac{Y^i_{68}}{Y^i_{63}}\right)\log Y^i_{68} + \lambda\left(\frac{Y^i_{68}}{Y^i_{63}}\right)\log Z^i_{64} + U_i. \quad (42)$$

Attempts were made to replace the ratios by growth rates; however, the results were definitely worse (lower R^2s and fewer variables significant). The fact that the adjustment coefficient is therefore illustrated as a function of $(1+g)$, which is entered multiplicatively, tends to indicate the existence of a certain constant element in the adjustment function. Efforts were also made to enter the level of profits as a 'feasibility' variable but multicollinearity resulted.

In the results presented it can be seen that either the ratio of output, sales or their multiple relative to earlier levels, when introduced, can improve the fit of an equation as measured by R^2 or $\bar{R}^2$. However, when there is no effective constant in the equation R^2 loses its meaning. The F statistics are thus also presented. Their ranking is the same as the ranking of R^2. In the three formulations where the performance is improved the power of Y in the function for the saturation stock would appear to be estimated at around 0.7, which it is felt justifies the efforts made to introduce increasing returns to scale in the analysis of the aggregate data.

Having found that one can introduce the growth in sales and the growth in output and thereby increase the explanatory power of the Gompertz hypothesis the next stage is to examine what this implies. First, it need not affect the conclusions at the aggregate level for it was found that the growth in output could be introduced there but the performance of the hypothesis did not improve. However, it would seem now that the industry with faster growth in output and sales will adjust faster to its saturation stock (the implication of the absence of sign reversal when these variables are introduced into the function). This result is in line with the results of the literature search, but is not necessarily a justification of the basic theory brought over from the previous chapter. In fact the role of output and sales growth can be rationalised in a number of ways.

(a) A fast expanding industry may require more equipment and as such becomes more aware of the possibilities of computer usage.

(b) An industry growing faster may have more contact with a tight labour market and thus be more aware of the need to save labour through computerisation.

(c) Fast growth may encourage computerisation through influence on evaluation procedures via expectations.

(d) The faster growth may be the result of better management and this better management may also cause more computer usage. All these factors can be rationalised in the framework of the behavioural theory, but the significance of the two variables does not necessarily imply the problem solving basis of that theory, and the sales variable would even seem to have the wrong sign.

Thus after attempts to find a role for certain economic variables connected with behavioural theory, it has been possible to introduce some of these variables. However, it cannot be guaranteed that it is the behavioural basis of technique choice that is causing them to be significant, so one cannot say that they support or disprove the conclusions of the previous chapter. In fact the results that have been achieved so far can be summarised thus:

(a) The Gompertz hypothesis best summarises the aggregate data.

(b) A Gompertz hypothesis spread over a four year time period with an adjustment coefficient varying with the growth in output and/or sales can be used successfully to describe the industry data.

The only common basis of both these conclusions is that the information proxy, the lagged stock of computers, consistently performs well. This does not, however, support any particular theory for practically every theory of diffusion ascribes a similar role to the lagged stock.

The reasons why the behavioural theory should not operate obviously well as an explanatory hypothesis of this data has been covered above, but it is still felt that the theory has something to contribute to the understanding of diffusion processes. As it has not been possible to apply it to the above data it was felt that it may be possible by use of the behavioural framework to rationalise the results that other researchers have found in their studies. These results are summarised in section 7.4 and listed as (i)–(v).

The first result on the effect of the lagged stock was covered in the previous chapter. The second result refers to faster diffusion for an innovation which is very profitable and requires a smaller investment relative to a less profitable and more expensive innovation. The explanation given by Mansfield [1968] (p. 138) for these results corresponds to the present discussion of the evaluation process – more profitable innovations can pass evaluation tests more easily and smaller investment can pass 'feasibility' tests more readily. Also included in the second result is a slight indication that diffusion rates are faster in less concentrated industries. This conclusion has been much disputed and will not be pursued.

The third set of results indicates that firms for which the innovation is most profitable, which are most liquid and which first used the new technique diffuse it faster over all possible applications in the firm. It would also appear that small firms are at least as fast as large firms to diffuse once they have begun to use the technique. The liquidity variable could reflect 'feasibility', the profitability variable reflect on evaluation procedures, and the date of first use has already been shown in the previous chapter to have influence, where it was rationalised as another aspect of the information variable. Little can be said on firm size, except that indivisibilities exist, and that large firms may have fewer problems with feasibility, which might imply faster diffusion for larger firms instead of the opposite.

Fourth, it might also be that a firm's growth rate and the durability

Table 7.12. *The proportions of EDP installations processing each of the types of work indicated* (%)

Type	1964	1969
Financial A/C	40	82
Management information	54	81
Payroll	59	69
Invoicing and billing	36	67
Stock control	40	64
General statistics	28	61
Production control	19	32
Other office work	12	45

SOURCE: D of E [1972] Appendix 11, p. 71.

of its previous equipment could have influence. The durability argument fits in well with the previous chapter, where it was shown that obsolescence promoted the re-evaluation of technology. Thus the less durable is equipment, the earlier is the stimulus to re-evaluate technology. The effect of a firm's growth rate has been discussed above in relation to our regression results.

Finally there is the existence of the S-shaped diffusion curves. It can be argued that with the influence of the information variable, these result from the fact that as time proceeds the amount still to be converted to the new technique is falling as the installations increase, but the chance of changing technique increases. These two pressures result in the S-shaped curves. There is nothing in the theory under discussion that would invalidate this.

Thus, although it was not possible to show the true nature of the theory in the explanation of the data available, that theory can be used to generate predictions that are in line with the pattern of diffusion processes that have been discovered by other researchers. When this is combined with the study of the previous chapter, it is felt that this theory provides a realistic view of the technique choice decision and thus the diffusion process.

An interesting postscript to this analysis can be provided by studying the spread of different computer applications, the data on which is summarised in table 7.12.

In addition to the spread of computer ownership there has been a spread of tasks to which computers have been applied. However, this spread of computer usage is even more intractable than that analysed above. It was shown in the previous chapter that there is a connection between the nature of computer applications and the department responsible for the computer. This can be now supplemented by some

Table 7.13. *Computer use and the period of ownership*

Average number of advanced techniques per organisation	Years since first installation				
	1	1–3	3–5	5–8	8
In use	0.6	0.6	0.8	1.1	2.1
Planned for 1974	2.1	1.9	2.4	3.3	4.6

SOURCE: NCC [1972] p. 46.

data on applications and the length of computer ownership. In table 7.13 the relation between the application of advanced techniques and the number of years since computers were first installed is illustrated. This data implies that experience generates further computer usage in a similar manner to numbers installed influencing search procedure. However, older installations tend to belong to larger firms, which it seems place greater demands on their machines (NCC [1972] p. 47). This in itself would imply some relation between firm size and the rate of diffusion that has not been found elsewhere, although it has been argued elsewhere that this may result from indivisibility and feasibility influences.

With these few comments on the spread of different types of applications it is now possible to draw the conclusions from the whole analysis of the demand for computers. The initial intention to explain the data available by the use of behavioural principles was not very fruitful because of data and conceptual difficulties. However, by the use of supplementary data on orders it has been possible to show that the aggregate data can be approximated by a Gompertz hypothesis if dummies are introduced to reflect the generation concept – but the function must be constrained if increasing returns to scale are to be apparent. This summary of the aggregate data implied a limited role for prices, as it was only possible to rationalise their influence if they were considered as included in the generation dummies.

In the search for more evidence to support the behavioural hypotheses an analysis was carried out on the industry data. At this level it was shown that a variable adjustment function could be included but the results could not be said to confirm or cause one to reject the behavioural approach.

Finally, it was illustrated that the behavioural approach to diffusion processes was consistent with the results generated from other studies of diffusion processes and as such may still represent a better indication of the economy's workings during diffusions than any statistical formulations that summarise the data.

7.6 THE SUPPLY OF COMPUTERS

The above discussion has been carried on in the absence of any mention of supply difficulties other than to argue that a variable that reflects demand must include orders. In this section the supply of computers will be considered in more detail.

In many econometric studies the approach is to posit a supply and demand curve and to assume that the market is cleared in every time period, which, assuming identification, allows one to estimate the coefficients of the supply and demand curves from one series on the total stock installed. We cannot do this, since we are not willing to assume that the market is cleared in every time period.

The approach to take, then, is to work on more direct information – what the companies tell the world about their output decisions. Unfortunately the computer companies are reluctant to divulge very much about their decision making (IBM suggested that such information was proprietary and worth £½m to their competitors).† It is possible, however, to build up a picture from Evidence to the Select Committee and non-attributable industry sources.

A computer takes approximately eighteen months to build, given the technology. The firm makes an estimate of the demand for its output at the beginning of a time period. ICL state specifically that they use a forecasting model to answer similar questions (SCST [1970a] p. 27). If at the time that a machine is nine months from completion it has not been ordered, construction work ceases and only those machines with a definite sale are finished. Construction work will restart when it is ordered. Thus if there is an overestimation of demand there will be an increase in inventories and work in progress. If, on the other hand, there is an underestimation of demand, or the desired supply cannot be produced, there will be an increase in orders and/or a decrease in inventories.

To test this hypothesis rigorously would involve the construction of a supply curve based on some expectations mechanism, combining it with one of the demand curves constructed above, and interposing an equilibrating system based on changes in the order level. The order data is insufficient to allow one to perform such an exercise, and the result moreover would depend crucially on the assumptions about expectations behaviour.

It is possible, however, to gain some insight by looking at the cross sectional distribution of orders. If the present hypothesis is correct then one would expect to find that the orders of each industry in a given time period are related to the demand of that industry. This demand

† Private communication from IBM.

should be measured by the change in stocks and order over the previous period and thus the hypothesis would state that

$$O^i_t = a_1 + b_1(S^i_t + O^i_t - S^i_{t-1} - O^i_{t-1}) + U^i_{1t}. \tag{43}$$

An alternative to this is that the computer industry will work in a contract supply manner, i.e. that the industry will only start construction once an order is received. This would imply that orders in time period t would be related to the increase in the stock in the following time period, i.e.

$$O^i_t = a_2 + b_2(S^i_{t+1} - S^i_t) + U^i_{2t}. \tag{44}$$

If, however, the demand variable should not include orders but should only refer to the changes in the stock, then the following hypothesis would result:

$$O^i_t = a_3 + b_3(S^i_t - S^i_{t-1}) + U^i_{3t}. \tag{45}$$

Finally one could argue that the industry works in a contract supply manner but is not always able to supply all that is asked of it and the orders will pile up. This would imply the hypothesis that

$$O^i_t = a_4 + b_4(S^i_{t+1} + O^i_{t+1} - S^i_t - O^i_t) + U^i_{4t}. \tag{46}$$

These hypotheses, labelled 1 to 4, were fitted to the whole set of the industry data (combining industries 9 and 10) for the years 1962 to 1970. The results are presented in table 7.14.

Of the results for the years 1963–9 the hypothesis that most closely relates to our discussion above, i.e. that orders in this period are related to demand in this period when this demand is measured by changes in stocks and orders, performs best in all but two years (1967 and 1968) in terms of R^2 and is second best in those two years. The contract supply hypothesis does not perform very well. If orders are not to be the base of a contract supply mechanism they must be used to mop up excess demand. However, in the results there is a high constant as well as a coefficient on demand significantly different from zero. This means that even if there is no excess demand some orders would exist. This can probably be explained by the production lag discussed above.

The results above can be used for yet another purpose. It has been argued that the distribution of computers across industries is related to their demands. It has also been argued that if an industry's demands cannot be met it must result in orders. Thus if computers were not being distributed in relation to demand one would expect to find that one industry always had more outstanding orders relative to its level of demand than another industry. Now the fact that the cross-sectional relation of orders to demand generates a high R^2 suggests that computers are distributed relative to demand. However, one can go

Table 7.14. *Order hypotheses*

	1962	1963	1964	1965	1966	1967	1968	1969
a_1		652.5	36.3	1435.8	591.2	2111.0	1248.7	1576.4
t		2.84	0.08	2.77	0.65	2.89	1.30	1.26
b_1		0.35	0.79	0.80	0.88	0.54	0.52	0.48
t		3.65	9.03	10.50	7.89	5.91	5.72	4.36
R^2		0.43	0.81	0.85	0.76	0.62	0.61	0.48
$\bar{R}^2$		0.36	0.79	0.83	0.73	0.59	0.57	0.42
a_2	284.7	864.1	1421.0	933.6	1311.0	1423.5	2521.0	1629.0
t	1.10	3.19	2.76	1.14	1.14	1.35	2.16	1.54
b_2	0.37	0.23	0.63	0.79	0.73	0.48	0.37	0.57
t	2.72	2.06	4.34	6.85	5.33	4.41	3.42	5.33
R^2	0.29	0.18	0.48	0.70	0.57	0.48	0.36	0.57
$\bar{R}^2$	0.21	0.10	0.43	0.67	0.54	0.43	0.30	0.53
a_3		1079.0	2500.0	2036.0	2365.0	984.9	1504.0	1978.8
t		4.20	2.40	2.53	1.85	1.26	1.27	1.31
b_3		0.19	0.30	1.32	0.75	0.62	0.51	0.44
t		1.43	0.74	5.77	4.11	6.72	4.25	3.16
R^2		0.10	0.03	0.62	0.46	0.68	0.16	0.32
$\bar{R}^2$		0.00	−0.07	0.59	0.40	0.65	0.41	0.26
a_4	847.0	1192.5	1697.8	775.6	4669.4	2491.0	2585.0	
t	2.43	4.41	2.86	0.78	3.26	2.15	2.45	
b_4	0.01	0.04	0.27	0.68	0.28	0.33	0.36	
t	0.06	0.69	3.10	5.62	1.58	2.96	3.85	
R^2	0.00	0.02	0.32	0.61	0.11	0.29	0.41	
$\bar{R}^2$	−0.11	−0.08	0.26	0.57	0.02	0.23	0.36	

Table 7.15. *Rank correlation coefficients*

Period	Coefficient
1963–4	0.355
1964–5	0.360
1965–6	0.487
1966–7	0.305
1967–8	0.347
1968–9	0.455

further. If the relativity existed one would expect to find that industries' orders, after the demand effect had been removed, would have completely different rank in each time period, i.e. the rank correlation coefficient of the errors from equation (43) for consecutive years would not differ significantly from zero (Hoel [1966] pp. 255–7). The ranks of each industry in these errors for each year were calculated. In cases where the number of industries changed between years the ranks were recalculated. The rank correlation coefficients obtained are presented in table 7.15. The null hypothesis can then be accepted at the 99% level for all years and at the 95 % level for all years except 1965–6 and 1968–9.

These results indicate that in fact computers were distributed relative to demand. It was felt, however, that it was possible to go one stage further. The most important question of distribution is whether the computer supply industry will always meet its own demands before its customers'. As this industry (number 5) always seemed to have a low rank, and thus low orders relative to its level of demand, it was felt that it was important to test whether its rank was always the lowest. Thus the rank correlation coefficient was calculated between its actual rank and what it would have been if it always had the lowest orders. The coefficient calculated was 0.506 with sample size 7. The tabulated value at the 95 % level is 0.714. Thus the null hypothesis cannot be rejected, and it is accepted that computers are distributed in relation to demand for all industries.

7.7   CONCLUSION

In this chapter it has been suggested that the supply of computers is based on expected demand and if that demand does not appear there is an increase in inventories or work in progress. If the actual level of demand is greater than supply then orders take up the excess. This implies that the actual measure of the level of demand for computers should be the change in the sum of stocks and orders. It has also been shown that computers are distributed between industries relative to their demands, there being no favouritism.

Using the change in stocks and orders as the demand variable where possible, attempts were made to explain the diffusion process in terms of the demand principles of chapter 6. This attempt was not successful at the aggregate level and only partly successful at the industry level. The reasons for this were discussed at length. It has been argued, however, that although it was not possible to use the theory to explain the data under discussion, the behavioural basis of our approach was in line with the findings of other researchers on diffusion processes and was therefore not totally contradicted. The actual data itself could be best explained by the use of the Gompertz hypothesis at the aggregate level (although it had to be modified to reflect increasing returns to scale and the generation dummies had a large role to play) and by a similar hypothesis with a variable adjustment coefficient at the industry level. The implications of these findings have been discussed. The argument that diffusions are a natural extension of the theory of technique choice as expounded in chapter 6, has therefore to be based on theory rather than verification through the data under consideration.

8. THE IMPLICATIONS OF COMPUTER USAGE FOR THE UK ECONOMY

8.1 INTRODUCTION

This study has so far considered the nature of activities, the appearance of new technology, the choice of techniques and the diffusion of a new technology. The next obvious stage is to investigate what effect the use of the new technique has had on the economy. The problem is with what can one make a comparison? Consider first what might be labelled the ideal approach. Postulate that one can observe two island economies that are completely self contained. On island A there exists a basic technology matrix, a given savings function, rate of growth of the labour force and a final demand vector with given proportions. Assume that this economy is in long run equilibrium, then there is associated with this state a total labour input, a level of output, wage and profit rates, and a certain level and composition of capital stock.

Consider now that there exists an island B that is similar in all respects to island A except that the technology matrix contains activities for the construction and use of computers. Assume that this economy is also in long run equilibrium. By definition long run equilibrium must imply full employment of labour, but there may be differences in other key indicators between the two islands at a moment of time. These differences will centre around,

(a) the activities of which the technique matrix is comprised, in the sense of whether the computer activities are included and whether other activities have also been replaced (trigger effects),

(b) changes in the distribution of income,

(c) changes in the level at which the final demand vector is run,

(d) changes in the distribution of labour between industries and

(e) changes in the size and composition of the capital stock.

These differences between the two economies can be considered to be the result of the existence of the new technology. However, it should be realised that this is a comparison of islands. No two economies are ever so alike, thus one must consider one economy at different moments in time. Assume that an economy starts in long run equilibrium with a constant labour force, and then the new technology is made available to it. From this date nothing else changes except that by some later date it has achieved a new equilibrium position. A comparison of these states could act as a proxy for the above comparison. However, in order to reach this new equilibrium state the economy has to go through a transition stage. The effects on employment, output, etc. in these transition stages are as much attributable to the new technology as are the differences between equilibrium states. Thus the effect of a new technology has to be considered on two levels.

In reality economies never achieve long run equilibrium states, they are always being subjected to shocks. Economies are therefore always in a process of transition, and the transition effects become of overriding importance. Moreover in reality the other factors considered for the purpose of this argument as constant over time never remain constant. So one can never really observe in the manner of the theoretical formulation. Thus if technological change and its effects are to be viewed in this way the only method open for analysis is theoretical. In the appendix some of the basic problems concerned with such an analysis are discussed in a simple theoretical framework.

If one is to observe and quantify the effects of technological change on an economy one has to be content with a much less exact approach. The literature on this subject has been concerned with two basic approaches.

(a) The aggregate production function approach in which it is attempted to estimate the contribution of technical change to the growth in output per head.† This is contrary to the whole multisectoral approach that has been implicit in this study and is too aggregative to be of any use in answering the sort of questions considered above.

(b) The second approach may be labelled the input–output approach. This is much closer to the theoretical concepts. The essence of this method is that one considers input–output tables for an economy at two different dates. One then compares the total requirements of primary and intermediate inputs for the generation of a given (usually that appropriate to the later table) final demand vector. These differences can then be attributed to changes in technology.‡ The major theoretical objection to this approach is that the level of the final demand vector is considered to be independent of the technology. This implies a certain type of savings function (see the appendix). The practical objections are that,

† Cf. Solow [1957].   ‡ Cf. Carter [1970].

it is impossible to separate out the effects of one technological change among many,

there is difficulty in separating out prices so that input–output coefficients actually reflect technology,

one has to consider that an input–output structure is realistic, e.g. constant returns to scale and no joint production,

the model does not separate out the distinctions between innovation, diffusion and changes in the technology matrix, e.g. if a diffusion is proceeding, the actual estimated coefficients at a moment in time will refer to some mix of activities, and

finally, the objection that from a practical point of view is most important – the data requirements are huge, and yet the size of the task is so large that details cannot be provided.

This means that yet another approach must be taken. A cross-section analysis between countries is not possible so the approach must refer to time series. The ideal would be to select certain sectors of the economy and consider what their time path would have been without computers compared to what it actually was. Apart from a basic difficulty of considering how such a comparison time path would be constructed, the sheer size of R & D expenditures on computers suggests that a role would have to be found for them if computers had not existed. The resulting possible time paths would be infinite in number. Thus it has been decided to proceed in a much blunter manner as follows.

We consider as our comparison path an economy with the same output as the actual economy and the same technology except that computers are not available. Then by isolating the effect of computers in the actual economy per degree of penetration we can project what the differences between the actual and the comparison economy would be at 100 % penetration, i.e. we can perform an exercise in comparative dynamics. Moreover if we can isolate transition effects per degree of penetration and then assume that the actual level of computer usage as a percentage of the total indicates what degree of penetration an economy would achieve that many years along its transition path, we can date the time path of transition effects. However, the fact that we have had to make assumptions about the nature of the comparison path indicates that we have not really isolated the true transition effects. This is a matter considered in the appendix.

This study will concentrate upon the implications of computer usage for the demand for labour. This has been the major concern of nearly all studies of automation.† We concentrate mainly on the

† As examples of other approaches to isolating the effect of computers see: OECD [1966], UN [1971], Taviss [1970].

level but can also comment on the skill composition of the demand for labour.

In addition we can comment on (a) the balance of payments by looking at the effect of computerisation on the UK balance of payments; (b) trigger effects by looking at the possibility of computerisation causing changes in techniques only related indirectly to computers; and (c) the effects of computers on organisation structure, wage levels and knowledge.

The analysis will proceed as follows. In section 8.7 the data on computer usage is analysed to investigate the nature of the costs and benefits realised by computer users. Our initial aim being to estimate labour savings per machine in computer use. These estimates are based on data referring to 1964 and 1969, and are assumed to refer to third generation computer technology. Changes in computer size over time are ignored at this stage. In section 8.3 computer manufacture is analysed and the net changes to labour requirements in capital goods construction are investigated, again with data relevant to third generation technology. In section 8.4 an estimate of the satiation stock of third generation computers is derived and the net effect on the demand for labour calculated. We then estimate the effects along the transition path on the assumption that all computers installed have had (and will have) the net labour saving characteristics of third generation machines. At this stage we discuss the importance of the above assumptions on size and technology and introduce other qualifications of the results. Finally, the conclusions are presented.

8.2 COMPUTER USAGE – REALISED COSTS AND BENEFITS

The first matter to consider is the pattern of computer usage in different sectors of the economy. We begin by presenting the pattern of computer usage for certain industrial sectors. Some of these sectors relate to the industrial breakdown of the previous chapter whereas others differ according to the data source. Only those sectors in which data is available are included. The aim of this discussion is to indicate the tasks to which computers are applied; the proportion of the total stock put to administrative use, process control and scientific and technical work, in each sector; the types of functions computerised; and the effects of computer application quoted by industry sources.

Aviation. There are two main groups in this industry, the manufacturers and the airline operators. The manufacturers held about 2% of the total national computer stock in 1970. Rolls Royce (SCST [1970b]

p. 236) detailed their applications as 40% to support research design and development, 40% to production control and 20% to administrative use and product support. Computers are also used extensively in flight simulation (CW [1971]). The airline operators use their machines for seat reservation systems, aircraft scheduling, and the general administrative functions (SCST [1970b] pp. 163–5). Their share of total computer ownership is not large, however. Computers are also used in air traffic control, the Linesman–Mediator system involving sixty-one computers and 250 man years of software effort (SCST [1971c] p. 77 and SCST [1971b] p. 185).

Armed services. This sector held about $2\frac{1}{4}$% of the computer stock in 1970 with eighty-one machines. The usage of these machines (SCST [1971b] pp. 180–2) was

Bureau	3	Pay and Personnel	8
Production control	1	Supply and movements	27
Engineering	3	Operations	3
Scientific and R & D	18	Training	13
Finance and accounting	15		

In value terms, machines valued at £6m out of the total of £21m were used on scientific work. In addition fifteen machines were used by the Ministry of Aviation Supply of which all but three were used for administration. These two departments used 45% of the whole of government computing power (SCST [1971c] p. 107). Further comments will therefore be left to the general study of government applications.

Atomic energy. The UKAEA had approximately 0.7% of the whole computer stock in 1970, eighty-two machines. Of these, fourteen large ones were used for management, seventeen for scientific work, four for data conversion, and sixty small machines for process control (there is some overlap). The scientific work concerns reactor design calculations, reactor physics, etc. The process control machines have replaced logging equipment (SCST [1970a] pp. 38–40).

Financial: banks, building societies and insurance. This sector owned about 11% of the total computer stock, used almost totally for office tasks and thus classed as administrative. The actual applications are processing accounts, cheque clearing, share registration and general administrative tasks, including payroll (SCST [1970b] pp. 201–2).

The savings the sector has effected tend to be concentrated on staff and office space. Both the Midland and National Westminster stress staff savings, the latter estimating a saving in staff upward of 5,000 (SCST [1970b] pp. 211–16).

Construction. Up to 1967 only a few of the very largest firms used computers and they were employed on architectural design, engineering design and services, quantity surveying and the usual management functions (MPBW [1967a], [1969]).

Oil and petro-chemicals. This industry, using $1\frac{1}{2}\%$ of the total stock in 1970, is similar to the atomic energy industry in that it uses a large number of process control computers and because of its technology is in the forefront of computer applications. This industry accounted for nearly 50 % of all process control equipment (CW [1972g]). The computers are used for the planning and scheduling of products between oilfields, processes and consumers. Linear programming is used extensively and computerised. However, Mobil said that accounting work still involved 75 % of total usage, but technical projects were increasing in importance (CW [1972g]). Esso had four large machines and one small machine for commercial work, and seven small machines for control and engineering work. Their evidence (SCST [1970b] p. 228) indicated that they managed to reduce costs and staff employed by the replacement of punched card equipment by computers in accounting work, and have reduced costs by applying computers to refinery planning and supply distribution. Shell indicated that they spent approximately £20m on computers each year, of which about 25 % went on system maintenance. Their management applications took up about 70 % of their total budget (SCST [1970b] p. 237).

Transport. This sector controlled about 2.3 % of the total stock in 1970. An NCC report detailed that if vehicle scheduling were used more widely savings of £35m could have been effected in 1966, but only 15 % of companies had computerised this function by 1969 (NCC [1969]). As examples of computer use, the National Freight Corporation use their machines for general accounting and administration (SCST [1970b] p. 187), and British Rail use their machines mainly in the accountancy field. British Rail estimated, however, that, using a 10 % discount rate, computerised freight scheduling could yield them a return of £22m on an investment of £37m (SCST [1970b] p. 167 and SCST [1971c] p. 15).

Textiles and clothing. Approximately 12 % of companies in the industry made use of computers, mainly in the growth end of the industry. In most cases the machines replaced accounting machines and were mainly used in commercial and general management applications (NCC [1968a]).

Hotels and catering. It is estimated that the break-even size for computer ownership is control of 400 rooms and for bureau use 200 rooms. Computer usage is very limited and where utilised they are mainly involved in the general management functions, although room reservation systems are feasible (NCC [1968b]).

Public utilities. The coal, gas, electricity and water industries controlled 3 % of the total stock in 1970. The Coal Board began computer use with payroll in 1957. Their machines are mainly used for administrative purposes, but are also applied to production management and support for engineering and technical services. The Board estimated that although they employed 1,250 people on computers they had been able to reduce staff needs by 3,500 (SCST [1970b] pp. 181–7). The Gas Board has made extensive use of computers in administrative tasks, scientific applications and process control, and the Area Boards, although mainly concentrating on customer billing, have used them for similar tasks (SCST [1970b] pp. 176–81). These patterns are reflected in the electricity supply industry as well (SCST [1970b] pp. 169–76).

Steel. The British Steel Corporation had forty-seven machines installed or on order on 1 January 1970 for business purposes. These were used for operational research, statistical studies, order handling, etc. They also had thirty-six process control machines used in steel construction (SCST [1970a] pp. 143–7).

Government. If one includes all branches of government a share of 15 % could be attributed to this sector. The larger part of the computing power is used for administrative purposes. Most of the computers have been justified on grounds of staff savings, although in certain cases the computer has enabled work to be done that otherwise could not have been. Departments have claimed savings in staff of 2,500 up to March 1968, and another 1,000 in the following year. A total saving of 13,000 for all working and planned systems was forecast (CSD [1971] p. 11).

Local authorities. This sector owned approximately 6 % of the stock in 1970, and by far the largest proportion of these machines was used for administrative tasks, mainly financial, although a few authorities used them for engineering and architectural applications (Baxter [1971]).

Universities. With approximately 5½ % of the total stock in 1970, the machines are applied mainly to scientific and technical tasks although the use of computers in university administration is quite widespread.

This review of the pattern of computer usage and some of its effects across different sectors covers approximately 50 % of the total computer stock in 1970. There is no reason to believe that other industries would differ markedly from the above patterns. The effect of the computers on the economy is going to depend to a large extent on the pattern of use of these machines. The general impression received from the above is that the administrative applications of machines predominate. In table 8.1 the breakdown of the use of all machines (costing more than £20,000) in 1969 is presented.

Table 8.1. *Nature of computer use 1969*

Application	No. of machines
Office, administrative	2,108
Scientific, technical and design	600
Educational	150
Process control	150
Others	100
Total	3,108

SOURCE: D of E [1972] pp. 10–11.

When it is also considered that, in general, process control machines are small machines, then the predominance of administratively used machines is adequately illustrated. Scientific uses come second and process control applications third.

To extend the analysis of the effects of computers each of these three types of computer use will be considered separately. Process control will be looked at first, then scientific applications will be studied. Finally administrative uses will be analysed.

It has been shown that process control applications are concentrated in certain specific industries (aviation, atomic energy, oil and petro-chemicals and public utilities), and that the oil and petrochemicals industries account for about 50 % of the total usage of such control equipment. The UKAEA illustrate the general attitude to the use of process control computers.

In many cases these machines carry out functions which were formerly the duty of special logging or control equipment. . . It is very often cheaper to use a computer in this situation. In general terms, the reason for using a small computer is to obtain an immediate response in a monitoring or control situation.

In all these applications the benefits are that a small computer can carry out the task more cheaply or more effectively than the alternative method. To this must be added versatility of function. (SCST [1970b] para. 26, p. 192.)

In control applications the computer is always a part, and usually only a small part of a complete system. In the case of industrial systems it is quite normal for the central processor to be only 10–20 % of the control system cost which in turn may be only 10–20 % of the cost of the whole plant (SCST [1970b] p. 78).

The influence of computers via process control applications will not be very large when the low level of usage and the specialised areas of applications are considered. The main effect will be improvements in efficiency and the speed of process control.

The scientific, technical and design applications are again concentrated in a few sectors, mainly universities and government, but the scientifically based industries (atomic energy, aviation, and petrochemicals) also make some use of computers for these tasks.

A large proportion of scientific work, especially in universities, involves 'number crunching', the carrying out of numerous simple calculations on small data sets. Computers are ideal for such tasks. Hollingdale [1970] and Tootill give as examples of areas making such uses of computers, high energy nuclear physics, molecular biology, space travel, and the aircraft industry. In many cases the sheer volume of calculations would make the task impossible without computers. However, in the aircraft industry, for example, stress calculations in the design stages of aircraft manufacture used to be carried out by large numbers of workers using slide rules. The computer has reduced the labour force and yields more accurate results faster.

The problem with estimating the effects of computers in such applications is that without computers much work would not have been done because of the sheer size of the calculations. Should one therefore consider the usage of computers as labour saving or expansionist? If the work was to have been done the labour requirements would have been very large, but it is felt here that it is best to consider that the use of computers in scientific applications has mainly enabled work to be done that was not previously feasible. This means that the computer's existence will have drastically affected the basic knowledge and capabilities of a society. This is not the place to pursue an economic appraisal of such changes, so when we come to investigate the balance of costs and benefits this sector will be considered to mainly contribute 'new knowledge', although some labour saving contribution could also be implied. We consider that 'educational' machines ought to be treated similarly.

Turn now to the administrative and office use of computers, involving approximately two-thirds of total usage by number (this proportion would increase after quality adjustment). The weight of numbers implies that the main impact of computers would arise from this area.

Although the administrative tasks performed by computers vary between industries it is not going to be possible, except by comments, to separate out the effects of computers on specific industries in any more detail that has been done already. It will therefore be necessary to talk of the effect of these computers in general.

To begin, it is interesting to investigate what benefits users feel that their computer has provided. The Miles Roman survey† details the extent to which the objectives influencing the decision to computerise have been achieved. Manpower utilisation was the most commonly recorded objective, and quality of service was more often mentioned than management control and was also more often achieved. In table 8.2 a mean index of achievement is presented for each objective. The sample was 340 installations and the index is constructed so that if expectations were exceeded it equals 1.5, if they were met exactly it equals 1.0, and if almost met 0.5.

Table 8.2. *The achievement of computer objectives*

Objective – to improve	Occurrences	Index
Services to customers	245	0.75
General administration	1242	0.73
Manpower utilisation	246	0.69
Financial planning and control	234	0.65
Departmental planning and control	189	0.63
Capital equipment utilisation	71	0.52
Corporate planning and control	102	0.45

A further tabulation refers to the satisfaction users have obtained from their systems using different yardsticks. The three yardsticks are,

A Quality of service: reliability, accuracy, promptness.
B Management information provided, improvement in efficiency or control of business.
C Economics of the office work itself: staff savings, cost comparisons, etc.

Many respondents quoted that they used more than one yardstick in the appraisal of the effectiveness of their computer systems. In terms of the prime yardstick the degree of satisfaction users achieved from their system varied as in table 8.3.

† NCC [1972]. Although it should be stated that this study reflects much greater satisfaction with computer usage than have other studies.

Table 8.3. *Satisfaction of computer users*

				Degrees of satisfaction			
Principal yardstick	No. using	% of sample	(a) Nil	(b) Not very	(c) Reason-ably	(d) Extremely	(c+d) as % of no. using
A	68	20	0	6	46	16	91
B	54	16	1	4	33	16	90
General	73	21	2	11	39	21	82
C	128	38	9	12	75	32	84
None	17	5	0	0	15	2	100

The conclusions to be drawn from these two tables are that users sought cost savings, improvement in services and improvement in control, in that order, from their installations. They have been most successful in generating the expected benefits in services, have improved control, but consider economies, especially in manpower, to have reached a better achievement level. It is not going to be possible to quantify improvements in service or management information and control; these are essentially intangible. They will, however, be held in mind while the study proceeds by concentrating on the economics of office work.

When a computer is installed it will either replace an existing method or perform new tasks. In chapter 6 the methods replaced were discussed; thus the first point to be made is that when a computer is installed there will be a fall in the stock of and investment in punched card and keyboard accounting machines relative to that which there would have been. This in itself will affect labour usage and will be considered below. As for expansion, there are two aspects to consider: (a) expansion that would have taken place even without the advent of computers; (b) expansion that is dependent on computer usage, i.e. work made practicable by computers for the first time. In the *Computers in Offices* surveys (M of L [1965] p. 19, and D of E [1972] p. 14) it is indicated that nearly 70% of all installations carry out some work of type (b), but the difference that it makes to manpower requirements is very small. It would seem therefore that one can proceed to look at manpower requirements and for practical purposes ignore this influence. The effect of expansion of type (a) can be dealt with during this analysis. The questions to be answered in looking at manpower requirements are:

(i) How many posts have been taken over by computers? This includes extra posts that would have been needed in the ADP area to

Table 8.4. *Estimated number of posts taken over by all ADP installations with computers installed or on order at 1 January 1964*

Occupation	Total	Per installation	Per computer	Per organisation
Managers and supervisors	700	1.2	1.0	1.5
Clerks	33,300	59.2	47.3	70.6
Machine operators	14,600	26.0	20.7	30.9
Typists	2,400	4.2	3.4	5.0
Total	51,000	90.6	72.4	108.0

SOURCE: M of L [1965] p. 19.

Table 8.5. *Office posts taken over by computers, 1954–69*

Occupation	Well established installations			Newer installations Total	All installations Total
	Total	Inst.	Comp.		
Management	1,250	1	1	500	1,750
Supervisory	5,800	6	5	2,450	8,250
Clerical	62,000	65	49	26,500	88,500
Typing	9,000	10	7	3,750	12,750
Accounting machine operators	14,800	16	12	6,400	21,210
Other machine operators	6,850	7	5	2,900	9,750
Other	900	1	1	400	1,300
Total	100,500	106	80	43,000	143,500

SOURCE: D of E [1972] p. 20.

cope with the expansion of business if ADP had not been available to cope with it.

(ii) How many posts were created by computers?

Consider question (i) first. The 1965 study presents data from which table 8.4 is derived, detailing posts taken over by computers. The figures are calculated on the basis of 562 installations, 703 computers and 472 organisations, and of the savings indicated it is estimated that 10 % are attributable to national government, 10 % to the gas and electricity boards and 20 % to insurance and banking (M of L [1965] p. 19).

Only a very small proportion of the 108 posts per organisation are due to expansion resulting from computerisation. Of these 108 posts, 58 were actually discontinued and 50 would have been necessary without computers. The results for 1969 are remarkably similar, and are presented in table 8.5.

Table 8.6. *Estimated number of posts created in ADP excluding service bureaux and computer manufacturers' services to customers, 1965*

Occupation	Permanent posts	Per			Total posts	Per		
		Inst.	Org.	Comp.		Inst.	Org.	Comp.
Data processing manager	565	1.0	1.2	0.8	565	1.0	1.2	0.8
Systems analyst	850	1.5	1.8	1.2	1,520	2.7	3.2	2.1
Programmers	2,360	4.0	5.0	3.3	3,090	5.5	6.5	4.4
Machine operators	4,725	8.4	10.0	6.7	10,725	19.0	22.7	15.2
Other ADP machine operators	—	—	—	—	2,600	4.7	5.5	3.7
Total	8,500	14.9	18.0	12.0	18,500	33.9	39.1	26.2

SOURCE: M of L [1965] p. 20, adapted.

In addition posts taken over by small computers are estimated at 2,000 and those taken over by service bureaux at 12,500, unfortunately not reduced to categories, making a grand total of 158,000 posts in 1969.

The averages from this data are higher per installation than in the earlier figures (106 as opposed to 90) and the average per computer is also higher. This may well be the result of larger machines introduced in the intervening years.

Work which could not be done without the computer was specifically excluded from these 1969 figures which were based on a questionnaire asking: if you did not have your computer installation, how many additional office workers would you require to maintain your present level of business? In this case it was not possible to isolate posts actually taken over from those that would have existed without computers.

Turn now to posts created by ADP. Although it was shown in an earlier chapter that computer manning requirements vary with scale, only averages will be considered in this context. In table 8.6 data is presented on the number of posts created by ADP up to 1965. This data separates out permanent from transitional labour in that the survey considered that some posts created by computers were not permanent, i.e. they were only concerned with the transfer of work to computers and would not be needed for maintenance of the system.

When the service bureaux and the manufacturers' services are included the pattern in table 8.7 results. This includes both permanent and transitional labour. As can be seen from table 8.6, the major differences in permanent and transitional labour centre around machine operators. The rationale for this is that to start a computer system all data has to be entered and this means a large coding task – thus

Table 8.7. *Staff employed on ADP in 1964 including service bureaux and manufacturers' services*

Occupation	Total	Per computer
DP managers	839	1.1
Systems analysts	2,836	3.7
Programmers	4,258	5.6
Machine operators	11,587	15.2
Other ADP machine operators	2,982	3.9
Total	22,502	29.5

the extra machine operators. There is also some allowance for analysts and programmers to write the initial applications software. When one compares the data with and without service bureaux employment the major increase is in programming and systems staff. As such institutions are mainly software houses this is as expected.

The data from the 1972 study has discarded the permanent and transitional distinction. It was found that the number of employees did not reduce as a system aged. The reason is that organisations are dynamic institutions and their continual development has required continuous employment of what might be considered transitional labour. In table 8.8 data is presented on estimated employment on computers including service bureaux and manufacturers' services to customers in 1972.

Table 8.8. *Posts in EDP, January 1972*

Occupation	Total	Per computer
DP managers	5,000	1.3
Systems analysts	21,000	5.4
Programmers	29,000	7.4
Machine operators		
Computer room	20,000	5.1
Data preparation	54,000	13.8
Other	5,000	1.2
Other EDP staff	20,000	5.1
Total	150,000	38.4

SOURCE: D of E [1972] para. 4, p. 18.
NOTE: Posts per computer are calculated assuming 3,640 machines installed.

One major difference between these figures and the 1965 figures is in the treatment of machine operators. In the 1965 figures attempts were made to separate machine operators who were employed on previous techniques from those who had to be employed as a consequence of computer usage.† The actual numbers cannot be separated out. In the later data this distinction was not made. It was therefore decided to consider the data without distinction.

In table 8.9 the results of this discussion are presented in terms of posts created and replaced by computers. The data used includes bureaux employees and manufacturers' services to customers in posts created, for this sector is used by many computer owners, and for 1965 the sum of transitional and permanent employees is considered, i.e. data from tables 8.4, 8.5, 8.7 and 8.8.

Table 8.9. *Posts replaced and created per computer installed,*
1964 and 1969

	Net increase in number of posts	
Occupation	1964	1969
Managers and executives		−1.0
Supervisors	−1.0	−5.0
Clerks	−47.3	−49.0
Typists	−3.4	−7.0
Calculating machine operators ⎱	−20.7	−12.0
Other office machine operators ⎰		−5.0
Other office workers		−1.0
DP managers	+1.1	+1.3
Systems analysts	+3.7	+5.4
Programmers	+5.6	+7.4
Machine operators		
Computer room ⎱	+15.2	+5.1
Data preparation ⎰		+13.8
Other EDP equipment ⎱	+3.9	+1.2
Other EDP staff ⎰		+5.1
Net reduction	42.9	41.6

The two sets of figures jointly therefore imply a saving per computer of forty-two staff. If one considered the data for 1965 which concerns only 'permanent' posts, separates machine operators into its two groups and ignores bureaux and computer manufacturers' services, the reduction in staff would be estimated as 60.4. For the reasons stated above the figure of forty-two per machine will be maintained for the rest of this chapter.

One interesting point, however, is that between 1964 and 1969 the

† This distinction was made only for posts considered permanent and did not extend to the service sector.

average quality adjusted value of a computer installed increased from £72,000 to £171,000. This may explain why six more staff were needed in the later period than the earlier. However, the fact that not much greater staff savings were generated tends to imply that the extra size must have been justified by greater unquantifiable benefits, e.g. better management information, control, etc.

Some other comments on these results are in order. First, the reduction in posts of forty-two per computer does not appear to have been reflected in redundancy, the reason being that many of the posts lost would have been the result of expansion and as such were never really created (M of L [1965] para. 4, p. 18). The other posts could be reduced by natural wastage. Second, the results above are averages and we know that employment does not vary proportionately with computer size and may also vary with the nature of applications in each industry. Also it has already been shown that those industries that formerly used the most clerical labour were able to reduce posts by the greatest amount. Third, in some cases changes were taking place from a base of clerical labour and in other cases from office machines to computers. The use of office machines in many cases had already affected considerable changes in the number of office posts. Thus the average figures also hide differences due to the nature of the prevailing technique replaced. Finally, there is some evidence that computer personnel tend to work more overtime and shift work than was the case under the replaced technique (D of E [1972] p. 40). As the figures do not reflect this, the true savings may be slightly different.

In addition to the staff savings directly attributable to the computer there will also be generated other savings that are the consequence of the staff reduction, for example reduction in overheads related to staff employment (e.g. personnel, payroll, etc.) and reductions in office space. One can generally assume that the office space occupied by forty staff will be less than that required by the computer, although the saving may be small. Over time, as computers have reduced in size, that saving may have increased. However, in many cases the environmental quality required by the machine is higher than that required by office workers so this may offset some savings. In certain cases computerisation has prompted a move to a lower rent area but this is not very important for a very large number of machines are still concentrated in the areas of high office employment, especially London.

Finally, in this section job content and training can be considered. The net changes in skill categories per machine installed are shown in table 8.10. There is a reduction in relatively unskilled staff and a smaller reduction in executive posts, but an increase in technically orientated posts. The implications for training centre on the need to

Table 8.10. *Net changes in skill categories per computer*

Skill category	Net change in number of posts
Management, executive, supervisory	−4.7
Systems analysts	+5.4
Programmers	+7.4
Computer operators	+5.1
Machine operators, typists, clerks, others	−54.1

produce systems analysts, programmers and operators. Thus one must answer, what staff is needed for training purposes? The *Computers in Central Government* survey (CSD [1971] pp. 93–6) gives some indication of training staff needs.

(a) It quotes one company with 1,000 computer staff with forty new graduate entrants each year that employs forty training instructors.

(b) It estimates that in government thirty-six training staff will be needed for 3,000 computer staff, but that this ought to increase to eighty-seven for 3,200 staff in 1974.

(c) It also estimates a staff–student ratio of 3:15. Evidence to the Subcommittee (SCST [1971b] p. 344) tends to suggest that computer staff in government get approximately six weeks formal training plus 'on the job' training. If one takes this figure of six weeks, assuming a staff ratio of 3:15, then one man with a forty-eight week working year ought to be able to train forty staff. If the on the job training, re-training, etc. are considered, an addition to posts created of one man year per annum of computer operation ought to take account of skill differences between staff employed and laid off.

To draw some conclusions from this section we can first state that computer usage was split into three categories, process control, scientific and technical applications and administrative uses. It has been suggested that process control machines generate benefits centred mainly on efficiency of operation but require better quality staff.

In the scientific area it was suggested that increases in knowledge are the main benefit but some labour saving could be identified. In administrative applications machines yield unquantifiable benefits of improved service, information and control, but a staff saving rounded to forty staff per machine can be identified. Some saving in other inputs is consequent upon this. It should be stated, however, that the saving could be estimated as high as sixty staff per machine.

If one allows a computer to have a working life of seven years, then the benefits can be detailed as, (a) savings of 280 man years of office staff per machine in office applications, over seven years, (b) increases in information, (c) increases in control, (d) ability to perform work not otherwise feasible, and (e) improvements in the quality of service.

8.3 CAPITAL GOODS CONSTRUCTION

Before one can finally analyse the effect of computerisation on the economy it is necessary to investigate the nature of inputs in computer construction relative to the inputs in replaced techniques. It was shown above that the production of computers has been very labour intensive, and thus for simplicity the labour aspects will be concentrated upon.

The estimates of labour input per computer produced are unfortunately very approximate. From the Census of Production 1968 the employees in the industry (including manufacture of central processors, peripherals and software) are as in table 8.11.†

Table 8.11. *Employment in computer manufacturing*

	Thousands	
	1963	1968
Operatives	6.0	10.4
Other employees	4.4	8.6
Total including working proprietors	10.4	19.1

To relate this to output per man an estimate of the total output of computers is required. The data used in the previous chapter indicated that there were 290 machines installed during 1963 and 1126 during 1968. It will be assumed that these were manufactured in the year in question. However, a number of these machines had been imported and some way must be found to reduce the data to reflect only home construction.

Ministry of Technology figures show that if none of the home production had been exported then 72 % of the British market could have been supplied from home production in 1968.‡ Thus of the 1126 machines installed, 810 could have been British made. This would have meant labour per computer as in table 8.12. As the import/export data did not exist for 1963 the same proportions are used and they

---

† Pratten (1971) does not like these figures because of the apparent discrepancy between the total workforce and the ICL workforce. It is felt that this discrepancy can be cleared up by considering that ICL also produce office machines.

‡ See below.

imply a total home production of 208 machines in that year. The labour per computer in 1963 is also presented in table 8.12.

Table 8.12. *Labour per machine produced, 1963 and 1968*

	1963	1968
Operatives	29.0	13.0
Other	21.0	10.6
Total	50.0	24.0

This data implies that between 1963 and 1968 the output per operative more than doubled whereas the output per head of other employees did not quite double. In the technological change chapter (chapter 5) it was suggested that changes in component technology were the major causes of technological change in the computer industry. In the present situation this can give us the lead into the explanation of this apparent increase in labour productivity. It was shown above that as technology changed the proportion of value added between sectors also changed. Figures were presented in chapter 4 that illustrate that in 1963 computer manufacturers spent 21 % of their sales revenue on inputs from other sectors. By 1968 this proportion had increased to 43.6 %. It is therefore suggested that the major fall in labour per unit of output can be attributed to the shift of work between sectors, even though it has also been shown that when components technology changed there were some minor repercussions on technology in the computer manufacturing sector.

The figure required in this study must refer to all labour input required in computer manufacture and consequently must also reflect the labour input in the component supplying sector. Thus an estimate is derived that fifty years of labour input are required per unit of computer manufacture. Our reasoning is as follows: an attempt is being made to discover labour inputs for third generation computer technology. The 1963 technology was second generation and the 1968 third generation. Between the two years the differences in labour input have been attributed to an increase in components bought in from 21 % to 43 % of sales. If we assume that the 22 % increase in the proportion of inputs bought in can account for an increase in labour requirements of twenty-six men *in toto*, then to use the figure fifty for labour requirements per unit of computer output is equivalent to assuming 1968 technology with 21 % of sales spent on inputs (and this 21 % is itself to be offset, see below). This is, of course, a rather approximate way to estimate labour inputs.

Before turning to the manufacture of alternative techniques two further comments on this result are in order: (a) the labour figures include R & D personnel that may not really be attributable to current production; and (b) some of the fall in labour requirements over time may have been the result of the interaction of rising levels of output and increasing returns to scale.

Amongst the equipment being replaced, office machinery is the major category although some logging and control equipment is also involved. The estimates made of labour requirements in this section are even more approximate than those above. First, the Census of Production figures for 1968 indicate that employment in office machine manufacture was as in table 8.13.

Table 8.13. *Total employment in office machine manufacture, 1963 and 1968 (thousands)*

	1963	1968
Operatives	21.4	19.9
Other	8.8	10.8
Total	30.2	30.7

The *Computers in Offices* survey estimates that office employment would have increased at 2.4 % p.a. without computers (D of E [1972] p. 8). If one assumes that each new employee would have been equipped with the same machines as older employees, then over the five year period an increase in labour in machine manufacture of approximately $12\frac{1}{4}$% would have been required. On 1963 productivity rates this would have meant 34,188 employees in office machine manufacture in 1968. However, only 30,700 were employed, which implies that computerisation prevented the creation of 3,488 jobs. During the period 2,647 computers were installed, so an average of 1.5 jobs per computer were not created in this sector. The comments to be made on this are as follows.

(a) Any complication through home versus foreign construction has been ignored.

(b) The figures do not include labour input into the products supplied to this sector, either current or capital. It is assumed that this will offset the purchases of the computer sector from outside (i.e. the 21 %).

(c) The figures will be compared with the extra labour required for computer manufacture. Fortunately there is little reason to believe that any adjustment will be required for different productive lives of equipment.

(d) These figures do not include the logging and control equipment

being replaced and make no allowance for productivity increases in
office equipment manufacture or usage.

Because of these comments the figure of 1.5 is rounded to 2.0, which
will also make calculations simpler.

8.4   THE COMPARISON OF CONCEPTUAL ECONOMIES
WITH AND WITHOUT COMPUTERS

Enough information has now been provided to enable one to perform
the comparison of economic states and to analyse an economic process
of transition between states.

First, this study will concentrate on the quantitative labour implications, initially by comparing states and then by analysing the process
of transition. When this has been done the balance of payments implications will be drawn, and then some comments made on trigger effects
and miscellaneous other factors.

The labour implications per computer installed have been worked
out on the basis of data on office computers. The discussion above
leads us to the following conclusions and derived assumptions.

(a) All computers, whatever their use, save 2.0 man years of labour
by the non-creation of posts in the manufacture of machinery for
alternative techniques.

(b) All machines require fifty man years of labour to construct and
this, it is assumed, is spread evenly over two years.

(c) Assume that scientific, educational and process control machines
do not save labour in use but yield greater efficiency in production
and new knowledge instead. Assume also that administrative computers
are 67 % of all computers installed; thus when the labour saved on
administrative machines is spread over all machines a total of twenty-
seven man years of labour are saved for each computer for each year
of its working life.

(d) Assume that a computer will work for seven years (based on
Computer Survey data) but takes one year to install and then works until
the end of its eighth year.

These assumptions imply that the net labour saving over the lifetime
profile of a computer will be

Year	-2	-1	0	1	2	3	4	5	6	7
	25	23	0	-27	-27	-27	-27	-27	-27	-27

where year zero is the year during which the machine is installed† and
the non-production of office machines is taken care of in the reduction

---

† There may be some need for labour for installation purposes but we assume that this is
offset by labour saved in this installation year.

of extra labour in year -1. During the seven year life the other benefits of computer use are also forthcoming.

To compare different states the first problem is to approximate the saturation stock of computers. In the previous chapter, looking at the aggregate data, we generated an expression for the satiation stock. Specifically we estimated,

$$Z_t^* = \exp{(7.06 - 5.57D_0 - 3.30D_1 - 1.87D_2)}Y_t^{0.7}.$$

As all our figures on labour usage refer to third generation technology, we will use the expression for the satiation stock of third generation machines, i.e.

$$Z_t^* = e^{7.06}Y_t^{0.7}.$$

However, Z_t^* is a value term and the labour usage figures relate to number of machines. To reduce Z_t^* to numbers of machines we can look at the average quality of machines installed during the third generation stage (1964–70). By 1970, when the majority of machines installed were third generation, the average machine had a 1963 introduction price of £181,000. This figure implies that Z_t^* represents

$$\left(\frac{e^{7.06}Y_t^{0.7}}{181}\right) \text{ machines.}$$

The presence of Y_t in these expressions means, as one would expect, that to compare economies we have to fix the output level at which the comparison is effected. We will choose $Y_t = Y_{1970}$ for our comparison. Then

$$Z_{1970}^* = 1{,}835{,}628,$$

measured in £'000 at 1963 introduction prices, i.e. 10,142 machines. Using this figure and the estimates of labour saving and usage generated above we can calculate the labour demand implications of this stock.

Assume these machines would have an even age spread so a constant proportion would come up for replacement each year. To produce these replacements the economy would require an amount of labour in excess of that required to produce the output under the previous technical regime of $\frac{1}{8} \times 10{,}142 \times 48 = 60{,}852$ men. The use of 10,142 machines would, allowing one year for installation, save in each year relative to the previous technology $\frac{7}{8} \times 10{,}142 \times 27 = 239{,}604$ men, a net saving of 178,752 men, which represents 0.79 % of the 1970 labour force.

To generalise, we can say that for an economy that is computer saturated with third generation computers its output can be produced with a net labour saving over its previous technology in each year of $17.62(Z_t^*/181)$ if the machines have an even age spread. Or to put it in terms of output, the net labour saving ΔL for any output level is

$$\Delta L = 113.3 . Y_t^{0.7}.$$

A similar exercise could be performed to generate the savings under the zeroth, first and second generation technologies.

If 28 % of all machines are imported (see below) the savings increase to 195,791 man years, for less labour would be required at home to produce the machines. This labour would have to be used to supply goods to the foreign market to take up the balance of payments deficit. If one now compares the labour saving to the total 1970 labour force the computer effect is in the region of 0.80 % of the total labour force. Considering the assumptions that have been made on the way to this conclusion the size of the reduction in labour demand relative to the total labour force is so small that it would require very large changes in assumptions to affect significantly the 0.80 % figure produced.

At the same time as this reduction was effected one would expect increases in efficiency, service, etc. Moreover from the discussions of separate industries above one would also expect to find

(a) a relatively greater fall in labour demand in the financial sector,

(b) increased efficiency in the sectors extensively using process control,

(c) a changing skill structure of the labour force,

(d) an increase in labour in capital goods construction relative to consumption goods construction,

(e) further developments in scientific knowledge, and

(f) a shift of labour from home to export construction.

Turn now to the transition path. Here one is concerned with the changes that the economy must go through in order to reach the computerised state. We make two initial assumptions. First, that the labour savings and requirements established above are the same whether we are considering first, second or third generation machines (this assumption we discuss below). Second, as we wish to extend our period of analysis beyond 1970, we assume that the computer stock will grow at the rates predicted by the Department of Employment (in D of E [1972] p. 10), i.e.

$$g_t = \frac{S_{t+1} - S_t}{S_t}$$

will be in each year:

Year	1970	1971	1972	1973	1974	1975	1976	1977	1978
g_t (%)	20	17	13	12	13	13	10	6	5

Using our figures on the computer stock generated elsewhere, and applying these growth rates, we can generate a series on the computer stock 1952–78. This is presented in table 8.14.

Table 8.14. *The transition path for computerisation in the UK*

Year	Stock at end of year (1)	Net additions to computer stock (2)	Gross additions to computer stock (3)	Net labour requirements in computer construction (man years) (4)	Net labour saving in computer usage (man years) (5)	Balance (4) − (5) (6)	Balance[a] 72% × (4) − (5) (7)
1952	—	—	—	300	0	300	216
1953	—	—	—	551	0	551	397
1954	12	12	12	678	0	678	488
1955	23	11	11	1566	324	1242	803
1956	40	17	17	2931	621	2310	1489
1957	87	47	47	3177	1080	2097	1207
1958	161	74	74	3507	2349	1158	176
1959	220	59	59	5103	4347	756	−672
1960	306	86	86	8450	5940	2510	144
1961	417	111	125	12379	7884	4495	1029
1962	620	203	223	16495	10719	5776	1157
1963	875	255	290	21139	15795	5344	−574
1964	982	107	393	26757	15903	10854	3362
1965	1424	442	484	36950	25380	11570	1224
1966	1956	532	625	49019	35937	13082	−643
1967	2595	639	903	57540	45684	11856	−4256
1968	3522	927	1130	66801	64584	2217	−16487
1969	4319	797	1262	69353	82539	−13186	−32605
1970	5470	1151	1151	69557	106893	−37336	−56812
1971	6564	1094	1384	71757	139860	−68103	−88195
1972	7680	1116	1509	75761	166617	−90856	−112069
1973	8678	998	1482	92491	194292	−101801	−127699
1974	9720	1042	1667	113768	217431	−103663	−135518
1975	10983	1263	2166	121409	238059	−116650	−150616
1976	12411	1428	2558	115819	266031	−150212	−182641
1977	13652	1241	2503	106290	301023	−194733	−224494
1978	14471	819	2330	97584	327807	−230223	−257547

(a) Column 6 estimates the balance of labour requirements on the assumption that all computers installed in the UK are manufactured in the UK. Column 7 allows for the fact that the UK industry only had capacity to build 72% of these machines.

With the above series we can generate total labour saving as

$$(S_t - x_t) . 27,$$

where x_t is gross additions to stock in time t. Total labour usage is calculated as

$$\sum_{T=-2}^{0} x_{t-T} . a_T,$$

where a_T is the net change to labour requirements per machine in time T and T is time internal to the process. Gross additions to the stock are taken from *Computer Survey* data where possible, and elsewhere calculated by assuming that machines die at the end of their seventh year of operation.† In table 8.14 figures on net additions and gross additions to the stock are presented. To these are added the calculated additions and subtractions to labour requirements, and also the resulting balance. Recalculations to allow for 28 % of gross additions to be imported are also added.

As can be seen, this data reflects that labour requirements in the early years increased and in the later years decreased. What we must ask, however, is: in relation to what can we make this statement? In fact the savings are relative to the demand for labour along our comparison path, which has the same output path as the actual economy. However, relative to the comparison path the actual economy would be experiencing increasing unemployment in the later stages of the diffusion process. This may seem unsatisfactory. In fact what we can argue is that the actual economy always reacts in such a way as to correct for labour redundancies by increasing its output level. Thus the actual economy does not reflect increasing unemployment.‡ This means that the output level is a function of the labour implications of computerisation and thus we could not have expected the economy to establish the comparison path if computers had not appeared. All this is equivalent to saying is that the theory of transitions is not adequately developed.§ Alternatively we could say that the comparison path is infeasible as it would have shown excess demand for labour.

We should also state that the transition path, although it has been detailed for twenty-six years has not reached any saturation level of computer usage. The advantages of trying to extend it further are, however, slight.

Two further comments on the derivation of the transition path results are in order. First, the calculated transition path is assumed to be made up of machines that replace alternative technologies, for this is how the pattern of changes in labour requirements was presented. If, however, some of the computers were installed not as replacements but as additions then their time profile of labour saving would have to be‖

Year	−2	−1	0	1	2	3	4	5	6	7
	+25	+25	0	+38	+38	+38	+38	+38	+38	+38

over the years of the life of the process.

† This assumption is not totally consistent with the relationship of gross to net in the actual data, and has the unfortunate outcome of producing 'echo' effects in the latter part of the series calculated. Attempts to estimate decay functions were unsuccessful and this necessitated the present assumption.

‡ D of E [1972] p. 40, indicates that very little actual unemployment results from computerisation.   § See the appendix.

‖ I.e. no labour will be laid off by the computer, only labour taken on.

Second, the import figures assume 28 % of all machines are imported thus generating balance column (7). The assumption of a constant proportion in each year is a slight inaccuracy.

These comments do not, however, materially affect the nature of the results. Concentrating on the first balance column (6), these results imply that if all computers were to be produced at home it would not have been until eighteen years after construction was started on the first machine that the savings in labour in computer use would outstrip the increased demand for labour in computer production. The reason is that the speed of diffusion of computers has been so fast that the required expansion in the output of computers more than catered for labour released through computer usage. Only as this expansion is reflected in the stock of machines do the labour savings start to build up.

Finally, in deriving our comparative statics and transition results we have made a number of assumptions about computer size and computer technology. We can at this point illustrate the effects of these assumptions.

Technological change in computer technology has been considerable. The main characteristics of this change are exemplified by the generation concept. Each generation refers to a specific computer technology, and corresponding to each generation is a specific technology of computer use – the zeroth generation and experimentation, the first generation and the automated clerk concept, the second generation and the integrated data processing approach and the third generation and the management information concept.

In our analysis the figures on labour demand in computer usage were derived from data relating to 1964 and 1969. The latter refers to third generation machines, the former to second generation. As we have shown, however, net labour saving in computer usage does not vary between these two years by more than one man year. In computer construction we have attributed the major changes in labour requirements to changes in 'bought in' inputs, and then calculated a figure for labour requirements relevant to third generation technology. Thus as far as the estimates of saturation effects are concerned there are no major problems. In the transition, however, we have assumed that machines installed in the early years also had similar characteristics with regard to labour usage. To the extent that this is wrong we would have overestimated labour saving in computer usage and underestimated labour usage in computer construction. Both errors would reinforce the conclusion that computerisation increased the demand for labour in the early years.

Our second assumption concerns computer size. Above we calculated the labour implications of computers by averaging over all computers. In computer usage we found that net labour requirements per machine did not change much between 1963 and 1968, but we do know computers increased in size between these years. This means that other benefits of computers must exist to justify the extra expense (see below). In looking at computer construction the size element has again been ignored, being swamped by the effect of changes in the level of 'bought in' inputs. Also there is considerable evidence for stating that there are scale economies in computer use and construction. This may mean in total that our estimate of labour usage in the construction of third generation machines is an overestimate. This will mean our comparative statics exercise underestimates the effect of computers. The effects of ignoring size changes and scale economies along the transition path ought also to be considered. First, we can argue that as more third generation than first and second generation computers were built, the effects of scale will mean that to use third generation labour input coefficients in computer construction for the analysis of first and second generation machines will underestimate labour required in computer construction. However, we may argue that as early machines were also smaller the scale effect is being offset by the size effect. In computer use we may argue that if the small size of early machines did mean less labour input, scale effects may offset this, their small numbers requiring more labour than our third generation estimates suggest.

The final point to discuss is that the proportions of computer usage as detailed in table 8.1 have changed over time, but we have assumed them constant. In the initial stages computers were used more in scientific than administrative applications and process control is relatively more recent. As scientific machines are not essentially labour saving, but still have to be built, one would expect the stage on the transition path showing labour saving to be underestimated in terms of the size of the increase in the demand for labour and also perhaps the length of the period for which there is an increase in labour demand.

From this discussion of labour requirements one can now turn to the other implications of computer usage. First, we will consider balance of payments implications.

The methods superseded by computers have already been detailed as office machines and clerical labour in the office field, and logging and control equipment in the process control field. Most can be said about the office machines. There are reasons to believe that the UK was self sufficient in office machinery, for IBM, the main foreign producer, did not operate in the British market. Prior to 1949 the British and Commonwealth franchise for Hollerith office machines was held by the British Tabulating Machine Co. which merged with Powers Samas,

Table 8.15. *Computer Imports and Exports*

	1965	1966	1967	1968	1969	1970
Exports (£m current prices)	7.2	15.0	37.8	47.6	56.8	51.7
Imports (£m current prices)	18.6	35.9	56.5	74.8	97.5	110.0
Balance (£m current prices)	−11.4	−20.9	−18.7	−27.2	−40.7	−58.3
Exports as % of UK manufacturer				35	40	41
% of UK market supplied by UK production		57	67	60	62	66

SOURCE: SCST [1970a] p. 355, and SCST [1971b] p. 30.

the producers of accounting machines, in 1958 to form ICT. There may have even been a surplus in the office machine trade balance.† With computers, however, the balance of payments is negative. The figures for the export and import of hardware and unbundled software for the years 1965–70 are presented in table 8.15. Thus between 35 % and 45 % of all machines installed are imported. If, however, one were to divert export production to home usage the figures imply that 72 % of the home market could be supplied by home production.‡ To this one ought to add that nearly all unbundled software is supplied from home production.

The interesting thing about these figures is that there is a worsening of the balance of payments position relative to the situation without computers. If the gap is to be closed resources must be diverted to production for export. In the comparison of states it was shown that labour would be released and this may be used for that purpose. However, the derived transition path, allowing for the foreign manufacture of certain machines installed, illustrates that in the example worked no labour would be released for that purpose until the seventh year of the transition and the example does not permanently reflect labour released until the eleventh year. This implies that the labour would not therefore be available to fill the balance of payments gap until the transition had proceeded some distance.

The next matter to consider is whether any trigger effects have been apparent. Simon defines a trigger effect as, 'through changes in the

† If this was so then the figures for numbers not employed because of non-production of equipment for alternative techniques would be biased. It is considered that this will be reflected in the rounding up process.

‡ This is derived as follows. If 60 % of the home market is supplied from home manufacture, 40 % must be imported; thus a figure of £187m is derived for the home market (74.8 × 2.5). As 35 % of home manufacture is exported total home manufacture equals £136m (47.6 × 2.857), from which one derives that total home manufacture is 72 % of the total home market. This figure may, however, be slightly biased because of a large cross-trade in parts within the multinational companies.

technological coefficients of an economical activity I...a previously uneconomical activity II becomes economical and replaces a previously economical activity II' (Simon [1951] p. 271). It is interesting that Carter [1970] in her study found that such effects are rare. It has been shown, however, that in certain cases the use of computers enabled work to be done that otherwise could not have been and if it could was prohibitively expensive. However, no effects have been discovered in which differing benefits to different industries have so affected the price structure that further changes in technique have resulted.

There has been, however, one related phenomenon. The computer industry has developed by the use of new components. The existence of the industry must have in some way promoted the development of those components if only in the sense of representing potential demand. Moreover the size of the computer industry's demand for those components must in some way have reduced costs in component manufacture through the increasing return to scale effects isolated. This will have produced repercussions in those other areas where components are used, e.g. other electronic capital goods and electronic consumer goods.

Finally, one can look at two other areas in which computers have had influence.

Organisational structure. It is often argued that to take advantage of the computer a firm must have a certain optimal organisational structure. This means changes in job contents, information channels and the interrelationships of departments within a firm. This is especially so in management information systems, for which the use of computers promotes and requires the reconsideration of data requirements, data standards and data accessibility. The formation of a data bank often requires the breaking down of old barriers that caused departmental independence.

Wages and skill level. It has been shown that computer employees are more skilled than the staff that they replace and thus the spread of computers will change the skill composition of the labour force. Moreover the skill levels of employees in computer production are likely to be higher than those in the production of equipment for replaced techniques. This means that the spread of computer usage must mean an increase in the economy's educational and training facilities. Moreover it is generally the case that computer employees are more highly paid than the men replaced. Thus *in toto* a low-paid low-skill section of the workforce is being replaced in part by a high-paid high-skill workforce.

8.5 CONCLUSION

The contents of this chapter have been concerned with the derivation of the effect of computer usage on an economy. This analysis proceeded on two levels. First, the realised costs and benefits of computer usage were estimated for the different application areas in which computers are installed. Apart from the unquantifiable benefits it was estimated that each computer would save approximately forty man years of labour relative to replaced techniques if used in administrative applications, and this figure reduced to twenty-seven if savings were spread over all machines. It was further calculated that the manufacture of computers required approximately forty-eight extra man years over the number required for the manufacture of equipment for replaced techniques. With these figures it was projected that if 100 % computer penetration was applied to the 1970 economy 0.80 % of the labour force would be made redundant. We have also derived from our study of the transition path that an increase in labour demand resulted for the first eighteen years of the transition process. These effects of computer usage have to be supplemented by the implications for the balance of payments, efficiency and increased knowledge. It should be stated however, that the quantitative estimates are made on a large number of unverified assumptions, although it is considered that these are not too crucial.

Thus the principal conclusions that we can draw from our analysis are twofold.

(a) If we effect a comparison of states then computerisation can be seen to reduce the demand for labour. Specifically, we estimate that if we compare a computer saturated economy to a non-computerised economy with the same level of output, then the change in labour requirements, measured in man years, is

$$\Delta L = 113.3(Y_t)^{0.7}.$$

This means that for the 1970 level of output $\Delta L = 178{,}752$ man years, which represents approximately 0.80 % of the 1970 labour force. If we allow for the machines that are imported ΔL increase to 0.870 % of the labour force.

(b) When we look at the transition path, we observe that not until the late 1960s was the computerisation process beginning to release labour, the rate of diffusion up to this date being so fast that more labour was required in computer construction than released by computer usage. The surplus was, however, small.

8

Overall, the effects of computers on labour demand have been small and are unlikely ever to reach large proportions. However, the whole of this analysis, apart from a few comments, has ignored any macro-economic repercussions of computer usage. For example, what effect would a reduction in the work force have on the level of demand thus through a multiplier process on the economy's time profile? These are exactly the matters considered in the appendix.

9. CONCLUSION

This study has covered a number of topics the main connection between which has been that they are all necessary for the investigation of the spread of computer usage in the UK. It was stressed in chapter 1, however, that the results arising out of this study also have implications outside their immediate context. It is therefore considered that in this conclusion the results can all be brought together to indicate what implications the results have for the different areas to which it has been claimed that the study can contribute.

To begin we will concentrate on those results the only relevance of which is for the understanding of computerisation. At different points in this work references have been made to the other studies of computerisation that have been undertaken. It has also been stated that all such studies refer to the United States. A major contribution of this exercise must therefore be the construction of quality adjusted price and quantity series for the computer stock in the UK. These series were presented in chapters 3 and 7. At the same time, with the help of these series, it has been possible not only to indicate the actual characteristics of the computerisation process in the United Kingdom and to detail the characteristics of the development of computer technology and the nature of computer technology, but also to illustrate the effects of computerisation in the UK economy.

These achievements are of interest in their own right, but a presentation of the characteristics of a process call for an explanation of those characteristics. It will be shown in the appendix, however, that if one can provide observations on certain economic variables and behaviour patterns, then one can also contribute to the understanding of the determinants of the time path of an economy being faced with new technological possibilities. To understand fully the process of computerisation one needs some comprehension of the process of technological change, innovative behaviour, technique choice decisions, imitation patterns, supply behaviour, distribution determinants and disequilibrium adjustment processes. Such understanding can, however, also contribute to the analysis of the time path of an economy undergoing technological change. The results that we have generated with respect to these topics can be neatly compartmentalised.

The study of technological change in many respects confirmed the findings of other researchers in the field, making allowances for the special nature of the industry in terms of both technological opportunities and the pressures of scale returns. On the main question of the effects of market structure on technological change it was found that the industry in some respects lacked the forces to turn invention into marketed innovation because of the market position of IBM. This market position, it was argued, also reflected on other aspects of the industry's innovative achievements. The other side of the coin was studied and it was observed that technological change also affected market structure. The influence of R & D expenditure was analysed and it was discovered that the expected relationship between the number of marketed innovations and the level of R & D expenditure was complicated by the failure of IBM to market all innovations, the importance of defensive R & D, the effect of specialisation and the nature of forecasting activity. However, the differing rates of advance in the UK and the US were attributed to a large extent to the effects of different levels of R & D expenditure in general, and in particular to the influence of Government contribution to R & D funds. A discussion of the forces influencing the decision to begin manufacturing computers was inconclusive and a major role was attributed to the realisation of potentially profitable activities although it was considered that the background of the market participants would have some role to play. This background, moreover, was considered important in determining the technological nature of competition in the industry and the bias in technological change.

This discussion of technological change centred mainly on the changes in computer manufacturing, it being argued that in computer use innovation could be considered as part of the general question of technique choice (an attempt to apply this philosophy to computer manufacture failed through the lack of appropriate data). An extensive study of the decision to computerise resulted in the rejection of a theory based on maximisation and continual re-evaluation in favour of a theory based on behavioural postulates. The nature of this theory is its separation of the timing of the choice decision and the actual choice made. The timing aspect of the theory led to the consideration of using it for a study of diffusion.

The application of general principles of technique choice to the theory of diffusion processes is considered to be necessary if one is to comprehend the nature of such processes. The fact that our conclusions are derived from the study of UK data further increases the relevance of the results, for both Phelps Brown [1972] and Kennedy [1972] stress the paucity of research referring to the UK on technological change in general and on diffusion processes in particular.

A major disappointment of this study was the inability to use adequately the theory of technique choice for the explanation of the data on the spread of computer usage that had been constructed. It was shown, however, that after considerable modification such data could be used to support a stock adjustment model based on the Gompertz hypothesis. This model had to be considerably modified to achieve a reasonable level of explanatory power. The results were, however, interpreted in line with the conclusions of chapter 6. It was also shown that the behavioural principles could be used to predict the findings of other studies of diffusion processes and it was therefore considered that this approach still had much to contribute.

In contrast to many studies of diffusion processes the analysis of the data on the spread of computer usage extended one stage further – into the discussion of supply and adjustment mechanisms. For a true analysis of diffusion this is considered important. The results indicate that the supply of computers is based on expected demand, they are distributed between industries in relation to demand, and inventories and orders reflect differences in supply and demand.

All these matters are considered essential to the analysis of the time path of an economy facing new technologies, and in the appendix an attempt is made to illustrate how these factors all link together. This appendix is intended to illustrate the effect of technological change on an economy by the use of a simple theoretical model. In chapter 8, however, some estimates of the effect of computer usage on the UK economy were derived. The interesting point about these results is that the economy was increasing its computer stock so fast during the early stages of the diffusion process that, as opposed to a reduction in labour demand in the comparison of states, the employment in computer manufacturing more than took up the labour released from computer use. This result is considered to be of equal interest in the analysis of the effect of technological change as results referring to the comparison of states that may never be reached.

The third stress of this study, it was stated in chapter 1, was the dependence where possible on direct observation. This aim has been pursued using data from a number of independent sources. With this approach it has been possible to make comments on a number of the economic phenomena mentioned above. Other results refer to scale returns and the bias and degree of embodiment of technological change.

194   **Technological diffusion and the computer revolution**

Thus our study has detailed the process of computerisation in the United Kingdom, and has attempted to explain the forces behind this process and to illustrate how the implications that are to be drawn from this analysis can be used to promote economic understanding.

Appendix. COMPARING ECONOMIES

A.1 INTRODUCTION

In this appendix an attempt is made through theoretical analysis to investigate the effect on an economy of the appearance of a new technology, i.e. the addition of a new activity to the technology matrix. This discussion proceeds on two levels – a comparison of long run equilibrium states involving techniques the coefficients of which approximate those of the computer and the technology prior to computers, and a study of the transition path between such states. Because new technologies are always appearing it is considered that the transition path is the most interesting but it is also the less amenable to analysis. It is possible to show, however, that the nature of the transition path is dependent on exactly those matters with which this monograph has been concerned.

The study proceeds as follows. In section 2 the choice of theoretical model is discussed, in section 3 a comparison of equilibrium states is carried out and then transition is looked at in section 4. Finally, the conclusions are drawn in section 5.

A.2 THE THEORETICAL FRAMEWORK

So far our analysis has advanced implicitly using the theoretical framework discussed in chapter 1. However, that presents analytical difficulties which make its usefulness limited in the present circumstances. There are three alternatives: multi-sector models, Neo-Austrian models and two sector models. All three have been used in the discussion of the characteristics of economies with heterogeneous capital goods.† It has been decided to use the two-sector model here because, compared to the multi-sector framework, a much simpler

---

† For example, multi-sector models are used by Sraffa [1960], the two sector model by Hicks [1965], and the Neo-Austrian model by Hicks [1970]. For a general discussion of the behaviour of heterogeneous capital good models see Harcourt [1972].

analysis can produce the important results and, compared to the Neo-Austrian framework, the inter-industry rather than the inter-temporal aspects of production are stressed. Both are considered to be advantages in the present context.

It should be stated at the outset, however, that attempts to represent real world technology in such a model involve considerable simplification in addition to that due to the aggregative structure. For example, it has been shown that increasing returns to scale and a time intensive production process can be observed in computer production. Both are assumed away in this model. Although this is realised it is considered that the amount of effort required even to attempt to introduce them into the model would not yield commensurate benefits. The model can be represented as follows.†

Let the economy consist of two sectors – the consumption good and the capital good sectors. The technology is such that the consumption good is produced by the capital good and labour, and the capital good is produced by itself and labour. The production relationships are linear and homogeneous. Initially we shall assume that there is only one technique of production available. The following terminology is defined:

π = price of the consumption good
α = input of machines per unit of consumption good output
β = input of labour per unit of consumption good output
C = output of consumption goods

p = price of a machine
a = input of machines per unit of machine output
b = input of labour per unit of machine output
t = number of machines produced

T = total stock of machines
L = total workforce
w = wage rate
r = rate of profits
d = depreciation coefficient
g = the growth rate

All prices are expressed in terms of an arbitrary unit. When one chooses a commodity as a standard of value and sets its price equal to one, all prices are expressed in terms of this commodity. In long period equilibrium the price relationships will be

$$\pi = \alpha p(r+d) + \beta w, \tag{1}$$

$$p = ap(r+d) + bw, \tag{2}$$

† The formulation is based on that of Spaventa [1968].

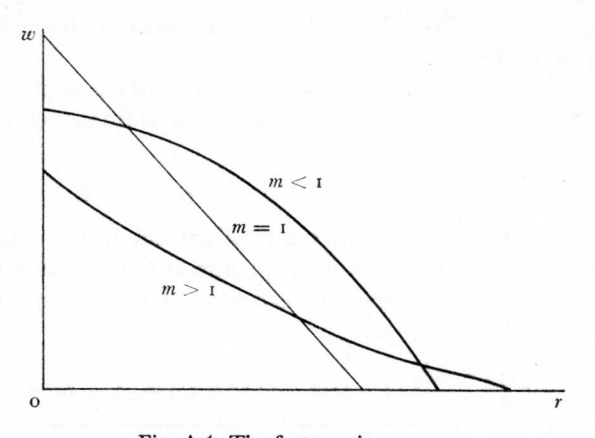

Fig. A.1. The factor price curve.

which when π is set equal to unity, making the consumption good the standard of value, yields

$$w = \frac{1-a(r+d)}{\beta(1+a(m-1)\ (r+d))},\tag{3}$$

where

$$m = \frac{\alpha b}{a\beta},$$

i.e. the ratio of sectoral factor intensities. Equation (3) is known as the factor price curve, and indicates the maximum wage that the given technology can support for any level of $(r+d)$. The curve is illustrated in fig. A.1. The curve is always downward sloping but the curvature depends on 'm', i.e. whether the consumption or capital good sector has the highest ratio of machine input to labour input.

The quantity equations are the dual to the price equations. If the economy is under a regime of steady growth at a rate g then

$$t = (g+d)\,T\tag{4}$$

so that

$$L = b(g+d)\,T+\beta C,\tag{5}$$

$$T = a(g+d)\,T+\alpha C.\tag{6}$$

If one assumes that $L = 1$, so that all quantities are expressed in per head terms, then (5) and (6) yield

$$C = \frac{1-a(g+d)}{\beta(1+a(m-1)\ (g+d))}.\tag{7}$$

This relationship between C and g (consumption per head and the rate of growth) is mathematically identical to that between w and r in the

factor price curve (FPC). Equation (7) is termed the optimal transformation curve (OTC).

The link between the price and quantity systems is provided by the
savings function and the savings equals investment condition. The
general savings function used is

$$S = s_p P + s_w W \quad 0 \leqslant s_w \leqslant s_p \leqslant 1, \tag{8}$$

where s_p is the propensity to save out of profits and s_w the propensity
to save out of wages. P equals total profits and W equals total wages.
Assuming that savings equals investment the resulting equilibrium
condition is that,†

$$g = \frac{s_w \left(\dfrac{1-ad}{a}\right)[1+a(m-1)(r+d)] + (s_p - s_w)\,mr}{m - s_w[m-1-a(m-1)(r+d)]} \tag{9}$$

in which g is externally determined such that in long run equilibrium g
equals n, the rate of growth of the labour force.

Consider now that a number of alternative techniques exist, all of
the same linear form and each requiring a specific capital good. For
each technique there is a factor price curve and the envelope of these
curves is the factor price frontier. This represents the maximum rate of
profits that the economy can achieve with a given wage rate when
the technique can vary. The equilibrium conditions for full-employment
steady-state growth at a rate equal to the rate of growth of the labour
force is that the technique in use should be on the factor price frontier
and that equilibrium condition (9) should hold with input coefficients
appropriate to the technique on the frontier for that value of r for
which $g = n$. Equilibrium condition (9) with variable technology does
not preclude the possibility of multiple equilibria.

A.3 THE COMPARISON OF STATES

Consider that the economy is in long run equilibrium growing at rate n
with a given technique. Consider that this technique is being replaced
by computers. In terms of the above coefficients sufficient has been
said in earlier chapters to indicate that this initial technique was very
labour intensive with few machines used in either consumption good
or capital good production. Let us for simplicity assume that the
initial technique has a ratio m equal to unity.

It is suggested now that the input of machines per unit of output
relative to the input of labour per unit of output is greater in the use of
computers than in the production of computers. Thus considering computers as the new technique it will have a value of m greater than unity.

† See Spaventa [1968] p. 26.

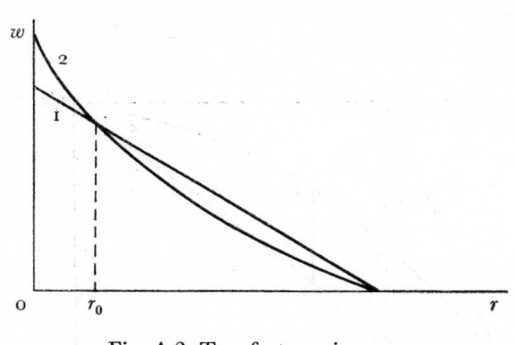

Fig. A.2. Two factor price curves.

For simplicity it will be assumed that the input of machines per unit of machine output is the same in each technique.†

One may now represent the factor price curves of the two techniques. As the coefficient for machine input in machine production has been assumed to remain constant, each technique has the same intercept on the r axis. The intercepts on the w axis will depend on the reduction in β relative to the increase in m comparing the old to the new technique. Given that the new technique must lie outside the old technique at some stage and for the new technique m is greater than one, the intercept of the new technique must lie above that for the old technique. Consider that the situation is as in fig. A.2. In terms of this diagram, if the original equilibrium position was such that the rate of profit was to the right of r_0 then the appearance of the new technology would not affect the equilibrium unless some other change occurred to push r to the left of r_0, i.e. into the area in which the new technique is on the factor price frontier.

To proceed we use a diagrammatic apparatus developed by Hicks ([1965] pp. 170–82). This procedure is based on the principle that in equilibrium the share of wages in output must be the same when predicted by the price and quantity equations as predicted by the savings relationship.‡ Thus it is possible to construct two curves relating the share of wages in output to the rate of profit, and the point at which they cross is the long run equilibrium point. If one lets

$$f = \frac{rpT}{wL + rpT}$$

† It was decided to proceed in the manner of comparing these two techniques rather than performing a comparison in general, because of the increase in the immediate relevance of the exercise and the difficulty of producing any general statements.
‡ This is equivalent to equilibrium condition (9).

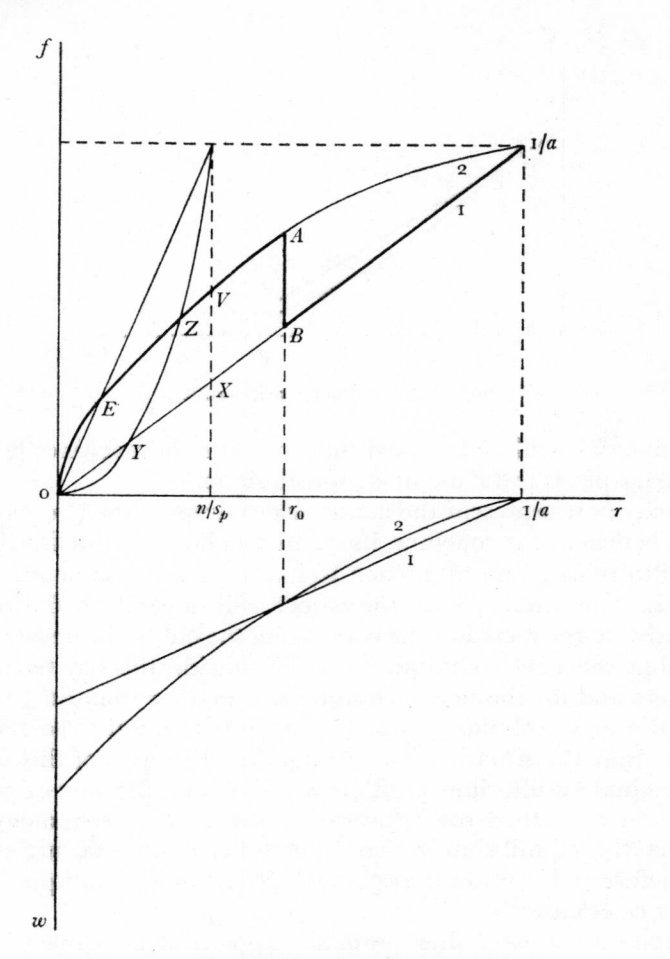

Fig. A.3. Long run equilibria.

then from the price and quantity equations, ignoring depreciation, with $g = n$,

$$\frac{1}{f} - 1 = \left(\frac{1-ra}{ra}\right)\left[\frac{1+(m-1)an}{m}\right].$$

If $r = 1/a$, the maximum rate of profits for a given technique, then $f = 1$. If r equals 0 then f equals 0. The curve between these points will be a straight line if m equals 1 and upward bulging if $m > 1$. Thus in fig. A.3 it is possible to represent the relationship between f and r for the two techniques under discussion (curves 1 and 2).

From the savings relationship three cases arise.

(a) If no saving takes place out of wages $g = s_p r = n$ in full employment equilibrium.

(b) If there is saving out of both wages and profits one can derive that

$$\frac{1}{f} - 1 = \frac{s_p}{s_w}\left(\frac{n}{s_p r} - 1\right).$$

If $r = n/s$, f equals 1, and as s_w is assumed less than s_p the curve must be downward bulging. It will also pass through the origin. This curve is independent of the technique in use.

(c) If $s_p = s_w$ the curve reduces to a straight line between the origin and (if the saving ratio is still s_p) n/s_p. In figure A.3 the three savings relationships are presented and the factor price curves are added.

Consider now that we have one economy that is in a long run equilibrium using technique 1. This economy is compared to a second economy that at the same moment in time is also in long run equilibrium, but although the same as the first in every other respect, has available to it both technique 1 and technique 2. First, the case with s_w equal zero, and s_p greater than zero but less than or equal to one is considered.

In this case $r = n/s_p$. If in economies 1 and 2, n is such that n/s_p is to the right of $1/a$ then no equilibrium will exist. If $r_0 < n/s_p < 1/a$ then the equilibrium will exist but the same technique is on the frontier in both economies, so the appearance of the new technique would not effect any differences between the economies. Consider the third case where n is such that n/s_p lies between 0 and r_0. In this case the economy with technique 2 available to it will be using this technique in long run equilibrium. Thus compared to the other economy it will have a higher wage rate but the same profit and growth rate. Also, in the economy with technique 2 available the value of f will be higher, i.e. the share of profits in output must increase. Thus with the same rate of profit the value of capital per man must increase. Moreover as the OTF† is the dual to the factor price frontier and the growth rate remains the same, consumption per head must increase. As the growth rate is defined as equal in the two economies, this particular conclusion must hold whatever the savings behaviour.

Consider now the case of the proportional savings function. In the one technique economy it would appear that the only equilibrium is at the origin. In the two technique economy a new equilibrium could exist if n/s_p is to the left of r_0. If n/s_p lies to the right of r_0 there is only an equilibrium at the switch point with both techniques in use, for to the right of r_0 technique 2 could support the growth rate but is the

† The Optimal Transformation Frontier which is the envelope of the Optimal Transformation Curves.

inferior technique, and the equilibrium for technique 1 (at the origin) is a point at which technique 2 is best. Consider, however, that the equilibrium in the two technique economy is at a point such as E. In this position the rate of profit has increased relative to the other economy and the share of profits has also increased. It is not possible to say from the diagram whether the wage rate will increase or fall.

Finally, the case with savings out of both wages and profits can be discussed. Considering only the case where the new technique will be used in the two technique island, the equilibrium in the first economy would be Y and in the two technique economy Z. Thus the new equilibrium in the present case would involve a higher rate of profit and a higher share of profits in income. The slope of the savings curve (dependent on the ratio of s_p to s_w) will determine whether w will also increase.

To generalise, if the growth of the labour force is such that the new technique will be used, then, whatever the savings function, the consumption per head will increase in the new equilibrium and the rate of profit will increase if wage earners save, and remain constant if they do not. In the latter case wages will increase and the share of profits and the value of capital per man will also increase. In the other cases it would seem that the share of profits will always increase but the wage rate need not necessarily do so.

This comparison has concerned two different economies at a moment in time. In reality two economies are never so alike, so a true comparison must concern one economy at two different moments in time. Once this case is considered the problem of getting from the original equilibrium to the new equilibrium must be analysed. Given that economies are always being presented with new opportunities and being subjected to random shocks, it is apparent that an economy will never be able to settle down to an equilibrium position and thus the study of an economy in transition must be more realistic than a study of an economy in equilibrium.

A.4   THE TRANSITION BETWEEN TECHNIQUES

The reaction of an economy to the appearance of a new technique has been studied by other researchers but in general the results are not too useful. The prime example is the work of Schumpeter [1934], who used the appearance of new technologies as the major determinants of the trade cycle process. Solow [1967] has discussed the process of transition in multi-sector models but assumes the existence of a central planning authority which precludes the derivation of results for a non-planned economy. Pasinetti [1969] has stated the nature of the problem with heterogeneous techniques. Spaventa [1973] has approached the problems but ignores the main problems resulting from heterogeneous capital, and Kregel [1971] (pp. 208–12) has detailed how a transition might work out but ignores certain of the problems considered below. Hicks [1965] (pp. 183–97) looked at the traverse in the two-sector model but his results are inconclusive, and he also studied the problem extensively in the Neo-Austrian model (Hicks [1970]), in which the main result is that the transition path will depend crucially on the number of new capital goods produced and installed in each time period. The Neo-Austrian model was first used for these purposes by Samuelson [1966] (pp. 579–81), but his approach leaves open the question of why an inferior technique should be started in a time period when the new best-practice techniques are also being started (in his approach it is necessary in order to ensure that the transition path involves the full employment of labour).

The unsatisfactory nature of existing theory, except for the Schumpeter approach perhaps, has led us to the reconsideration of the problem here in the context of the two-sector model. It has not in this study been possible to provide a generalisation of the transition process but what has been possible is to detail some of the problems involved in the determination of the time path of an economy under transition and to indicate how the present study of computers can yield some solutions to these problems. This time path should detail the path of employment, output, consumption, prices, income distribution, etc., during the stages in which the economy is changing its basic technique matrix.

It will be considered, unrealistically, that the economy starts in a position of full employment long run equilibrium using technique 1. There is then a change in the technology matrix such that technique 2 becomes available. It will be assumed that this new technique can support a new long run equilibrium position and that at the wage rate appropriate to the old equilibrium the new technique can yield a higher rate of profit. This sudden appearance of a new technology is a simplification that is not supported by the facts; it would seem that, to an extent at least, new technologies are the result of endogenous processes and not provided exogenously.

Proceeding on these assumptions there are three stages to the transition. First, there is the start of the new technique, i.e. innovation in the production and use of computers. The second stage is the running of an economy with an increasing stock of the new capital good and a decreasing stock of the old capital good. The third stage is the running of the economy with just the one new capital good, but this stage will not be discussed because it has been covered extensively in other investigations of two sector growth models,† and it may well be that at some time during this stage – if not before – another new technology might appear.

First, the initial stages will be considered. To start the transition it is necessary to discuss where the initial stock of the new capital goods for capital goods production appears from, what forces determine the beginning of production of the new capital good, and what forces determine the beginning of use of the new capital good.

In the present formulation of this model the new type capital goods must be produced with new type capital goods. Thus to start the transition one must go outside the model to generate this initial stock. There are three possible sources for this stock. First, it may come from another unconnected geographical area. This would suggest that the change in technique is the result of substitution and not technological change. Apart from the fact that this was argued to be an unlikely occurrence, to make this assumption would only shift the problem to a different place and time. The second possibility is that the new capital goods should be constructed using old capital goods. This would be a useful result, but in the present context with only one capital good in an equilibrium, it would mean that there are as many ways of producing each capital good as there are different capital goods if a transition can start from any point on the factor price frontier. If this were not the case it would be necessary to know *a priori* with what capital goods the new one could be produced. The third possibility is that the initial stock of new capital goods would be produced by labour alone. This would allow a transition to start from any point. It would also appear that if one abstracted from intermediate products then the earlier computer prototypes were hand built. It would therefore seem a reasonable assumption to allow the first of the new capital goods to be produced by unaided labour. This, however, is a problem that is special to this type of model. The more important question is what forces start the production and use of the new capital goods.

Schumpeter attributes this start to the influence of the entrepreneur but studies of innovation have provided further detail. Our own results of the start of computer usage commercially show that Lyons as a customer first decided on computer usage and then went off to construct one. It was also suggested that the first commercial computer producers tended to be either producers of equipment for an alternative technique, new companies or producers in related business. The main point must be their realisation of a potentially profitable activity. In the user sector it was suggested that the innovators happened to be those with problems whose search behaviour extended to the new technology. An acceptance

† See, for example, Hahn [1964].

of this technology would be conditional on its expected rate of return meeting targets set by the innovator. One could therefore suggest that it must be able to meet a target that the existing method could not, i.e. yield a higher expected profit than the replaced technique. Unless the whole transition is to proceed on the basis of misplaced expectations it must mean that it must be more profitable than the old technique at the prices relating to the old technique in the initial position. This has been assumed to get the transition started.

It would seem therefore that the existence of a potentially more profitable new technique is not in itself a sufficient condition to get the transition started; the major point must be the realisation of this potential. One can therefore only ascribe the start of a transition to the characteristics of technology re-evaluation and search behaviour.

There is, however, a further complication. If the users are to innovate it has been suggested that the new technique must yield a higher rate of return than the old technique. However, it can only yield such a return to users if the producers do not set the prices of new machines so high as to increase their own rate of return to such a level that the old machines are still cheaper to use. In fact there is a whole area of indeterminacy here in the price behaviour of the producers of new and old machines. The superiority of the new techniques at the old wage rate would allow a greater rate of profit in both production and use. If the use of capital goods is dependent on their price then the relative installations of old and new types would depend on how the profit in each technique is varied between user and producer. It will be assumed that with a given wage rate the prices of old and new capital goods are always set such that the same rate of profit is available in production and use.

Consider now that the economy can enter stage two. Some capital goods are available for the production of new capital goods and there is also the old stock of capital goods still available ready for productive use. The characteristics of the economy in a time period will depend on how these capital stocks are used. The producers of capital goods will determine the level at which they wish to utilise their capital stocks and the producers of consumption goods will decide what output of consumption goods to produce. These decisions will determine output, the total demand for labour in that period and, once a real wage rate† is found, there will be a certain demand for consumption goods if we work in terms of the 'all wages consumed, all profits saved' saving function.

Whether this involves the full employment of either labour or

† In such models there is a certain indeterminacy involved in that there is no adequate theory for the determination of real wages.

machines will depend on how the output decisions are made and on what capacity is available in each sector for use. It is assumed that, once installed, capital goods are specific to the sector in which they are installed.

In the next period the capacity available will depend on the output of capital goods in the previous period and the distribution of those capital goods between industries. As the long run is made up of short run periods, the capacity available at any time on the transition path will depend on the time path of the output of capital goods and their distribution between industries, and the employment, etc. at any point on this path will depend upon the capacity available at that point in time and the decision on what output to produce with that capacity. Thus the output decision at a moment in time determines the employment at that time, and the output decision at different time periods combined with the distribution of the output determines the time path.

The speed at which the transition will proceed, in the sense of the time that it takes to reach the end of stage 2, will depend on the ability of the capital goods industry to re-equip the whole of the consumption goods industry with the new capital good and the desire of the consumption goods industry to take the new capital good, i.e. the output and distribution of new type capital goods. Thus one may argue that these two variables determine the speed of the transition and, combined with similar decisions for the old type capital goods, determine the time path of the economy and the employment of capacity at a moment in time.

Our study has indicated that the output of new type capital goods depends on expected demand, and the distribution between industries depends on the relative demands of each industry. As there is no reason to believe that other goods should be treated differently, one can specify that the output of all goods depends on expected demands and that capital goods are distributed between sectors in proportion to their demands.

Using this framework, let us consider how an economy in transition may develop. Consider that in a time period, t, the economy produces certain outputs of capital goods of each type and a certain output of consumption goods, using a specified money wage and quantity of labour. There is no reason for all capital goods to be fully employed or for all labour to be fully employed.

Given a set of prices, a real wage will exist at which all consumption goods may or may not be demanded. This apparent difference between supply and demand must be closed in some way. There are two main classes of adjustment processes, one based on price variation and the other on quantity variation. Recent work on price behaviour implies that 'prices move with long run costs and do not change because of variations in demand or cost that are thought to be temporary' (Godley [1972]). In the study of the computer market it was found that support could be found for the proposition that orders and inventories take up the variation in supply and demand. This implies the existence of quantity adjustment mechanisms. The nature of the mechanism will influence the time path of the economy, for the price mechanism under certain circumstances will yield automatic adjustment, whereas the quantity mechanism is the basis of the multiplier process. Thus we can say that in addition to knowledge of output and distribution determinants one needs information on adjustment mechanisms.

It will be considered that, in a position of non-equality of supply and demand, inventories must change. This change in inventories will influence the demand for new type capital goods for use in the production of consumption goods. The level of inventories, it may be said, will determine the level of output the industry wishes to produce in the following period. The demand for new type capital goods will depend, according to chapter 6, on the proportion of this output that the producers are willing to generate with their old capital goods and the share of the technology re-evaluation that yields a demand for new type capital goods. Combined with this demand for new and old type capital goods from the consumption goods industries the capital goods industries will form their demands for new capital goods which may or may not depend on the demand from the consumption goods industry in the present period. Thus a sum is produced for the demand for both types of capital goods. This sum may be greater than the output of the previous periods for one or both of the types of capital goods, in which case they are distributed in proportion to the demands of each sector, and orders increase. If the demand is less than the supply, both sectors get the desired amount and inventories build up. This build up in inventories, however, may reduce the demand for capital goods in the capital goods sector.

These demands for capital goods are consequent on certain output decisions that will now be put into effect. If at the end of the period t there were excess demands for capital goods one would expect to see full utilisation of capacity in period $t+1$. If, however, there was excess supply to the extent that some industries were adding no capital goods and perhaps through depreciation reducing their stock one might possibly see a reduction in output in period $t+1$. However, the balance of supply and demand in different sectors in period t via quantity adjustment mechanisms will influence the output and thus capital stock decisions in period $t+1$. At the beginning of period $t+1$ production will begin which, with the distribution of capital goods, will imply certain desired total employment which may or may not involve full employment. At the end of the period $t+1$ outputs of the different goods will be apparent and the same process of demand arising from different industries will occur. However, in period $t+1$ the consumption goods industry will increase the proportion of its technology being re-evaluated that is transferred to the new capital good. This will affect the labour requirements in this industry in period $t+2$ for a given output level and also reflect through on to the demand for each type of capital good. In each period a similar process will be gone through, an increasing proportion of re-evaluated technology being transferred to the new type capital good until all new capital goods are of the new type and then, after the old type left in consumption production have depreciated away, one has entered stage 3.

Attempts were made to formalise this' process into a more general model but they were not successful, and for this reason the analysis has been relegated to this appendix. Sufficient has been said, however, to indicate that the determinants of the time path of an economy undergoing transition must depend on the output decision in different sectors and the distribution of capital goods between sectors. Once this is combined with a theory of diffusion to separate out the relative demands for each type of capital good and a mechanism for dealing with non-equilibrium situations it is possible to discuss an economy under transition. In the study of computers it was possible to gain insights into all these requirements. Moreover it was possible to investigate also to some extent the nature of the innovation process which must be considered as stage 1 of the transition.

A.5   CONCLUSION

In this appendix an attempt has been made to look at the reaction of an economy to a new technique through the use of a simple theoretical framework. The first point that is apparent is the difference between the theoretical comparison of equilibrium states and the empirical comparison of states. The reason for this was explained in chapter 8. In the study of transition at the empirical level the determination of the transition path was simply solved by using the realised diffusion path and the effects were concentrated mainly on localised labour implications. In the theoretical study it is argued that the nature of the diffusion has implications for the whole economy. The actual time path of the economy under transition will depend on the determinants of the output decision, the distribution of capital goods, the choice between capital goods, and the nature of equilibrating mechanisms. These are all matters that have been considered in the main body of this study.

It can also be stated that the sources of technological change and the nature of innovative processes are also important for the determination of the path of an economy over time. Finally it must also be argued that the means of analysing that time path is via a theoretical model. The assumptions of that model ought to reflect reality. It has been argued that this study can also throw light in that area. Thus the implications for areas outside the immediate context of this monograph can be said to provide some further justification for the study of this one process of technical change.

BIBLIOGRAPHY

This bibliography is intended neither as an exhaustive bibliography of the subject nor as a listing of all the works consulted in writing this study, but as a list of work referred to in the text and the major works consulted.

Notes

1   A bibliography of the literature on computing is provided by: National Computing Centre, *The International Computer Bibliography*, NCC, Manchester 1968.
2   A bibliography of the literature on technical change can be found in C. Kennedy & A. P. Thirwall, 'Technical Progress: A Survey', *Economic Journal*, March 1972, pp. 11–72.

Aldous [1973]   D. Aldous, 'Soundings', *Hi-Fi News*, April 1973, p. 739.
Arrow [1962]   K. J. Arrow, 'The Economic Implications of Learning by Doing', *Review of Economic Studies*, 1962, pp. 155–73.
Atkinson [1969]   A. B. Atkinson and J. E. Stiglitz, 'A New View of Technological Change', *Economic Journal*, 1969, pp. 573–8.
Baxter [1971]   R. Baxter, *Computers in Local Authorities*. Technical note No. 3, Centre for Land Use and Built Form Studies, University of Cambridge Department of Architecture, Cambridge, 1971.
Carter [1970]   A. P. Carter, *Structural Change in the American Economy*, Oxford University Press, 1970.
CCL [1962–70]   Computer Consultants Ltd, *British Commercial Computer Digest*, Richard Williams and Partners, Llandudno, 1962–70.
CCL [1963–70]   Computer Consultants Ltd. *European Computer User's Handbook*, Editions 1–7, Richard Williams and Partners, Llandudno, 1963–70.
CCL [1969–71]   Computer Consultants Ltd, *Current Computers*, Richard Williams and Partners, Llandudno, vol. 1, 1969; vol. 2, 1971.
Chow [1967]   G. C. Chow, 'Technological Change and the Demand for Computers', *American Economic Review*, 1967, pp. 1117–30.
Cowling [1970]   K. Cowling & A. J. Rayner, 'Price, Quality and Market Share', *Journal of Political Economy*, November 1970, pp. 1292–30.
CS [1962–71]   *Computer Survey*, United Trade Press, London, 1962–71.
CSD [1971]   Civil Service Department, *Computers in Central Government Ten Years Ahead*, CSD Management Studies 2, HMSO, London, 1971.
CW [1971]   *Computer Weekly*, 'Computers in Aviation', 7 October 1971.
CW [1972a]   *Computer Weekly*, 'Efficiency Creates Right Environment', in 'Ancillaries and Accessories', Supplement, 23 March 1972.

CW [1972b]   *Computer Weekly*, 'Controlling ICL Production', 13 July 1972, p. 10.

CW [1972c]   *Computer Weekly*, 'Providing a Service to Benefit the User', 17 August 1972.

CW [1972d]   *Computer Weekly*, 'Computational Theatre is the Key', 26 October 1972, p. 2.

CW [1972e]   *Computer Weekly*, 'The Dawning Era of the Soft Machine', 12 December 1972, p. 2.

CW [1972f]   *Computer Weekly*, 'What Price when the LSI Chips are Down?', 28 December 1972, p. 2.

CW [1972g]   *Computer Weekly*, 'Oil and Petrochemicals', 16 March 1972.

CW [1973a]   *Computer Weekly*, 'Data Preparation', Supplement, 22 February 1973.

CW [1973b]   *Computer Weekly*, 'The Progress of Discs and Drums', 26 April 1973, p. 14.

CW [1973c]   *Computer Weekly*, 'Data Preparation Report Forecasts Decline of the Punched Card', 10 May 1973, p. 15.

CW [1973d]   *Computer Weekly*, 'ICL's new Range gets aid of £25.8m', 12 July 1973, p. 1.

Cyert [1963]   R. M. Cyert & J. G. March, *A Behavioural Theory of the Firm*, Prentice Hall, Englewood Cliffs, NJ, 1963.

Diebold [1959]   J. Diebold, *Automation: Its Impact on Business & Labor*, National Planning Association, Washington, 1959.

D of E [1972]   Department of Employment, *Computers in Offices 1972*, Manpower Studies No. 12, HMSO, London, 1972.

DTI [1971a]   Department of Trade and Industry, *Computer Bureaux*, June 1971.

DTI [1971b]   Department of Trade and Industry, *Study of Small Computers*, HMSO, London, 1971.

ECE [1971]   Economic Commission for Europe, *Symposium on the Use of Electronic Computers in the Coal Industry*, United Nations, New York, 1971.

Economist [1971a]   *Economist*, 'Is ICL in Trouble?', 27 February 1971, pp. 56–7.

Economist [1971b]   *Economist*, 'The Accident Prone Miracle; A Survey of the Computer Industry', Supplement, 27 February 1971.

English [1972]   L. English, 'The Remote Terminal – its Growth and Development', *Computer Weekly*, 27 January 1972, p. 6.

Enticknap [1972]   N. Enticknap, 'Demand Creates the End User Main Memory Market', *Computer Weekly*, 6 April 1972, p. 5.

Enticknap [1973]   N. Enticknap, 'The Strong Challenge of Bubble Memories', *Computer Weekly*, 29 March 1973, p. 12.

Freeman [1965]   C. Freeman, 'Research and Development in Electronic Capital Goods', *National Institute Economic Review*, November 1965, pp. 40–91.

Frielink [1965]   A. B. Frielink, *Economics of Automatic Data Processing*, North Holland, Amsterdam, 1965.

Godley [1972]   W. A. H. Godley & W. D. Nordhaus, 'Pricing in the Trade Cycle', *Economic Journal*, September 1972, pp. 853–82.

Goldberger [1964]   A. S. Goldberger, *Econometric Theory*, John Wiley & Sons, New York, 1964.

Griliches [1957]   Z. Griliches, 'Hybrid corn: an exploration in the economics of technical change', *Econometrica*, October 1957.

Griliches [1971]   Z. Griliches, *Price Indexes and Quality Change*, Harvard University Press, Cambridge, Mass., 1971.

Hahn [1964]   F. H. Hahn & R. C. O. Matthews, 'The Theory of Economic Growth: A Survey', *Economic Journal*, 1964, pp. 779–902.

Hahn [1966]   F. H. Hahn, 'Equilibrium Dynamics with Heterogeneous Capital Goods', *Quarterly Journal of Economics*, 1966, pp. 633–46.

Hahn [1970]   'Some Adjustment Problems', *Econometrica*, January 1970, pp. 1–17.

Harcourt [1968]   G. C. Harcourt, 'Investment-Decision Criteria, Capital-Itensity and the Choice of Technique', *Czechoslovak Economic Papers*, 1968, pp. 77–95.

Harcourt [1971]   G. C. Harcourt & N. F. Laing (eds.), *Capital and Growth*, Penguin Modern Economic Readings, Harmondsworth, 1971.

Harcourt [1972]   G. C. Harcourt, *Some Cambridge Controversies in the Theory of Capital*, Cambridge University Press, 1972.

Harman [1971]   A. J. Harman, *The International Computer Industry*, Harvard University Press, Cambridge, Mass., 1971.

Harrod [1948]   R. F. Harrod, *Towards a Dynamic Economics*, Macmillan, London, 1948.

Hawkins [1970]   D. G. Hawkins, *Computing for Power*, Central Electricity Generating Board, 1970.

Hicks [1965]   J. R. Hicks, *Capital and Growth*, Oxford University Press, 1965.

Hicks [1970]   J. R. Hicks, 'A Neo-Austrian Growth Theory', *Economic Journal*, June 1970, pp. 257–81.

Hoel [1966]   P. G. Hoel, *Elementary Statistics*, Wiley, New York, 1966.

Hollingdale [1970]   S. H. Hollingdale & G. C. Tootill, *Electronic Computers*, Penguin, Harmondsworth, 1970.

Humphries [1970]   J. D. Humphries, 'Future Staff Needs', *National Computing Centre Newsletter*, February/March 1970, p. 12.

ICL [1971]   International Computers Ltd, Advertisement Launching 1900S Series, *Times*, 28 April 1971.

ICT [1968]   International Computers and Tabulators, *ICT 1900 Series*, 1968.

IDC [1961–9]   International Data Corporation, *Computers and Automation*, 1961–9.

Johnston [1963]   J. Johnston, *Econometric Methods*, International Student Edition, McGraw-Hill, Kogakusha Ltd, Tokyo, 1963.

Jorgenson [1971]   D. W. Jorgenson, 'Econometric Studies of Investment Behaviour', *Journal of Economic Literature*, December 1971, pp. 1111–47.

Kennedy [1972]   C. Kennedy & A. P. Thirwall, 'Technical Progress: A Survey', *Economic Journal*, March 1972, pp. 11–72.

Kmenta [1971]   J. Kmenta, *Elements of Econometrics*, Macmillan, New York, 1971.

Knight [1966]   K. E. Knight, 'Changes in Computer Performance', *Datamation*, 1966, pp. 40–5.

Kregel [1971]   J. A. Kregel, *Rate of Profit, Distribution and Growth: Two Views*, Macmillan, London, 1971.

Lamb [1973]   G. M. Lamb, *Computers in Public Service*, Allen and Unwin, London, 1973.

Lamberton [1971]   D. M. Lamberton (ed.), *Economics of Information and Knowledge*, Penguin Modern Economics Readings, Harmondsworth, 1971.

Lancaster [1968]   K. Lancaster, *Mathematical Economics*, Macmillan, New York, 1968.

Leijonhufvud [1968]   A. Leijonhufvud, *On Keynesian Economics and the Economics of Keynes*, Oxford University Press, 1968.

Leontief [1971]   W. Leontief, 'Theoretical Assumptions and Non-observed Facts', *American Economic Review*, March 1971, pp. 1–7.

McDonough [1963]   A. M. McDonough, *Information Economics and Management Systems*, McGraw-Hill, New York, 1963.

McKinsey [1968]   The McKinsey Consulting Organization, *The 1968 McKinsey Report on Computer Utilization*, McKinsey and Company, 1968.

McRae [1971]   T. W. McRae (ed.), *Management Information Systems*, Penguin Modern Management Readings, Harmondsworth, 1971.

Malinvaud [1966]   E. Malinvaud, *Statistical Methods of Econometrics*, North Holland, Amsterdam, 1966.

Mann [1960]   F. C. Mann & L. K. Williams, 'Observations on the Dynamics of a Change to Electronic Data-Processing Equipment', *Administrative Science Quarterly*, 5, 1960, pp. 217–56.

Mansfield [1968]   E. Mansfield, *Industrial Research and Technological Innovation*, Longmans Green, Harlow, 1968.

Miles Roman [1971]   Miles Roman Ltd. *Computer Analysis '71, A Summary of Preliminary Conclusions*, 1971.

M of L [1965]   Ministry of Labour, *Computers in Offices*, Manpower Studies No. 4, HMSO, London, 1965.

Morishima [1964]   M. Morishima, *Equilibrium Stability and Growth*, Oxford University Press, 1964.

MPBW [1967a]   Ministry of Public Building and Works, *The Application of Computers in the Construction Industry*, HMSO, London, 1967.

MPBW [1967b]   Ministry of Public Building and Works, *Computers in the Construction Industry*, HMSO, London, 1967.

MPBW [1969]   Ministry of Public Building and Works, *Computers for Contractors in the Building Industry*, HMSO, London, 1969.

Muellbauer [1971]   J. N. J. Muellbauer, *Testing the Cagan-Hall and the Hedonic Hypotheses*, Warwick Economic Research Papers, No. 19, University of Warwick, Coventry, 1971.

NCC [1967]   National Computing Centre, *Computer Aided Production Control*, NCC, Manchester 1967.

NCC [1968a]   National Computing Centre, *Computers in Textiles*, NCC, Manchester, 1968.

NCC [1968b]   National Computing Centre, and National Economic Development Office, *The Use of Computers – Hotels and Catering*, NCC, Manchester, 1968.

NCC [1969]   National Computing Centre, *Computers in Vehicle Scheduling*, NCC, Manchester 1969.

NCC [1970]   National Computing Centre, *Management of Computer Based Data Processing*, NCC, Manchester, 1970.

NCC [1971a]   National Computing Centre, *Economic Evaluation of Computer Based Systems*, NCC, Manchester, 1971.

NCC [1971b]   National Computing Centre, *Computers in Business*, BBC Publications, 1971.

NCC [1972]   National Computing Centre, *Analysis of Computer Usage in the U.K. in 1971*, NCC, Manchester, 1972.

Nell [1967]   E. J. Nell, 'Theories of Growth and Theories of Value', *Economic Development and Cultural Change*, 1967, pp. 15–26.

Nelson [1973]   R. R. Nelson & S. G. Winter, 'Toward an Evolutionary Theory of Economic Capabilities', *American Economic Review, Papers and Proceedings*, May 1973, pp. 440–9.

Nelson [1974]   R. R. Nelson & S. G. Winter, 'Neoclassical vs. Evolutionary Theories of Economic Growth', *Economic Journal*, December 1974, pp. 886–905.

Noakes [1973]   H. W. Noakes, 'Buffered Punching Flexibility', in 'Data Preparation – a Computer Weekly Supplement', *Computer Weekly*, 22 February 1973.

Nuti [1970]   D. M. Nuti, 'Capitalism Socialism and Economic Growth', *Economic Journal*, March 1970, pp. 32–51.

Observer [1971]   *Observer*, 'Is ICL Next for the Knacker's Yard?', 18 July 1971.

OECD [1966]   Organisation for Economic Co-operation and Development, *Manpower Aspects of Automation and Technical Change*, OECD, Paris, 1966.

OECD [1968]   Organisation for Economic Co-operation and Development, *Gaps in Technology – Electronic Components*, OECD, Paris, 1968.

OECD [1969]   Organisation for Economic Cooperation and Development, *Gaps in Technology – Electronic Computers*, OECD, Paris, 1969.

Owen [1971a]   K. Owen, 'Peripheral, but Critical, Challenge for IBM', *The Times*, 21 July 1971.

Owen [1971b]   K. Owen, 'Microcircuit, Mini Demand, Maxi-Depression', *The Times*, 23 July 1971.

Owen [1971c]   K. Owen, 'British Rail Confirms IBM Freight System', *The Times*, 23 November 1971.

Owen [1971d]   K. Owen, 'Sperry Rand Joins RCA in New Deal', *The Times*, 21 December 1971.

Owen [1972]   K. Owen, 'Honeywell Tries Harder', *The Times*, 13 October 1972.

Owen [1973]   K. Owen, 'How Transistors Transformed Electronics', *The Times*, 16 February 1973.

Pasinetti [1969]   L. Pasinetti, 'Switches of Technique and the Rate of Return in Capital Theory', *Economic Journal*, September 1969, pp. 508–31.

Phelps Brown [1972]   E. H. Phelps Brown, 'The Underdevelopment of Economics', *Economic Journal*, March 1972, pp. 1–10.

Pratten [1971]   C. F. Pratten, *Economies of Scale in Manufacturing Industry*, University of Cambridge Department of Applied Economics, Occasional Paper 28, Cambridge University Press, 1971.

Pyatt [1971]   F. G. Pyatt, 'The Analysis of Demand', in F. G. Pyatt & A. S. C. Ehrenberg, (eds.), *Consumer Behaviour*, Penguin Modern Management Readings, Harmondsworth, 1971.

Ray [1969]   G. F. Ray, 'The Diffusion of New Technology: a study of ten processes in nine industries', *National Institute Economic Review*, May 1969, 40–81.

Read [1968]   L. M. Read, 'The Measure of Total Factor Productivity Appropriate to Wage-Price Guidelines', *Canadian Journal of Economics*, May 1968, pp. 349–58.

Robinson [1962]   J. Robinson, *Exercises in Economic Analysis*, Macmillan, London, 1962.

Robinson [1969]   J. Robinson, *The Accumulation of Capital*, Papermac, Macmillan, London, 1969.

Robinson [1972]   J. Robinson, *Economic Heresies*, Macmillan, London, 1972.

Rogers [1962]   E. M. Rogers, *The Diffusion of Innovations*, Free Press, New York, 1962.

Rose [1969]   M. Rose, *Computers, Managers and Society*. Penguin, Hardmondsworth, 1969.

Rosenberg [1971]   N. Rosenberg (ed.), *The Economics of Technological Change*, Penguin Modern Economic Readings, Harmondsworth, 1971.

Ruttan [1959]   V. Ruttan, 'Usher and Schumpeter on invention, innovation and technological change', *Quarterly Journal of Economics*, November 1959, pp. 596–606.

Rymes [1971]   T. K. Rymes, *On Concepts of Capital and Technical Change*, Cambridge University Press, 1971.

Salter [1969]   W. E. G. Salter, *Productivity and Technical Change*, second edition, Cambridge University Press, 1969.

Samuelson [1966]   P. A. Samuelson, 'A Summing Up', *Quarterly Journal of Economics*, November 1966, pp. 568–83.

Schumpeter [1934]   J. A. Schumpeter, *The Theory of Economic Development*, Harvard University Press, Cambridge, Mass., 1934.

Schumpeter [1954]   J. A. Schumpeter, *History of Economic Analysis*, Oxford University Press, 1954.

SCST [1970a]   Select Committee on Science and Technology, *U.K. Computer Industry*, vol. I, *Minutes of Evidence*, HMSO, 1970, HC 137 (Session 1969–70).

SCST [1970b]   Select Committee on Science and Technology, *U.K. Computer Industry*, vol. II, *Appendices*, HMSO, 1970, HC 272 (Session 1969–70).

SCST [1971a]   Select Committee on Science and Technology, *The Prospects for the United Kingdom Computer Industry in the 1970's*, vol. I, *Report* HMSO 1971, HC 621-I (Session 1970–1).

SCST [1971b]   Select Committee on Science and Technology. *The Prospects for the United Kingdom Computer Industry in the 1970's*, vol. II, *Minutes of Evidence*, HMSO, 1971, HC 621-II, (Session 1970–1).

SCST [1971c]   Select Committee on Science and Technology, *The Prospects for the United Kingdom Computer Industry in the 1970's*, vol. III, *Appendices*, HMSO, 1971, HC 621-III (Session 1970–1).

Sen [1970]   A. Sen (ed.), *Growth Economics*, Penguin Modern Economic Readings, Harmondsworth, 1970.

Sharpe [1969]   W. F. Sharpe, *The Economics of Computers*, Columbia University Press, 1969.

Shell [1967]   K. Shell & J. E. Stiglitz, 'The Allocation of Investment in a Dynamic Economy', *Quarterly Journal of Economics*, November. 1967.

Shirley [1969]   D. Shirley, *Choosing a Computer*, third edition, Business Publications Ltd, London, 1969.

Simon [1951]   H. A. Simon, 'Effects of Technological Change in a Linear Model', in T. C. Koopmans (ed.), *Activity Analysis of Production and Allocation*, Chapman & Hall, London, 1951.

Smythe [1970]   C. Smythe, *Choosing a Computer*, fourth edition, Business Publications Ltd, London, 1970.

Solow [1957]   R. M. Solow, 'Technical Change and the Aggregate Production Function', *Review of Economics and Statistics*, August 1957, pp. 312–20.

Solow [1967]   R. M. Solow, 'The Interest Rate and the Transition between Techniques', in C. H. Feinstein (ed.), *Socialism, Capitalism and Economic Growth, Essays Presented to Maurice Dobb*, Cambridge University Press, 1967.

Spaventa [1968]   L. Spaventa, 'Realism without Parables in Capital Theory', *Récherches Récentes sur la fonction de Production*, Centre D'Etudes et de Récherches Universitaire de Namur, 1968, pp. 15–45.

Spaventa [1973]   L. Spaventa, 'Notes on the Transition between Techniques', in J. A. Mirrlees and N. H. Stern (eds.), *Models of Economic Growth*, Macmillan, 1973.

Sraffa [1960]   P. Sraffa, *Production of Commodities by Means of Commodities*, Cambridge University Press, 1960.

Statland [1965]   N. Statland, R. Proctor & J. Selznick, *An Approach to Computer Installation Performance Effectiveness Evaluation*, US Dept of Commerce, 1965.

Steiber [1966]   J. Steiber (ed.), *Employment Problems of Automation & Advanced Technology*, Macmillan, New York, 1966.

Stone [1957]   R. Stone & D. A. Rowe, 'The Market Demand for Durable Goods', *Econometrica*, 1957, pp. 423–43.

Stoneman [1973]   P. Stoneman, 'On the Change in Technique – A Study of the spread of Computer Usage in the U.K.', PhD Thesis, University of Cambridge, October 1973.

Sunday Times [1973]   *Sunday Times*, 'The IBM Indictment' 13 May 1973.

Taviss [1970]   I. Taviss, *The Computer Impact*, Prentice Hall, Englewood Cliffs, NJ, 1970.

Taylor [1972]   J. Taylor, 'The Advantage of On Line Systems in the World of Modern Business', *Computer Weekly*, 18 May 1972, p. 6.

Theil [1967]   H. Theil, *Economics and Information Theory*, North Holland, Amsterdam, 1967.

Times [1971a]   *Times*, 'Whatever Happened to RCA?', 29 September 1971.

Times [1971b]   *Times*, 'Computer Users – A special report', 7 October 1971.

Times [1973]   *Times*, 'U.K. Computer Market Records 6 p.c. Increase Over Previous Quarter', 24 January 1973.

UN [1971]   United Nations, *Economic Aspects of Automation*, New York, 1971.

Whisler [1967]   T. L. Whisler & C. Myers, *The Impact of Computers on Management*, MIT Press, Cambridge, Mass., 1967.

Wigley [1966]   K. Wigley, *The demand for fuel 1948–1975*, Program for Growth no. 8, Department of Applied Economics, University of Cambridge, 1966.

Williamson [1965]   O. E. Williamson, 'Innovation and Market Structure', *Journal of Political Economy*, February 1965, pp. 67–73.

Wilkinson [1973]   W. Wilkinson, 'House Prices and the Measurement of Externalities', *Economic Journal*, March 1973, pp. 72–86.

Wooldridge [1963]   R. Wooldridge & J. F. Radcliffe, *Algol Programming*, English Universities Press, London, 1963.

INDEX